DIGITAL MANIFESTO

Principles and Practices for Orchestrating an IT Value Chain

FRANÇOIS ZIELEMANS

ISBN-13: 978-1-60427-134-8

Printed and bound in the U.S.A. Printed on acid-free paper.

10 9 8 7 6 5 4 3 2 1

Please visit the WAV section of the J. Ross Publishing website at jrosspub.com/ wav for the Library of Congress Cataloging-in-Publication data.

Phone: (954) 727-9333
Fax: (561) 892-0700
Web: www.jrosspub.com

CONTENTS

To Jamie, my wife

To Hendrik, my friend and mentor

PREFACE

The journey resulting in this book started in 2009 when Hendrik Wester and I decided to start a boutique consulting firm that specialized in advising CIOs on the impact of digitalization on their operating models. We thought that the worst of the financial crisis from 2007 was behind us and that we would be able to catch the next wave of economic growth. It turned out that fortune telling was not our forte. In 2011, we decided to close the firm; and we joined two different IT service providers in executive positions.

This book is the sole survivor of our short but extraordinary period as entrepreneurs. I started working on it in July 2011, and over a period of more than five years, and several rewrites, it eventually resulted in the book you are holding in your hand.

WHY THIS BOOK?

Sustainable success in digital markets requires more than adopting agile Scrum or replacing the business IT alignment paradigm with business IT fusion. These are point solutions, while digitalization starts with the business and IT reframing their current belief set and operating model. A successful transformation of an analog business model into a hybrid or digital equivalent touches on companies' leadership style, culture, skill sets, strategy, business model, sourcing strategy, and process model. Technology-rich markets are too dynamic and competitive for half-measures.

The same forces also translate into a need for flexibility. Companies are too diverse to be captured in one universal management framework. For this reason, this book is structured around six principles, each supported by several models and practical examples. The principles are concrete enough to translate into actionable improvement initiatives, but leave enough room for company-specific adaptations.

This book is written for business-savvy technologists and business executives who are leading digitalization initiatives—professionals who understand that business and IT have to stand side-by-side to be successful in new, and often digital market spaces, and realize value from disruptive technologies.

Due to the broad scope of this book, it is not possible to cover all of the topics in the detail they deserve. For that same reason, it would be helpful for readers to be already familiar with concepts like agile, waterfall, the Information Technology Infrastructure Library, the business model, and enterprise architecture—or at least don't mind doing a few internet searches regarding the concepts here and there while reading this book.

In case you want to know more about the topics covered in this book, feel free to visit my website at www.digital-manifesto.org.

François Zielemans

ABOUT THE AUTHOR

François Zielemans has 20 years of IT management and international consulting experience. He is currently an IT executive who is responsible for the solution engineering business unit of the Centric organization located in the Netherlands and Romania. Centric is a European IT provider that delivers infrastructure and software solutions for a variety of markets such as financial services, supply chain, healthcare, construction, and government in the Nether-  lands, Germany, Switzerland, Norway, and Sweden. It also provides business process outsourcing and staffing services.

Mr. Zielemans' business unit applies both emerging and mature technologies to solve complex business challenges in the areas of digitalization, big data, advanced automation, the cloud, and the Internet of Things. While planning and executing these projects, Mr. Zielemans applies the principles and practices covered in this book—reshaping and further refining them in the process.

Prior to joining the Centric organization, François advised numerous large multi-national organizations regarding the digitalization of their business models, leading several organizational transformations in complex and dynamic environments. He worked abroad for extensive periods in the United States, Singapore, India, and Malaysia.

A few of his other areas of experience and expertise include defining and executing (sourcing) strategies, and defining and launching new value propositions to help organizations realize sustainable operational excellence. Early in his career, he gained experience leading successful IT support and operations teams using performance management frameworks and Information Technology Infrastructure Library best practices.

François Zielemans has a bachelor's degree in mechanical engineering and a master of science degree in business administration, along with being a well-published author in the IT-related Dutch media. His current area of focus is the impact of digitalization on companies and society and, more specifically, the fact that the accelerating impact of technology is forcing companies to boost their capability to sense more quickly and act more decisively than ever before in history; they must disrupt or be disrupted.

François has had a popular blog for several years and recently developed a new website and blog called *The Digital Manifesto* (www.digital-manifesto.org) where you can find valuable information.

ACKNOWLEDGMENTS

First and foremost, I would like to thank my wife, Jamie, for supporting me in chasing my dreams. I would also like to thank Drew Gierman at J. Ross Publishing for the chance to turn my ideas into an actual book. To Benjamin Woo, I am grateful to you for introducing me to Kenny Tan, my editor. To Kenny, thank you for turning my personal interpretation of English into proper American English. Thank you Jasper Alleman for your review and your valuable comments. Most of all, I am thankful for all of the writers, academics, practitioners, colleagues, and other thought leaders whom I either had the pleasure to work with or read their books and articles.

At J. Ross Publishing we are committed to providing today's professional with practical, hands-on tools that enhance the learning experience and give readers an opportunity to apply what they have learned. That is why we offer free ancillary materials available for download on this book and all participating Web Added Value™ publications. These online resources may include interactive versions of material that appears in the book or supplemental templates, worksheets, models, plans, case studies, proposals, spreadsheets and assessment tools, among other things. Whenever you see the WAV™ symbol in any of our publications, it means bonus materials accompany the book and are available from the Web Added Value Download Resource Center at www.jrosspub.com.

Downloads for *The Digital Manifesto* include IT business model canvases for foundation and entrepreneurial IT, and an Excel template to calculate net present value of an outsourcing deal, with and without real options.

1

THRIVING IN DIGITAL MARKETS

We tend to underestimate the future, demonstrated by this internal memo from Western Union (1876): "*This 'telephone' has too many shortcomings to be seriously considered as a means of communication.*"

The telegraph was invented in 1792. It took almost 100 years for its successor, the telephone, to arrive. Today, the pace of one technology being replaced by another is exponentially getting faster, dramatically impacting both our working and private lives. Food and clothes are only two examples of what may be next in line to be transformed by the miniaturization of sensors and the internet. The transformation that many traditional or *analog* products go through is well demonstrated by observing the automobile.

Since the introduction of the anti-lock braking system (or ABS) in 1978 by Mercedes-Benz, the car has slowly become less automotive and more *IT-motive*—including motor management systems, cameras, lasers, radars, heads-up displays, and other high-tech equipment. Many systems are dedicated to improving the safety of both the driver and others who are using the roads, while increasingly complex motor management software is used to comply with (or even circumvent) stringent pollution laws and their requirements. In the near future, cars will be equipped with car-to-car communication allowing them to react to each other's behavior and interact with a larger traffic control infrastructure. After that, the next logical step of riding in fully autonomous cars could be just around the corner.

For farmers, IT holds the promise of sleeping in instead of getting up at 5 a.m. to milk and feed the cows. The newest generation of milk robots allow cows to be milked whenever they feel like it—a cow just has to walk up to the machines. They recognize each individual cow by the tag she is wearing before feeding her and disinfecting her udders prior to milking her. Data regarding her health and the quantity and quality of milk she produces is stored and is accessible to the farmer whenever and wherever he wants. Business intelligence tools transform the data into actionable information, such as the producible number of cheese wheels or cartons of milk from an individual farm's milk production, for both the farmer and the downstream factory. As a result, the farmer can spend his time on exceptions, like calling the vet, and initiatives to further improve productivity and quality.

Movie and game rental company Blockbuster is on the other side of the equation. It was unable to compete effectively with the disruptive business model of Netflix. The latter streams movies over the internet, removing the cost of renting local floor space and employees. Unable to transform itself in time, the former rental giant had to file for Chapter 11 bankruptcy protection with a debt of $1.46 billion.

IT used to be a utility—today it is a game changer. More specifically, closed customer data[1] and software are the jokers stacked in an IT team's deck. The former is relatively scarce in a world that is dominated by a small number of ecosystems—for example, Apple, Google, Amazon, and Microsoft—while the latter has become so powerful that it is reshaping the job market even now. However, there are a few snags. For starters, technology itself is abundant and has to be combined with business capabilities to become a strategic differentiator. This in turn requires the IT team to act less as a faithful servant (*business, tell me what to do*) and more as a business partner (*business, this is what I suggest we should do*). In native digital and hybrid markets, business and IT domains may even have to fuse to create a frictionless operating model.

Equally important is not to get carried away by technology-related buzzwords. The Internet of Things (IoT), social media, big data, and the cloud are all very important trends, but they are no reason to forget everything from the past. Agile Scrum is taking the development world by storm, but there are still plenty of cases where waterfall development is preferable. Similarly, the business IT alignment paradigm from Henderson and Venkatraman remains the best choice to collaborate with the business for the stable, efficiency-driven part of the IT portfolio.[i]

The need to differentiate can also be observed at company and industry levels. A manufacturer of roof tiles relies far less on IT for its financial success than Google. Or, consider a start-up company versus an established company: the first starts with a clean sheet while the century-old company has a mountain of legacy to consider.

---

[1] Closed data refers to data that companies don't want to share due to commercial reasons (e.g., competitive advantage) or regulatory compliance (e.g., personal data of customers).

The world is too complex and diverse to think only in black and white. It consists of many shades of grey, too. The digitalization of markets and business models requires companies to execute certain things less, and others more. These practices are embodied by the following six principles:

- Less defensive, more offensive
- Less inside, more outside
- Less uniform, more differentiated
- Less static, more flow
- Less isolation, more cohesion
- Less cost, more value

The similarity to the Agile Manifesto is obvious, as is the following concept applicable in this book: "*while there is value in the items on the left, we value the items on the right more.*"[ii] Every year, product life cycles become shorter, products more complex, and markets more uncertain. This requires companies, regardless of their industry and age, to invest in capabilities embodied by the items on the right.

The remainder of this chapter is dedicated to the concise introduction of the six principles and a map to guide the reader through this book.

To stimulate the mind, every chapter includes statements like the ones in Table 1.1. These invite the reader to form an opinion before and after reading the chapter. They cover both the book as a whole and the six principles. Some may seem cryptic now, but I will help you decode them as we go along (see Table 1.1).

Table 1.1   Statements to think about when reading this chapter

Statements
Processes, role descriptions, and reward systems cannot change an introvert into an extrovert.
The protective shield between the market and IT provided by the business has evaporated.
Technology by itself is a non-distinctive asset; a business-technology concept is a moderately distinctive asset; and closed customer data is a distinctive asset.
A one-size-fits-all IT operating model forces the business to invest in shadow IT.
The hottest technology today is the legacy of tomorrow.
The mainframe and the IoT can and should coexist.

1.1 CAPABILITIES TO LEAD IN A DIGITAL WORLD

The environment in which we live and work today is more uncertain and complex than ever before. To survive, let alone thrive, companies have to boost their capability to sense and act on both foreseen and unforeseen events quickly and decisively. According to Rita McGrath,[iii] the downfall of Sony, Black-Berry, Blockbuster, Circuit City, and even the New York Stock Exchange can be attributed to failing to do so:

> *"Their downfall is a predictable outcome of practices that are designed around the concept of sustainable competitive advantage. The fundamental problem is that deeply ingrained structures and systems designed to extract maximum value from a competitive advantage become a liability when the environment requires instead the capacity to surf through waves of short-lived opportunities. To compete in these more volatile and uncertain environments, you need to do things differently."*

Of the 500 largest companies in 1957, less than eighty were still part of the S&P 500 forty years later. Some were taken over by other companies, but most shrunk or simply went bankrupt.

Even today, Facebook, Twitter, LinkedIn, and other young multi-billion-dollar companies aren't exempted from these economic forces. Yahoo was one of the pioneers that turned the internet into a billion-dollar business. Today, it is no longer an independent company—Verizon bought it in 2016 after a months-long bidding process. Facebook had attracted a huge teen following, an important demographic group for marketeers, at its inception. However, privacy concerns in combination with Mom, Dad, Aunt Edna, Uncle Jim, and the rest of the uncool lot joining Facebook are affecting engagement with this age group. Consequently, they move on to apps like WhatsApp, Snapchat, or others to communicate with their peers. *For now*, between today and a couple of years from now, a start-up introduces a new value proposition, starting a new cycle. Technology is therefore both a key enabler of new business models, and at the same time, a major source of strategic risk.

Data follows a similar path. The continued miniaturization of sensors, CPUs, and other components turns *dumb* products into *smart* ones. This, too, is a potential source of billions of dollars in revenue for both IT service providers and the companies that are using their solutions. Downsides include bankruptcy for companies ignoring the IoT and big data altogether, and waste for companies that are unable to effectively realize the potential value represented by these buzzwords. Combine data with advanced algorithms and you have a tool to automate knowledge-intensive work, create robots maintaining other robots, and autonomous driving trucks, cars, and airplanes. However, until artificial intelligence becomes mature enough to dynamically solve myriad situations, both foreseen and unforeseen, weaknesses in either data set or algorithm could result in dramatic distortions in the value chain or in a car ending up in the ditch.

It is important to note that the changing role of technology does *not* equal asking the CFO to double the IT budget or adopt every new technology entering the market. The success of Apple's iPad doesn't come from any introduction of a new disruptive technology—it is a winner because Apple combined easy access to a wide variety of books, music, games, and movies with a good looking, high quality device. Additionally, the iPad actually provided so much more functionality than the average e-reader that it created a new market. Consumers did not know they had the need until Apple launched the product. As a result, the iPad sold more than three million units in its first 80 days, making it the fastest selling electronic device at the time. Coming in at number two, a considerable distance back, was the DVD player with 350,000 units in its first year.

In their book *Blue Ocean Strategy*, Kim and Mauborgne describe the creation of new (uncontested) market spaces as a means to break away from traditional competition models. They argue that the traditional fighting for competitive advantage, battling over market share, and struggling for differentiation has resulted in a bloody *red ocean* of rivals fighting over a shrinking profit pool. The authors argue that tomorrow's leading companies will succeed not by competing head-to-head with competitors, but by fulfilling a new demand in an uncontested market space, creating a *blue ocean*—an ocean that will, in most cases, be full of technology and data.

The need for technology and business departments to act quickly and decisively is amplified by the infusion of IT into our day-to-day lives. Today, there are four billion people using mobile phones—approximately 450 million of them have internet on their mobile phones, and that number is expected to grow rapidly. We can consume information 24 hours a day, purchase a book at 3:00 a.m., and read a memo from a colleague at the breakfast table. IT is not only changing business models, but also the way we spend our free time (e.g., checking our Facebook account, playing mobile games).

Technology overcomes many boundaries, enabling companies to tap into new markets and enriching the private lives of billions of people. We are part of a global ecosystem—with all of its opportunities and challenges. To thrive as a company in this world, companies need to invest in the capabilities reflected by the six principles described in the following sections.

1.1.1 Less Defensive, More Offensive

The lack of scarcity inhibits technology from being a sustainable strategic differentiator by itself. It requires a specific mix of business and technological capabilities to create value propositions that are both attractive to customers and difficult to copy by the competition. Entrepreneurs show the way by launching a constant stream of new business models that leverage advances in sensor technology, powerful but energy efficient processors, and clever software to enter or even create new markets like e-health and smart homes. While market dynamics ensure that most of these companies will vanish before ever reaching maturity, Google, Facebook, Twitter, Box, and Salesforce demonstrate the inherent *business* potential of technology.

Some digital or hybrid start-ups create completely new markets while others disrupt existing ones. For instance, the introduction of fitness tracking devices from companies like Fitbit and Garmin did not replace any analog substitute. This is very different from the impact that 3-D printing has on the manufacturing industry. Here, the commoditization of 3-D printing is democratizing the production of physical products. Customization and build-to-order take on a whole new dimension now that printers and materials have become cheap and durable enough for individuals to design and produce their own products.

The longer the history of a company and its stability in the market, the wider and deeper the canyon that has to be bridged when game-changing technologies turn up on the horizon. To make matters worse, adopting a new strategy and the associated operating IT model takes time. Depending on the industry or market, there is little or no time when nimble start-ups enter the market with their new and disruptive business models. The first principle is therefore primarily about the right mindset. To be more than a mere utility provider, the IT team of established companies has to be open minded, curious, proactive, and constantly ready to adapt to change. *Less defensive, more offensive represents the attitude and skills required to lead in digital markets.* The performance management framework, IT business model, and concepts from the other principles are instrumental in nature. By themselves, they cannot change a shy introvert into a confident extrovert.

1.1.2 Less Inside, More Outside

The one thing that did not change between 1950 and 1989—the year that the worldwide web was invented by English scientist Tim Berners-Lee—was the number of customer segments IT had to service. While the business consisted of multiple functions, the demand profile was homogeneous, stable, and moderately complex. Technological breakthroughs including the internet, wireless networks, and ongoing transistor miniaturization dramatically changed both the number and diversity of IT's customer segments. They enabled the business customers to become IT customers.

Digital and hybrid markets elevate technology to the heart of the business model. To be considered a business partner, the IT team has to do more than supply customer relationship management or e-commerce applications—this is something any external vendor can do. Only by adding tangible value (e.g., smoothing a cross-channel experience, turning a *dumb* product into a *smart* one) will the business refrain from removing the internal IT team from the equation.

The fun does not stop here, however, as the value chain, as a whole, digitalizes. The complexity and diversity of today's products require companies to specialize. Only as part of an interdependent network of business partners can a company produce and service an end-to-end value proposition from a customer perspective. Due to the strategic impact of these so-called *key partners*, the business expects effective collaboration tools, end-to-end actionable business intelligence, and flawless data exchange between devices (e.g., machine to machine, IoT). This effectively turns the key partners of the business into a VIP customer segment for IT.

Today's customer segments of IT are both internal and external, along with being heterogeneous, dynamic, and highly complex. With both the upstream and downstream parts of the digital value chain crossing company boundaries, *less inside, more outside represents the ability to manage multiple heterogeneous customer segments.* Only when IT embraces the fact that it happens *out there* instead of within the four company walls, indistinct technology can be turned into a company asset. No more hiding behind the business's skirt, but embracing the marketing and business concepts required to thrive in hybrid and digital markets—markets that all have their own demand profile affecting the positioning of IT and its value propositions.

1.1.3 Less Uniform, More Differentiated

Google and Apple dominate the mobile market using different approaches. Apple's success is based on a centralized, designer-centric corporate culture, while Google relies on distributed teams consisting of highly skilled individuals to make the right decisions. The product portfolio of Google is very broad, with a constant flow of new entrants and (premature) exits. In comparison, Apple's portfolio is narrow, but more stable.

FedEx and UPS also dominate their markets, again using slightly different value propositions. Compared to UPS, FedEx offers its customers more flexibility at slightly higher price points. More price-sensitive customers opt for UPS and the more standardized value proposition that comes with it. Even more pronounced is the difference between Walmart and Amazon. The first has its roots in physical retail outlets while the second started as a native digital business model.

Differentiation can also be observed at an operational level. Marketeers want to try new things on a daily basis, while the controllers and bookkeepers of the finance and administration department prefer stability and predictability.

Marketeers enjoy rally and off-road racing, while controllers tend to take the train for its excellent safety record. When it comes to IT, the marketeers want to be behind the steering wheel with IT as the co-driver, knowing that only as a team can they win. For the controller, a commercial off-the-shelf software-as-a-service (SaaS) solution will do just fine.

The higher the technology density of the market, the more important it becomes for IT to sense and act on the relative importance of co-creation, speed-to-market, flexibility, robustness, efficiency, or other sources of contextual value. In hybrid and native digital markets, this value can be equal to or even surpass the base value represented by the functional requirements. *Less uniform, more differentiated represents the ability to deliver contextual IT solutions.* At the company level, think of effectively positioning IT as either a faithful servant, business partner, Average Joe, or prima donna. At an operational level, the two key archetypes are entrepreneurial IT and foundation IT, as seen in Figure 1.1. The first is also known as *strategic IT* or *enabling IT*; but in hybrid and digital markets it is entrepreneurship that is required from IT. Being an entrepreneur means *one who undertakes an endeavor* or an *enterpriser*,[2] a far better term when business and IT are together in pursuit of more revenue, profit, or less strategic risk.

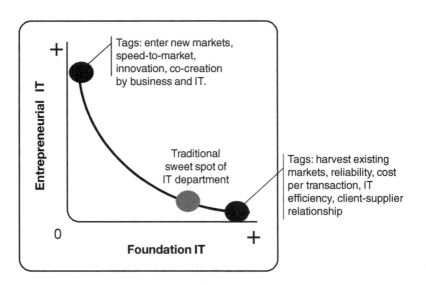

Figure 1.1   The continuum between entrepreneurial IT and foundation IT

---

[2] Technically, the term should be intrapreneur as IT would be acting as an entrepreneur within the company. As this term is not widely used, this book will use the more common term.

Foundation IT, also known as *transactional IT* or *factory IT*, is the traditional sweet spot of the IT department. Even though most consider it less sexy than entrepreneurial IT, the majority of companies' revenue and margin are generated by business processes that are enabled by this part of the IT portfolio. Entrepreneurial IT is, in most cases, a source of expected *future* cash flows funded by *current* cash flows that are enabled by foundation IT. The latter's portfolio also contains the capabilities required to *glue* IT systems together—like the enterprise service bus and the platform required by lean and business process management initiatives. As such, it acts as the solid foundation required by other initiatives to succeed.

To survive, companies need both flavors, differing only in the relative amount. Besides the usual suspects— such as specific industries, business strategies, and business models—one more factor drives the mix of entrepreneurial IT and foundation IT: time. Nothing ever stays static; everything flows.

1.1.4 Less Static, More Flow

Several years ago, I supported the CIO of a media company to clean up the mess left behind by an uncoordinated technological investment spree. This story will be all too familiar for many.

The IT department had gone through the classic evolution of mainframe to client-server solutions. The service portfolio consisted of core business applications that were required in order to edit, print, and distribute printed magazines and newspapers; the applications required by the shared support functions (e.g., HR, finance, accounting); and office automation. None of these applications provided the business with any strategic advantage and, consequently, IT was treated as a utility—not any more or less important than the quality of food served by the cafeteria for lunch.

When the internet and mobile platforms disrupted the company's business model, the CIO was barely consulted by the business on how to move forward. The IT team was not considered capable of driving the transition from printed to digital media. Caught off guard and fearing that they were going to be left behind by the competition, the heads of the business units did what they thought was best for their own team—they bought several start-up companies at the top of their valuation curve and embraced a wide variety of new technologies and platforms.

The results were underwhelming to say the least. Three years later, a new CEO was appointed to stop the bleeding. On the IT side, the lack of orchestration had resulted in a heterogeneous archipelago of shadow IT teams and technologies. To make matters worse, the hodgepodge made it impossible to quickly scale those few initiatives that were successful.

Looking back, it was easy to identify the root cause of the problem. Both business and IT were too focused on maximizing the revenue and margin of the existing business model to sense and act on the imminent disruption. They forgot that, even after decades of relative stability, every status quo eventually ends. Quoting Nike's CEO Mark Parker: *"Business models are not meant to be static. In the world we live in today, you have to adapt and change. One of my fears is being this big, slow, constipated, bureaucratic company that's happy with its success. That will wind up being your death in the end."*[iv]

Nothing can escape time. Business models, technologies, and individual value propositions are all conceived, grow, mature, and decline. Many don't even make it to the mature phase. In 2007, everybody talked about the virtual world known as Second Life. Businesses opened virtual shops and some colleges organized virtual lectures. By 2015, Second Life had become a ghost town. Other hyped initiatives that flopped include the satellite network Iridium, WebTV, 3-D televisions, the mini disk, BetaMax, HD DVD, and the Zune MP3 player. The jury is still out on Windows 10 Mobile, smart watches, and virtual and augmented reality—turning them into risky bets for now.

As risk and return go hand in hand, unproven business models and technologies should not always be avoided. Entrepreneurship is equivalent to risk taking. What they do require is proactive decision making and effective portfolio management. The previously mentioned media company was neither proactive nor in control—ending up with their back against the wall.

In hybrid and digital markets, regularly evaluating if and when to invest in or divest a business model or technology only gets you halfway. The close interdependence between business and technology life cycles requires an integrated approach. For companies like Amazon, Apple, Google, and other tech companies, this comes naturally. Facebook was launched in 2004 and captured market share while the underpinning technology platform was still under construction. Ten years later, both their business model and platform entered the mature phase, which enabled the company to spend more time on diversification like virtual reality (through the buyout of Oculus Rift, the leader of the industry at the time), and augmenting core parts of its business mode, such as online video advertising (through the purchase and integration of LiveRail).

The capability to closely integrate multiple life cycles is new to companies that are in the process of transforming their analog business model into a hybrid or digital one. It is nevertheless a crucial ability if they are to become successful players in their respective markets. *Less static, more flow represents the ability to integrate multiple, interdependent life cycles*—life cycles that become shorter, more complex, and more dynamic with each passing year. It is a complex challenge that cannot be solved by one isolated initiative.

1.1.5 Less Isolation, More Coherence

When a train that is loaded with chemicals derails near a village, all emergency response teams within a 50-mile radius scramble to get to the site. Depending on their role, they need critical information to be readily available: the fire chief wants to know the type and scale of the spill; ambulance crews need information regarding the expected number of victims; the local council has to determine whether to evacuate the nearby school; and the police need to know which roads should be closed. However, reviews of urban disasters show that these isolated efforts are not enough to minimize the impact on people, the environment, and the assets. A truly effective response requires all parties to collaborate and exchange information in a structured and prearranged manner. The more they collaborate, the less they lose their individual strengths and, consequently, more lives are saved.

Companies face a different, but not necessarily less difficult, challenge. The time where customers were happy with any color for their car as long as it was black has come and gone. Today, both choice and supply are abundant, shifting the power balance toward the customer.[3] Only through a complex network of interdependent external stakeholders (e.g., external business partners, government agencies) and internal stakeholders (e.g., division heads, IT director, CFO), can a company hope to produce a successful value proposition.

The larger and heterogeneous the network, the more difficult to realize the desired end-to-end flexibility, predictability, and efficiency. To overcome this challenge, companies implement both *vertical* and *horizontal* governance and management practices. The first represents the hierarchical line and accompanying distribution of authority. It divides the company in three layers[4]— strategic, tactical, and operational. Respectively, they focus on direction setting, control, and execution. Porter's value chain and Osterwalder's business model are popular models to structure the horizontal axis, supplemented with three types of integration capabilities.

A business model describes the rationale of how an organization creates, delivers, and captures value: economic, social, or other forms of value.[v] Coincidently, the IT department has the same objective. Also similar are the presence of customer segments, channels, customer relationships, value propositions, key activities, key partners, key resources, revenue streams, and cost structures.

---

[3] There are still (digital) value propositions that enjoy relative high switching cost for customers and barrier of entry for competitors, but their numbers are dwindling. See also Chapter 8.

[4] The three layers can be condensed to two by combining control with direction setting. In general, the larger, more stable, and more diversified the company, the more layers there will be.

Only minor adjustments, such as changing revenue streams into value streams, are therefore required to turn Osterwalder's business model canvas into an IT business model canvas, as seen in Figure 1.2. It is easy to explain to any business executive, and it can be applied to analog, hybrid, and digital markets by varying the level of forward integration and convergence of both domains.

The vertical axis has to be equally flexible, as entering a new market requires fast and decisive decision making—achieved either by delegating mandates to the managers who are operating at the front lines or leveraging on advances in business intelligence tools. The latter allows senior executives control that is broader and more effective than previously possible. For mature and declining markets, the usual key objective of speed-to-market is replaced by efficiency and asset recovery, translating into a different design of both the vertical and horizontal axis.

In short, to prevent value leakage from investments in technology, the business and IT have to be organized in a way they can get close-distant, informal-formal, fluid-robust, or any other property related to the entrepreneurial IT and foundation IT dichotomy. *Less isolation, more cohesion reflects the ability to operate multiple IT business models simultaneously.* To achieve this, the business models used by the business and IT have to be flexible, comparable, and coherent enough to drive joint value propositions throughout their life cycle. Simply stated, the shift from entrepreneurial IT by a value proposition to foundation IT should not take a year and cost three times the original investment.

At the strategic level, the name of the game is *positioning*, and includes the capability to act as a business partner and prima donna simultaneously or to

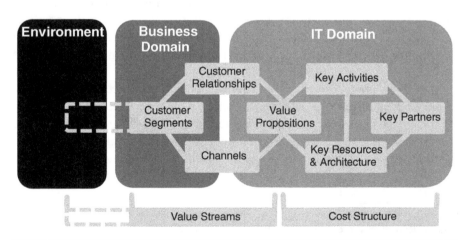

Figure 1.2   The IT business model (adapted from Osterwalder 2010)

quickly evolve from faithful servant to business partner when an analog market digitalizes.

This fifth principle therefore represents the tools and practices required to translate the previous principles into a working organization. Digital leadership, differentiated value propositions, and life-cycle management need an adaptable and scalable organizational *landing platform*. Only when all of the building blocks of the IT business model work in tune with each other can the gap between potential and realized value be closed. Ideally, the end result of all the hard work will be value.

1.1.6 Less Cost, More Value

For the first 40 years since its inception, IT was solely used to automate internal business processes in order to reduce cost. The association with cost was further reinforced by the soft relationship between company revenue and money spent on IT. The difficulty of tying IT capital expenditure and IT operational expenditure to business benefits in combination with large sums of money resulted in many IT managers reporting to the CFO. Even today, it is still common for the CIO of a company with an analog business model to be treated as a *junior* board member.

There is good news though—digitalization removes many of the layers that cause the dilution between $1 invested in IT and $1 in additional business revenue. Pandora, LinkedIn, and Facebook have no analog or even hybrid value proposition or channel—their business models only exist in cyberspace. It is therefore relatively easy to foresee and measure the return of increased investments in IT (e.g., one extra server can support x users, averaging y dollars in additional advertisement revenue). This does not make IT costs any less significant, but with digitalization, its relative importance changes.

For starters, in hybrid and digital business models, the business expects IT to report its contribution in business terms. The objectives of the business are increasing revenue, margins, flexibility, and customer satisfaction, while decreasing competitive risk, unexpected fluctuations in customer demand, and other challenges. These are very different objectives compared to the IT classic *monthly server availability* or an initiative whereby IT signs a rigid, long-term outsourcing contract to negate its own costs and any effects that that decision might have on the business domain (e.g., investments in shadow IT by the business, foregone revenue).

Less cost, more value represents the ability to realize value from a business perspective. The principle reflects IT's capability to define, measure, report, and optimize the performance of the end-to-end information value chain. When done well, it leads to quotes like this one from H&R Block's CIO Marc West:[vi] *"It's way beyond alignment, it's when a president of a retail tax business unit stands up and says 'here's the top five things my IT team is doing for me, (. . .) those guys in IT understand how we make money.'"* In order to get more quotes like this one, Chapter 7 introduces a new way to calculate the business value of IT, supplemented by practical tools like (joint) benefit and risk universes and differentiated value trees.

1.2 INTERDEPENDENT CHAPTERS

The sequence in which the principles are listed is no coincidence. There is a rationale, depicted in Figure 1.3. It starts with embracing at personal, team, and department levels that the raison d'être of IT is adding value to customers. In hybrid and digital markets, this requires an eagerness, focus, soft skills,

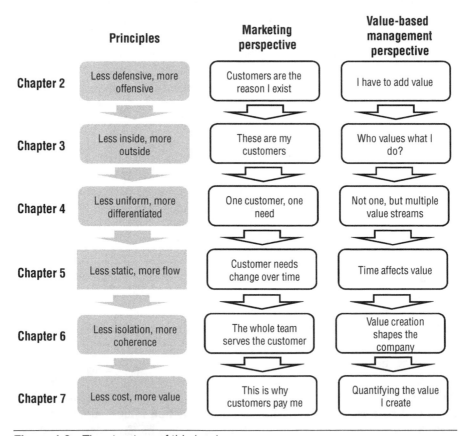

Figure 1.3   The structure of this book

and expertise untypical for an IT department that has been spoiled by decades of forced sourcing by the business. A business that was liberated by the commoditization of web applications and SaaS delivery models left the internal IT department no choice but to shape up or ship out.

With the notion that IT has to be run as a business and regarding the soft and hard skills that come with it as a solid foundation, the next step is identifying the customer segments. With digitalization, both the number (e.g., business-to-business customers, business-to-consumer customers, key partners of the business) and complexity (e.g., focus on user experience, business wants, virtual reality pilot) of the segments increases. Besides an increase in scope breadth, IT also has to deal with an increase in depth. Marketing demands a top-notch user experience for visitors of the website that offers a virtual reality experience for the product they plan to launch in the next quarter. The production department wants to further converge their industrial IT systems with the enterprise resource planning suite and start an IoT pilot project. In other words, one customer equals one need: or less uniform, more differentiated.

Translated to value-based management lingo, IT has to generate multiple value streams. Lowering the cost-per-business transaction through automation gets you almost all the way in an analog market, but it would get you barely beyond the starting line when the business model digitalizes. Increasing the challenge further is the fact that the demand of those multiple heterogeneous customer segments is not static. One person can be a teenager interested in getting insurance for his first car and later, a young parent looking for insurance to protect the financial future of the family and even later, an elderly person worried about the cost of healthcare insurance. In other words, the needs of a customer evolve, driven by the inevitable flow of time.

Chapter 6 provides the necessary paper, pencils, and glue to turn everything into a coherent and effective functioning organization. The marketeer may say something along the line of *the whole team serves the customer*, while the finance specialist argues that the *all management processes should be geared toward value creation*. The intangible and tangible value streams from the customer are the outcome of doing the *right things* through effectiveness and doing them the *right way* through efficiency. The accompanying performance management framework is part of the last principle—less cost, more value.

The last chapter of this book covers the Digital Manifesto itself. The Digital Manifesto is a growth path, consisting of six *interdependent* principles that *together* generate business value.

1.3 INDEPENDENT THINKING

Before continuing on with the following chapters, there are two more points to remember—the first being that paradigms, models, and best practices allow us to simplify and structure complexity. That is the reason we all love them so much. However, simplification inevitably results in omitting potentially relevant context and other information. Hence, one should never allow simplification to replace critical thinking and pragmatism—there are already enough demagogues out there who reject anything that does not fit their favorite paradigm, model, or best practice.

The second point is related to the fact that the principles become irrelevant when the market is fundamentally disrupted. Uber and Airbnb completely ignored the existing business models and the teaching of academic gurus. Taleb[vii] described the extreme impact of random events with a very low likelihood on our private lives and companies in his book *The Black Swan*. It refers to a bird that nobody believed existed until the discovery of Australia—requiring all ornithologists to adjust their statement that only white swans existed. Only by regularly challenging the fundamental beliefs underpinning the existing business model can a company hope to reduce this strategic risk—although, it can never be completely mitigated.

Hence, always be ready to disrupt your beliefs.

REFERENCES

   i. Henderson, J. C. and Venkatraman, N. (1993). Strategic Alignment: Leveraging Information Technology for Transforming Organizations.
   ii. Beck, K., et al. (2001). Manifesto for Agile Software Development. Link: http://agilemanifesto.org/.
   iii. McGrath, R. (2013). *The End of Competitive Advantage*. Link: http://www.europeanbusinessreview.com/?p=9705.
   iv. Carr, A. (February 14, 2013). Death to the Core Competency: Lessons from Nike, Apple, Netflix. Link: http://www.fastcompany.com/3005850/core-competency-dead-lessons-nike-apple-netflix.
   v. Osterwalder, A. and Pigneur, Y. (2010). Business Model Generation: A Handbook for Visionaries, Game Changers, and Challengers.
   vi. Tuck School of Business and Brimstone Consulting Group, LLC (2006). The CIO as Strategic Business Partner: Leading Change and Driving Results: An Executive Workshop.
   vii. Taleb, N. (2010). *The Black Swan: The Impact of the Highly Improbable*, Second edition. New York: Random House Trade.

2

LESS DEFENSIVE, MORE OFFENSIVE

Less defensive, more offensive represents the attitude and skills required to lead in digital markets.

Uber and car sharing are part of a trend whereby owning a car becomes less important. A growing number of people (mostly younger ones) just want to go from Point A to Point B at a certain moment in time. They want a service that—contrary to a physical good—is intangible, perishable, and consumed at the same moment it is produced, thereby requiring direct interaction between the customer and the company delivering the service.

The shift from owning physical goods to consuming a service can be observed in several markets. We stream music and videos instead of owning CDs and DVDs, sign up for all-you-can-read book subscriptions and rent designer bags. Ownership is replaced by a customized, enjoyable, and reasonably priced experience. It is only one of the developments that is part of the broader *as-a-service economy* trend. What all of these developments share is *technology as an important enabler*.

Throughout the whole value chain, progressively complex manual tasks are being automated and thus, driving down cost. The retained business teams are highly skilled, focusing on high added-value activities like objective and strategic settings, research and development, business development, marketing, and customer service. Translated to IT teams, the following to-do list emerges:

- Enable the transformation of internal business processes
- Provide the tools to (partially) digitalize business channels, value propositions, and customer relationships
- Deliver to internal business users an experience similar to the one delivered to external customer segments
- Automate as many IT tasks as possible, allowing a core IT team to focus on activities that add tangible value to the business

It takes vision, leadership, courage, drive, and a specific set of soft and hard skills from the CIOs and their teams to realize the required change within the time frame allowed by twitchy customers and cocky competitors. Without them, change will either be too slow, or worse, not even progress beyond good intentions, long presentations, and reports written by expensive consultants.

This chapter consists of three parts. The first one describes several trends emphasizing the IT employee as a key resource instead of a disposable company asset. The second part provides several pointers to implement the principle. And last but not least, the third part presents a small case study. Table 2.1 shows three statements that cover the chapter as a whole.

Table 2.1   Statements to think about when reading this chapter

Statements
Technology has become capable enough to influence the unconscious behavior of people.
With the digitalization of business models, employees become more valuable.
Agile, ITIL, and other best practices should be implemented as is. There are no company specific adaptions required.

2.1 WHY THIS PRINCIPLE MATTERS

In non-digital markets, customers incur an out-of-pocket expense when buying a product or service. The nature of digital markets allows for more variation. E-mail, music, and news are free when the customer does not mind looking at or listening to advertisements. To be a viable business model, a certain percentage of those advertisements have to result in an actual sale. This drives companies like Google, Facebook, LinkedIn, and Yahoo to invest billions in technology to collect as much data as possible about us. The more these companies know about their users, the more precise ads can be targeted, and the more money they can charge companies that want to advertise.

Customer data is not only used to prevent ads for sunbeds being served to people living in the Sahara. It is also used to appeal to our desire for individuality. With seven billion people on planet Earth, it is not easy to stand out; the increasingly fine-grained profiles of users on company servers allows for what marketers call hyper-personalization. Ginni Rometty, CEO of IBM, referred to it when discussing the ways that technology is changing our lives:[i] *"What you will see with rapid data and social sharing is the death of the average and the era of you. Businesses will be able to truly serve the individual."* Game developers embrace similar technology to optimize the gaming experience itself and the ability to target ads. People playing bingo and poker games from GSN Games leave a data footprint that provides details on their energy level (e.g., getting tired means slower screen presses) and how they react to losing a game. Using complex algorithms, the game proactively adjusts itself based on the constant flow of data generated by the user.[ii]

Predictive analysis is a dynamic and fast-evolving practice, with personal digital assistants like Siri, Google Now, Alexa, and Cortana pushing personalization to the next level. But knowing a lot about a customer is of no value if there is no attractive value proposition to sell. And even here, technology is disrupting traditional patterns. Companies like Facebook, LinkedIn, and Twitter created value propositions that influence our behavior. A combination of enabling technologies (e.g., the smart phone, the internet, apps), mental *hooks* (e.g., desire to see who liked or commented on your post), positive network effects (e.g., the more friends, the more likely to receive replies), and no out-of-pocket cost for the customer created a new category of value propositions.

The difference between the traditional use of technology and value propositions based on so-called habit-forming technologies is depicted in Figure 2.1. In the old days, the whole development budget was spent on coding business rules and database structures. The user experience was considered of secondary importance at best, resulting in application windows literally crammed from top to bottom with fields and menu buttons. With the rise of the internet and mobile

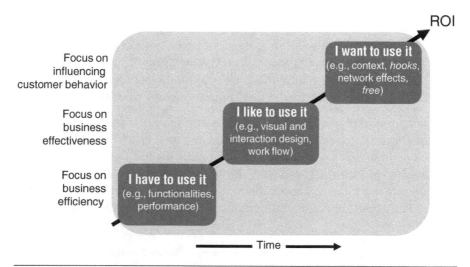

Figure 2.1   From conscious to unconscious use of technology

platform, companies started to pay more attention to graphic design, intuitive workflows, and all other elements that make an application (web or otherwise) pleasant to interact with for both current and potential customers.

The logical next step was to look for ways to convert *potential* customers into *actual* customers and maximize the revenue streams from digital channels. When done well, habit-forming value propositions can be a huge source of both revenue and profit. Many companies are happy when one employee generates $100k–$150k in revenue per year. Compare that with the $1,355,434 per employee for Facebook in 2014 ($12.47 billion in revenue; 9,200 employees).[1]

Technology can be a huge business multiplier in the right human hands.

The introduction of virtual reality and augmented reality is likely to take the impact of technology on our habits to the next level, as do technologies that provide more insight into our health (e.g., DNA mapping, continuous calorie and blood pressure tracking), and the ability of 3-D printing to turn every individual into a creative manufacturer.

The consumer as a creator of goods or services is part of a broader trend whereby companies are part of an interdependent network. Enabled by the widespread adoption of the internet, everybody on this planet is both a potential customer and supplier for a company. Called crowdsourcing, Boudreau and Lakhani[iii] identified four ways that companies can use the skill sets of individuals to realize value:

- **Contests**—solving complex or novel problems through large-scale and diverse independent experimentation
- **Collaborative communities**—aggregating a large number of small contributions into one value proposition
- **Complementors**—encouraging innovative solutions to users' many different problems with the companies' value proposition
- **Labor markets**—allocate discrete tasks more efficiently and flexibly than is possible internally (also known as the *gig economy*)

The first three skill sets in the list are more or less related to innovation, *the key source of future company revenue and margin.* In 2006, IBM organized an idea contest called *Innovation Jam*, and then invited their customers and employees to participate. The more than 140,000 participants yielded more than 46,000 ideas at a much lower cost than possible with an internal R&D department.[iv] The American defense research institution, Defense Advanced Research

---

[1] Revenue does not equal profit, but the large gap combined with labor cost being a large cost driver for any company is a clear indicator that habit-forming value propositions have the potential to be very lucrative.

Projects Agency, invited the public to play with an ACTUV tactics simulator—a submarine simulator. The objective was to integrate some of the best anti-submarine warfare (ASW) tactics and maneuvers that have been observed in-game into the software of the ASW continuous trail unmanned vessel (ACTUV). To connect companies and institutions that are less well-known by the general public, intermediate platforms like Innocentive, IdeaConnection, and Innoget were created to crowdsource research and development. Other platforms focus on marketing (e.g., CMNTY Corporation, Zooppa) or intelligence and prediction (e.g., Lumenogic, Ushahidi).

For TaskRabbit and Uber, individuals are a source of labor, allowing the company to focus on their core activities: marketing, legal, and IT teams that are responsible for the platform that matches demand and supply. Airbnb, Facebook, and Twitter can also be considered crowdsourcing business models as none of them supplies the service consumed by the customer. Private individuals, and sometimes companies, are the ones that provide the rooms (e.g., Airbnb) and content (e.g., Facebook and Twitter).

Technology allows the company to access an infinite set of skills and knowledge.

Besides increasingly advanced technology-enabled business models and capitalizing on the opportunity to leverage on the skill sets of seven billion people, IT also needs to formulate an answer to open source. Like crowdsourcing, it is part of a broader trend called share economy. Besides access to additional value streams (e.g., freemium business models), releasing software code or hardware designs raises the attractiveness as an employer, improves allocation of scarce resources, boosts brand awareness, disrupts the competition, and expands the size of the ecosystem or platform.

How much to open source depends on the business model and overall vision of the company. Apple prefers to keep their cards close and is not flattered by other companies copying their designs,[2] while Red Hat shares all of its code with the community, relying on value-adding support services for its revenue streams. Open source is also a powerful tool to disrupt the revenue streams of competitors. People used to pay for e-mail and storage services before Google introduced a business model whereby ads are used to cover the cost instead of monthly subscription fees. IBM followed a similar path when it was unable to compete with Microsoft in the server space. It adopted Linux, an open-source operating system, to undercut the licensing prices of its competitor and regain lost market share.

---

[2] There are exceptions, including the Swift development language and the Darwin operating system.

For companies with a platform business model, it is crucial to quickly attract a large group of both producing and consuming users. Sharing code lowers the entry barrier for developers to build on top of a platform and improve its overall quality. In 2014, more than 1,000 developers contributed to the 107 open source projects initiated by Facebook.[v] By July 2015, Google had released 20 million lines of code and over 900 projects as part of their open-source initiative.[vi] Another way to boost a platform business model is setting the standard—like the way Rackspace and NASA did with their OpenStack project. By being first, or at least early, in combination with adopting an open-source policy, a company can create a community and hence, momentum that makes it difficult for competitors to catch up.

The share economy and the emphasis on renting and sharing instead of owning have been embraced by Gen Y. It is the fastest growing customer and labor segment—challenging habits, rules, and other structures that older generations take for granted. The habits of Gen Y are shaped by social media sharing, such as Google (*Why learn facts?*) and instant gratification (*I'll get it when I want it.*). In order to lead in digital markets, companies not only have to create value propositions tailored to this customer segment, but also find ways to be attractive as an employer.

Technology can fundamentally change the way companies do business.

Regardless of the technology density of the business model, humans are and will always be at the center of the value realization process. Only people can turn the share economy into a market opportunity and turn the potential added value of habit-forming and other disruptive technologies into realized value. The principle of being *less defensive, more offensive* is therefore an invitation to regularly answer the following questions.

Considering the impact of new technologies on companies' market position, strategy, and business model:

- What are the new priorities of the leadership team? What can be done to ensure that the managers *walk the talk*?
- Which soft and hard skill sets decrease in value, and which are the ones to invest in? What can be done to attract and retain the professionals who are vital to future success?
- Which skills sets should be part of the business domain, and which should be part of the IT domain? What should be sourced externally?
- At what velocity should the business and IT move toward the desired direction? What is the optimal change approach?

The next part of this chapter is dedicated to providing at least some answers.

2.2 HOW TO BECOME LESS DEFENSIVE, MORE OFFENSIVE

Technology is abundant, easy to copy, and therefore unsuitable as a source of sustainable competitive advantage. It requires creativity, intelligence, perseverance, and all those other traits that only humans possess to turn technology into a differentiating hybrid or digital value proposition. Brian Solis, principal analyst at Altimeter Group made a similar observation:[vii] "*We already found that companies that lead digital transformation from a more human center actually bring people together in the organization faster and with greater results.*" Transformation is equal to change and only leaders can effectively influence the behavior of the people surrounding them—managers and bureaucracy cannot.

2.2.1 Leadership

Soon, all but the most complex and creative activities will be automated; reshaping the composition of the workforce—large, homogeneous, and moderately skilled will be replaced by small, heterogeneous, highly skilled, and motivated. The leadership style has to evolve accordingly.

According to Libert, Wind, and Beck Fenley,[viii] digitalization requires an open and agile organization, instead of an operating model whereby "*all insight and direction comes from the top. In short, the autocratic Commander, whether brilliant or misguided, just won't cut it anymore.*" Highly educated employees want to take ownership and expect their leaders to trust them to stay within pre-agreed boundaries. The added value of highly skilled team members is also reflected by the following quote from Angela Ahrendts, senior vice president at Apple: "*Everyone talks about building a relationship with your customer. I think you build one with your employees first.*"

One only has to look at Silicon Valley to see the impact of people as a key driver of company value. In her book *Regional Advantage: Culture and Competition in Silicon Valley and Route 128*, Anna Lee Saxenian, professor at the University of California, Berkeley, points out that the success of Silicon Valley is firmly based on people, culture, and connections. She explains why other regions aspired but were never able to replicate its success. In Silicon Valley, job hopping, peer networking, and sharing were the norm—fostering innovation and consequently, value creation.

Innovation is a key driver of change and the most valuable trait of leaders is their ability to remove the natural tendency of people to resist change. Resistance occurs when people feel they have lost control and/or pride, feel insecure about their competency, or are confronted with excessive uncertainty, surprises, or new routines.[ix] However, that is exactly what happens when an analog business model has to reinvent itself. Leading a team faced with this challenge requires somebody with a high intelligence quotient (IQ) and emotional quotient (EQ). People will utilize a high IQ to formulate a tantalizing vision and the strategy to get there, while people with a high EQ will excel when it comes to self-awareness, self-regulation, motivation, empathy, and social skills.[x]

Traditionally, IT is considered a suitable career path for students with high IQs, so the importance of EQ may at first sight seem overrated. But consider the following trends: more emphasis on user experience and habit-forming technologies; the convergence of business and IT domains; the automation of increasingly complex standard tasks; and the emphasis of the business on innovation and speed-to-market. These trends can only be dealt with effectively by business-savvy, assertive, highly skilled, adaptable, and creative people. That is the type of employees that every company wants—and they know it. To lure and retain them, the company needs to inspire and support them in their self-actualization and personal development. Employers aspire to hire leaders who score high on IQ *and* EQ.

More to the point, digitalization requires a renaissance of charismatic leadership, reversing its decline. The larger and older the company, the more likely *"charismatic authority is succeeded by a bureaucracy controlled by a rationally established authority or by a combination of traditional and bureaucratic authority."*[xi] Hybrid and digital markets are too dynamic and complex for finely grained and strictly enforced governance and control frameworks.

However, before a leader can channel the right inspiration and knowledge to the right person at the right moment, she or he first has to define the future direction and key objectives. Hale mentions two key skills to point a high-performance team in the right direction:[xii]

- **Focus on results**—this aspect includes clearly stating the goals and strategy; what the ground rules are to achieve them; what is open for discussion and what is not; the translation of team goals into personal objectives; and defining how benefits and success are measured.
- **Consistency of focus**—the communication message of the leader has to be consistent and she or he has to *walk the talk*. Too much change leads to distraction, confusion, and frustration while people change their behavior based on observable acts by their leaders. The visible rules have to match the invisible ones.

At the same time, market realities demand a certain level of flexibility. Technology, customer demand, and competitor behavior are in a constant flux, affecting both the present and future market position. Microsoft struggled for years to reinvent itself when mobile and consumerization disrupted its traditional business model. With the appointment of Satya Nadella as CEO, defending existing market spaces was replaced by a strategy based on the *mobile first, cloud first* principle. While Microsoft's new direction seems to hit the right mark, the CEOs of Acer, BlackBerry, AMD, and HTC are still struggling to revitalize their business models, demonstrating the difficulty of such an undertaking.

Besides adjusting the key objectives and strategy to stay connected to the market realities, a CIO also has to demonstrate situational leadership in two other areas. The first area covers the CIO's role toward the business. McLean and Tanner (1993) identified these four key roles (see Figure 2.2) after conducting a five-year study: technologist, enabler, innovator, and strategist.[xiii]

The technologist is focused on efficiency, optimizing the current technology, and the IT service portfolio. This is the traditional CIO who was focused on stability and technology, yet is all but extinct today. *Technology first* remains relevant only for an enterprise service bus, electronic data interchange, or other kinds of solutions that are invisible to the business.

The enabler is the CIO who acts as the ambassador of the mature business processes within the IT domain.[3] Due to the relative stability of the business demand and the technology portfolio, these first two IT leadership roles are closely related to foundation IT. When the business model is (or will be) technology rich and targets dynamic markets, the innovator and strategist leadership roles become important.

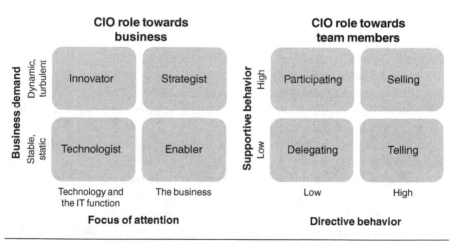

Figure 2.2   The CIO as a situational leader (adapted from McLean and Tanner [1993] and Paul Hersey and Ken Blanchard [1972])

---

[3] As mentioned in Chapter 1, these mature primary business processes are the moneymakers of the business and should be treated accordingly by the CIOs and the IT team.

The innovator provides the business with one or more platforms for experimentation and innovation, proactively updates technologies (e.g., replace Flash with HTML5 on the corporate website) and reengineers proof of concept when they turn out to be successful (e.g., from Mendix app to Microsoft.net app).

When the CIO puts on the hat of strategist, the objective changes to that of ensuring that the business understands both the strategic upsides (e.g., new market opportunities) of new technologies and their downsides (e.g., disrupts existing business model).

The CIO as a jack-of-all-trades does not stop here. Situational leadership is also expected when interacting with individual team members. When the business digitalizes, the IT team has to become less of a technologist and more of an enabler and strategist. The two archetype leadership styles available can be labeled *velvet glove* and *iron fist*. The latter refers to leaders that have a dominant and extroverted personality, and combined with a clear vision, they can be successful entrepreneurs. In large corporations, *iron fist* leaders are those who openly aspire to the position of a C-level executive due to the status that comes with it and the mandate to dictate what others have to do.

Mature companies that employ highly skilled individuals are better off with a leader who focuses on enabling the rest of the team to be productive and successful. Robert K. Greenleaf introduced the term *servant leadership* for leaders who scored high on EQ. They use charisma, soft skills, and inspiration to achieve the desired results, instead of sticks and carrots. Servant leadership emphasizes serving others, a holistic approach to work, promoting a sense of community, and sharing of decision-making rights.[xiv] It is very similar to the operational leadership role of Scrum Master in agile development teams.

The ideal leader is able to mix elements from both archetypes to maximize the effectiveness of the team and its individual members. The iron fist is a blunt instrument, demoralizing the team when used too often, while the velvet glove encourages laziness and complacency.

At the team level, it is the culture that requires considerable attention of the leader, as it is an important source of both positive momentum and resistance. When engaged in a one-on-one conversation with an individual team member, it is the maturity of the individual (e.g., knowledge, skills, self-confidence) and properties of the task that shape the optimal leadership style.

A popular model for situational leadership at team and individual levels is depicted at the right side of Figure 2.2. Besides offering differentiation, this model by Paul Hersey and Ken Blanchard also recognizes the ability of individuals and teams to mature from being incapable and insecure to being very able and confident.[xv] In other words, individuals and teams go through a life cycle when offered the right guidance and support by their leaders.

The situational leadership concepts described here are applicable to analog, hybrid, and native digital business models; however, this does not make them of equal importance. In hybrid and digital markets, advances in automation allow for a reduction in IT headcount (e.g., cloud, software-defined data center, application containers) while these companies rely on an increasing amount of company revenue and profit on digital value propositions and channels. Combine both and a small but highly skilled and motivated core IT team emerges.

A similar trend can be observed at the company level. The average revenue per employee tends to be much higher for native digital business models as compared to analog business models. The time and resources dedicated by Google and Amazon on getting and retaining productive, successful employees is no coincidence. If anything, the human factor becomes even more important for future success than it is today.

2.2.2 Culture

When digitalization meets an analog culture, things get interesting. The better the past and current financial result, the larger the coalition resisting any change. Change calls for embracing new patterns in strategy, processes, and behavior as a team and as individuals, inviting a sense of loss. Behavioral patterns can take years to change, making them a force to be reckoned with.

Company-specific behavioral patterns bond individuals together into a group. Newcomers are taught how to behave, formally or informally, reinforcing the *this-is-how-we-do-things-around-here* pattern. The culture of a company is shaped by:

- **The external environment**—when a team is used to easily satisfy customers in a stable market with few competitors, they will lack the habits required to fend off newcomers with disruptive business models
- **The primary process**—a team building handmade custom cars for wealthy customers share different do's and don'ts than a team that is employed by a mass production car manufacturer
- **The leadership and management style**—a mistake can be treated as a source of learning or reason for dismissal
- **The strategy and key objectives**—internationalization, mergers and acquisitions, entering new markets, or investing in new business models all expose the group to new cultural influences

A classic but still relevant model of business cultures is the typology described by Harrison[xvi] and Handy.[xvii] It identifies four basic culture types: power (Zeus), role (Apollo), task (Athena), and person (Dionysus). Person-focused cultures can be observed in many consulting firms, as consultants require little managerial oversight and are, or at least consider themselves to be, capable and confident. Hierarchy is frowned upon in a role culture—very different from companies with a power culture. In a power culture, one or two people make the decisions while the rest of the organization executes.

Within a role culture, bureaucratic structures and rules dominate. Large corporations in stable markets and government agencies are typical examples of this category. As long as the employee follows the procedures to the letter, slow but steady advancement is almost guaranteed. A task culture is prevalent when influence is based on skill and expertise. The whole team is dedicated to serving the customer. Everything else (e.g., from structure to learning, from mistakes to preventing waste), is of secondary importance.

The negative side effects of a culture and how one leads to another are depicted in Figure 2.3. Most start-ups are based on the energy and vision of one or two people. Their 100+ hour workweeks push the company from the incubator to an initial public offering.

Despite their efforts, there is a point in time when direct oversight has to be supplemented by structural elements in order to scale further. Role descriptions, procedures, governance, policies, controls, and everything else that most entrepreneurs dislike allow a business model to grow and mature. As the business model and market matures, companies tend toward spending more time on standardizing the value proposition, business process, and underpinning IT systems. The company slowly adopts a role culture.

It was this culture—optimized for efficiency—that caused market leaders to become laggards when their analog business models were disrupted by

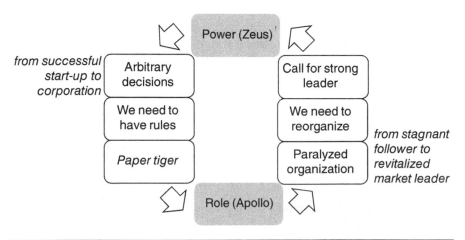

Figure 2.3   Culture as a flow (adapted from Harrison [1972] and Handy [1976])

digitalization. They became paralyzed, bankrupt, forcibly restructured, or an acquisition of other companies.

Just as cultural transformations have to be proactively managed, so too, do cultural differences. Most marketing departments have a task culture, very different from the role-oriented bookkeepers. With the need to differentiate between foundation IT and entrepreneurial IT, cultural clashes can even be expected within the confines of the IT department. Zoom in further to foundation IT, and one can observe that project and development teams tend to be more task-oriented than the colleagues who are responsible for operations and support.[xviii]

Cultural differences are a source of friction and delay that is unacceptable when speed-to-market is a key business driver. Teams that are responsible for entrepreneurial IT had to find a way to address this threat. One of the solutions that subsequently emerged is called DevOps; it closely integrates the business, software development, and operations into one task-oriented team, which minimizes friction. Authority (power), procedures (role), and the individual (person) are of secondary importance. What counts is deploying the most valuable features as quickly as possible and having someone knowledgeable available when a business user calls with an issue.

Besides pragmatism, task-orientation, constant learning, and speed, digitalization also requires an above-average risk appetite. Considered almost a poison in companies with a role culture, the shift from analog to hybrid or native digital business models increases the uncertainty and complexity of the business model. Teams with a task or power culture are therefore better suited when confronted with change, as they are more adaptable. Furthermore, uncertainty is a source of downside *and* upside —a fact that is often forgotten in large and stable organizations:[xix] "*Risks are random variables, mapping unforeseen future states of the world into values representing profits and losses.*"

But then again, even digital business models mature and a task-oriented team today may well turn into a role-oriented laggard in five years, given the chance. Only constant vigilance can prevent complacency from seeping in when times are good. Nobody is looking forward to the Biblical seven bad years that follow the seven good ones, as found in Genesis 41.

Changing a culture when it has time to embed itself within the company is difficult due to its intangible nature. A memo, presentation, or new policy may give a manager the impression that things have changed, but the painful truth is that things tend to continue glacially the same way as they did before. Hence the question: what can be done to effectively change the behavior of a team or individual?

2.2.3 Change

Rationally, every executive, manager, and employee understands that the company they work for has to remain in touch with market realities and act accordingly. The constant stream of companies that are struggling with some type of crisis—strategic, earnings, liquidity, or even a *Chapter 11*—is therefore counterintuitive at first sight. However, even at a personal level, something similar can be observed. The more ordinary the skill set of the employee, the more likely the job can be automated. Despite the widespread public attention for this trend, many employees still lack a sense of urgency. It is part of human nature to think that bad things only happen to others[4]—market and technology shifts don't affect them or the company they work for. Until, eventually, the pink slip arrives. Then the need to change is no longer an abstraction.

When a company or individual hits the proverbial wall, radical change is required. This type of change is infrequent, disruptive, forced, and of strategic importance. When the company or individual remains aligned with its external environment, change can be incremental. Incremental change[5] is continuous, focused on improvements, bottom-up, and emergent. Lean, *Kaizen*, the Deming circle, and agile methods and philosophies all fit in this category. Tools that are available to companies that require a radical change program include business process reengineering, rationalization of the product-market portfolio, large-scale outsourcing, and selling parts of the company. Some of the negative side effects of radical changes include losing highly skilled workers, low employee morale, and consequently, poor customer service. Radical change is therefore something best avoided.[6]

In some cases, companies have no choice but to restructure, due to things like unforeseeable technological disruption. Nevertheless, the majority of the

---

[4] This behavior is known as optimism bias, unrealistic optimism, or comparative optimism.

[5] Please note that one person may perceive a change as incremental, while the same change is perceived as radical by another. The account manager uses a new tool for expense reporting once a month (incremental change), while the bookkeeper uses it four hours a day for expense reporting (radical change).

[6] As the world is not black and white, a few words of caution from Benner and Tushman (2003): "*Thus, while process management activities drive innovation, the focus on variation reduction, search for incremental improvements in routines, and increased proficiency through repetition of organizational activities ensures that this innovation will be in the neighborhood of existing capabilities.*" In other words, too much focus on processes affects the capability of both business and IT to engage in radical innovation over time, such as being able to act quickly on disruptive start-ups. Source: Exploitation, Exploration, and Process Management: The Productivity Dilemma Revisited, Mary J. Benner and Michael L. Tushman, The Academy of Management Review, Vol. 28, No. 2 (Apr. 2003), pp. 238–256.

crises can be avoided by converting awareness into action—more specifically, the ability to take *appropriate* action. According to Donald Sull, most leaders and managers recognize threats early and initiate a series of responses, but fail to overcome the company's *active inertia*.[xx] Closely related to culture, active inertia is the team's tendency to follow ingrained patterns even when confronted with dramatic environmental shifts. To prevent failure, the leaders and managers should be vigilant so that:

- Strategic frames don't become blinders,
- Processes don't become routines,
- Relationships don't become shackles, and
- Values don't become dogmas.

Technology can also be a source of active inertia. It took Google Apps years to gain a foothold in the market that had been dominated by Microsoft Office, due to the following three characteristics of IT:

- **Increasing returns**—the initial investment in a new technology platform is high. With that said, once the developers become familiar with a programming language, the cost per function point, epic, or user story decreases. The application of lessons learned and the reuse of functional components, templates, and front-end designs further drive down cost, in time.
- **Network effects**—with so many people using Facebook, Twitter, and Adobe pdf documents, alternatives become less interesting. Within companies, application rationalization initiatives pursue similar effects by reducing the number of applications with overlapping functionalities, reducing both direct cost, such as licensing, and indirect cost brought on by things such as incompatibility issues.
- **Scalability**—when operations teams are familiar with Linux hosting, adding a virtual server is a matter of a few mouse clicks. The same applies to adding database capacity and accommodating the needs of additional development teams. However, ask that same Linux team to install a Windows server and things may take a while.

Embedding a culture that champions incremental change requires more than a shared sense of necessity, as seen in Figure 2.4.[xxi] Without a clear objective or vision, the team initiates well-meant but ultimately ineffective actions. The team as a whole has to move in one direction at a time. Closely related to the confusion that results from a lack of vision is chaos. The right person has to execute a specific task or decide on a topic at a certain moment in time.

Besides a plan to provide the necessary structure, change also requires resources. When the team is already regularly burning the midnight oil to finish

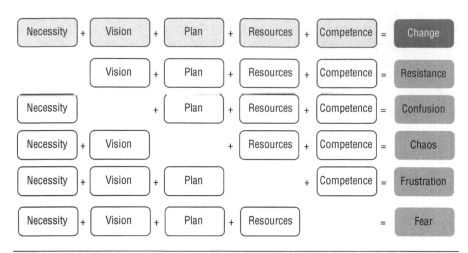

Figure 2.4   The many facets of effective organizational change (T. Knoster 1991)

the existing to-do list, expect frustration when adding several more items. And last but not least, there is fear—the emotion that pops up when an individual or team is asked to do something they don't feel comfortable with or are under-equipped to deal with. Unfortunately, fear of the unknown is often interpreted by the manager as resistance.

Another beginners' mistake is taking short cuts. One of the major contributions of the Information Technology Infrastructure Library (ITIL) is the emphasis on delivering user-oriented end-to-end services—like transaction processing instead of technology components, such as applications, databases, servers, and housing. Both the user and business executive get their own single point of contact, shielding them from the kitchen where all the magic happens. It is the quality and price of the dining experience that counts.

Bringing this kind of a paradigm shift to a successful conclusion requires more than writing procedures, implementing a service management tool, and training the staff. Implementing end-to-end processes requires a redistribution of mandate—upsetting the existing power balance. The larger and more stable the company and the more time mid-level managers have had for turf wars, the more likely the initiative will be frowned upon. An ITIL-in-name-only implementation is the result.

More recently we observed similar results with agile. Employees were appointed product owner or Scrum Master, sent to one or more training sessions, and agile was assumed to be implemented. Let us elaborate with a case study.

2.3 IT SERVICE PROVIDER ADOPTS AGILE

A mid-size IT service provider was founded 30 years ago and specialized over the years in developing and maintaining custom software. The employees in their 50s and early 60s, about half the population, regularly recalled a time when customer demand for IT outstripped supply (*the good old times, when life was better*). They knew everything there was to know about function point analysis, waterfall software development, and project management. Until five years ago, the company was led by a dominant leader who implemented strict procedures and controls. Hence, the culture was a mix of power (Zeus) and role (Apollo).

Around eight years ago, the financial performance of the company started to decline. For three years the leadership team was able to mask several structural weaknesses by postponing investments in new technologies and other areas. Eventually, the board of directors intervened and a new leadership team was appointed. Around the same time, several younger developers and project managers approached their managers with the request to attend an agile training course. Customers also started to inquire about this new development approach. What happened next was a period where the pendulum swung from one extreme to the other, to eventually settle somewhere in the middle.

The developers and project managers that attended the agile training came back with a fire in their eyes. Everything from the past was declared obsolete; the future was to use agile software development. Agile was also an easy sell for the account managers as it:

- Puts the customer first,
- Delivers rapidly (e.g., develop and deploy most-valuable requirements first),
- Strives to eliminate waste (e.g., elaborated requirements analysis for a proof of concept),
- Amplifies learning (e.g., customer feedback after every sprint demo),
- Makes decisions as late as possible (e.g., adjust priorities backlog along the way),
- Empowers the team (e.g., encourage instead of motivate),
- Has built-in integrity (e.g., soft controls, authority based on expertise, not hierarchy), and
- Sees the whole picture (e.g., work toward a shared business goal).

Hence, there is a lot to like about agile. Implementing agile turned out to require more than sending employees to a training, however. It also failed to be the silver bullet the agile demagogues declared it to be.

2.3.1 Risk Averse Customer Segment

There are two ways an IT service provider can realize a custom application for a client. The first involves the client hiring resources (e.g., Scrum Master, developers) who realize the solution while under the client's supervision. The key advantage of this sourcing model for the client is flexibility; the main downside is a higher risk profile (e.g., pay for lower than expected velocity and wrong design decisions). The responsibility of the IT service provider is limited to providing skilled resources at a pre-agreed hourly rate.

This mid-size IT service provider had a different value proposition. It targeted customers that were outsourcing fixed-scope, fixed-price projects. This customer segment expects the vendor to deliver a fully-functional application for a certain price, thereby transferring part of the inherent risks related to software development to the vendor, including reworks due to quality issues or access to the right skill sets. It is a type of project that is popular among companies with a relatively stable and predictable business model. Here, the bonuses and advancements of senior managers depend on avoiding nasty surprises like IT projects with large cost overruns. Procurement officers love this sourcing model for similar reasons; they want to minimize the financial uncertainty of their contract portfolio. In short, the key decision makers of this customer segment tend to be risk averse and they want to be in control.

For years, the IT service provider had the perfect tool to fulfill the needs of these customers: waterfall software development. To use the comparison of building a house, every nook and cranny was specified and agreed upon up-front, allowing for an accurate budget and planning estimation. Then, agile started to take the development world by storm.

Agile development is based on the premise that the external environment is too uncertain and complex to specify all requirements up-front. The application evolves based on a continuous flow of new information from things like customer feedback and competitor behavior that becomes available over the duration of the project. For this reason, the project is divided into iterations or *sprints* that take two or three weeks to complete. During this period, requirements are specified, coded, tested, demoed, and deployed. Furthermore, those requirements that are most valuable to the business are developed and deployed first, improving speed-to-market.

The benefits of agile were so obvious that even risk-averse senior managers and procurement officers showed interest. They also saw signs that start-ups with disruptive business models were about to enter their market. Agile was considered to be an easy fix. It turned out to be more complex than that, as agile represents a different organizational paradigm.

Neither decision makers on the client side nor the decision makers at the IT service provider grasped this fact when signing the contract that combined fixed-scope, fixed price, and agile.

2.3.2 What Went Wrong

When the IT service provider replaced waterfall with agile, it initially only disrupted the software development process at the *operational level*. Developers and project managers attended the agile and Scrum Master trainings and persuaded the managers who were responsible for software development and account managers to give it a try. The account managers were easiest to convince as *agile* was easy to sell (at least at first; later on they had to go back to the client to request a budget increase). Most mid-level managers were skeptical, but knew that organizational momentum was against them. Their lack of buy-in combined with the emphasis of agile on self-organizing teams soon resulted in isolated development islands. None of the responsible managers knew what the teams were doing until it was too late.

Summary: agile is more than a new toy for a developer.

As mentioned, decision makers can operate under a different set of rules than are required for a successful agile project. The decision makers of the IT service provider were desperate for new business while their clients' decision makers had stringent budgets and targets to meet that drive the design of the contract. After involving their legal department, the end result was a contract with the flexibility of a concrete wall. Every conceivable risk was covered in clauses, thereby implicitly assuming a stable and predictable future. Agile represented the exact opposite of that assumption: the future is uncertain and complex, requiring flexibility, adaptability, and continuous innovation.

When both the IT service provider's and the client's decision makers failed to board the agile train, it was bound to derail (see Figure 2.5).

Summary: agile software development requires an agile sourcing relationship and contract.

Consequently, the client's decision makers also underestimated the impact that agile had at the operational level. The product owner is the team member with the vision and is the owner of the product backlog. She or he translates the need of the business users into prioritized epics and user stories. Hence, it is the product owner who determines whether a sprint should be dedicated to adding a roof to the house or repainting the windows.

When the product owner prioritizes the latter for the last sprint of the project, it is not the fault of the IT service provider if the house is uninhabitable.

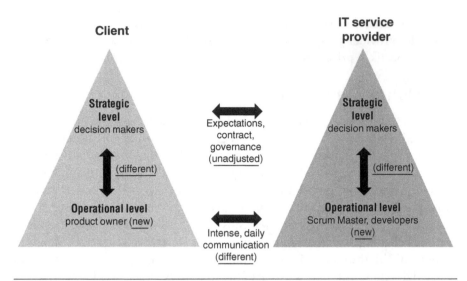

Figure 2.5 Impact of agile development on the communication structure

It is the fault of the client who appointed the product owner and therefore is responsible to reappoint somebody with the right skill set and mandate. Nevertheless, the client's decision makers expected the IT service provider to deliver a house they could actually live in. It was what they received the previous times and was formalized in the contract. Hence, the IT service provider soon found itself stuck between a rock and a hard place.

> *Summary*: the client underestimated the impact of agile on their own organization.

> *Summary*: the IT service provider failed to enforce the appointment of an effective product owner.

The communication and collaboration gap between the operational level and strategic level at the client side was not the only problem. Instead of organizing the resources in separate teams to optimize utilization, agile promotes teams that include all of the skills and expertise—such as business analysts, interaction designers, developers, testers, and operational leadership—that are necessary to produce working software. Combined with self-organization, the desire to create a safe learning environment, and focus on the customer, the Scrum teams of the IT service started to avoid management oversight. Initially, they even refused to report to the manager responsible for software development on their velocity or other basic performance criteria.

The disconnect and lack of trust prevented early warning signs that the project was in trouble from reaching the account managers. After the fifth sprint, the teams knew they were never going to reach the velocity required to deliver the desired end result. Neither the product owner nor the Scrum Master raised a red flag until three weeks before the planned go-live date. At that point, the Scrum Master deposited the problem on the desk of the software development manager, demanding additional budget and time. In one day, the project went from *on schedule* to *in crisis*.

Summary: the Scrum team was allowed to act as a black box.

Effective agile development requires mutual trust and close collaboration between all hierarchical levels. It is a culture whereby project managers are considered a source of help, instead of control. The shift from a mixed power (Zeus) and role (Apollo) culture to a pragmatic and effective task (Athena) culture at the IT service provider took several years. Some team members were afraid to take responsibility after years of solely executing tasks. Others seized the opportunity to create isolated fiefdoms. These and many more had to be addressed before the team eventually stabilized again.

2.3.3 Lessons Learned

In the wake of some expensive failures, the IT service provider steadily became more proficient in selling and executing iterative software development projects. People were assigned new roles, and in some cases reassigned a second time when the skill gap turned out to be too wide to bridge.

When assigning the role of product owner to a business analyst, he or she becomes the key delegate of the business. The product owner makes decisions on behalf of the business domain, representing both operational and strategic stakeholders. In the case of conflicting interests, it is the product owner who plays a vital role in smoothing things out. However, most business analysts are not used to decision making; they are business subject matter experts who advise and facilitate the business on the effective use of technology. Similarly, an excellent project manager or developer is not necessarily a good Scrum Master.

In general, it is the soft skill gap that is most difficult to bridge. Subject matter expertise is something a person can learn by reading, talking to people, and training. Communication, collaboration, and managerial skills are far more difficult to improve. They are based on deeply ingrained behavioral patterns.

Another generic lesson learned is appointing a pragmatic agile coach. Demagogues tend to be blind in the organizational and commercial context that agile has to operate in. Software development is not a sterile, isolated activity, but part of a complex and dynamic business model. A pragmatic agile coach knows when documentation, processes, and plans are unimportant (e.g., like proof of concept) or quite important (such as, software to run a nuclear power plant).

When working with distributed teams (e.g., nearshoring, offshoring), it is the agile coach who ensures that team members are aware of cultural differences, and intervenes when it affects the quality of interaction. In short, the agile coach stimulates, helps, guides, and teaches the team to be effective across a wide variety of situations.

Managers are not solely a source of control, but also of support—both direct and indirect. With the latter, the sales manager of the IT service provider took a liking to the agile process and introduced weekly stand-up meetings with the account managers. His objective was to stimulate team performance and utilize positive peer pressure by openly discussing the status of every individual lead, prospect, opportunity, win, and loss. Combined with the introduction of a team bonus, it increased the conversion rate of the sales funnels, as account managers started to help each other to be more successful. During stand-up meetings, the sales manager participated as an equal team member, providing his thoughts and ideas, but never judging.

Besides increasing the performance of the sales team, the initiative also increased the awareness within the company for agile. The perception started to shift from a toy to keep the developers happy, to a genuine company-wide source of added value.

After several project recoveries by line and project managers, the Scrum teams stopped acting like a clam shell that was hiding a valuable pearl. They finally understood that success required the IT service provider to act as part of one coherent team. It was no longer the Scrum team versus the management team, but one team with one shared goal. They found their new equilibrium.

REFERENCES

i. Goudreau, J. (March 2013). IBM CEO Predicts Three Ways Technology Will Transform the Future of Business. Link: http://www.forbes.com/sites/jennagoudreau/2013/03/08/ibm-ceo-predicts-three-ways-technology-will-transform-the-future-of-business/.

ii. Byrnes, N. (March 2015). Technology and Persuasion. Technology Review. Link: http://www.technologyreview.com/news/535826/technology-and-persuasion/.

iii. Boudreau, K. J. and Lakhani, K. R. (April 2013). *Using the Crowd as an Innovation Partner*. Harvard Business Review.

iv. Leimeister, J. M., Huber, M., Bretschneider, U. and Krcmar, H. (2009). Leveraging Crowdsourcing: Activation-Supporting components for IT-Based Ideas Competition. In: Journal of Management Information Systems (JMIS), Number: 1, Vol. 26, pp. 197–224.

v. Pearce, J. (2014). 12 Days of Open Source, Facebook. Link: https://code .facebook.com/posts/766306873424443/12-days-of-open-source.

vi. Source: https://developers.google.com/open-source/projects.

vii. Kapko, M. (July 2014). Enterprise Collaboration Will Drive Digital Transformation. CIO.com. Link: http://www.cio.com/article/2456097/ collaboration/enterprise-collaboration-will-drive-digital-transformation .html?source=CIONLE_nlt_enterprise_2014-07-23#tk.rss_itstrategy.

viii. Libert, B., Wind, J. and Fenley, M. Beck. (February 6, 2015). Is Your Leadership Style Right for the Digital Age? Knowledge at Wharton. Link: http:// knowledge.wharton.upenn.edu/article/the-right-leadership-style-for-the -digital-age/.

ix. Kanter, R. M. (September 2012). Ten Reasons People Resist Change, Harvard Business Review. Link: https://hbr.org/2012/09/ten-reasons-people -resist-change.

x. Goleman, D. (1995). *Emotional Intelligence, Why It Can Matter More Than IQ*

xi. Kendall, D. (1997). *Sociology in Our Times.*

xii. Hale, J. (2004). *Performance-Based Management: What Every Manager Should Do to Get Results.*

xiii. McLean, E. R. and Smits, S. J. (1993). The I/S Leader as "Innovator." In: J. F. Nunamaker, Jr. and R. H. Sprague, Jr. (Eds.), Proceedings of the Twenty-Sixth Hawaii International Conference on Systems Sciences, pp. 352–358.

xiv. Smith, C. (2005). Servant Leadership: the Leadership Theory of Robert K. Greenleaf. Link http://www.carolsmith.us/downloads/640green leaf.pdf.

xv. Hersey, P. and Blanchard, K. H. (1969). Life-cycle Theory of Leadership, Training and Development Journal 23, pp. 26–34.

xvi. Harrison, R. (1972). *Understanding Your Organization's Character.* Harvard Business Review.

xvii. Handy, C. B. (1976). *Understanding Organizations.*

xviii. Andersen, E. S. (2001). Understanding Your IT Project Organization's Character: Exploring the Differences between the Cultures of an IT Project and Its Base Organization, Proceedings of the 34th Hawaii International Conference on System Sciences.

xix. McNeil, A. J. (May 1999). Extreme Value Theory for Risk Managers, ETH Zentrum.

xx. Sull, D. (July–August 1999). Why Good Companies Go Bad. Harvard Business Review. Link: https://hbr.org/1999/07/why-good-companies-go-bad.

xxi. Knoster, T. (1991). Presentation in TASH Conference. Washington, D.C.

3

LESS INSIDE, MORE OUTSIDE

Less inside, more outside represents the ability to manage multiple heterogeneous customer segments.

Most people no longer distinguish between a product and marketing; the bottle *is* The Coca-Cola Company. A company and its products blend together, and the comments on Twitter and the number of *likes* on Facebook may well decide the future of a new product. On internal discussion forums, business users and executives share their thoughts on the progress of the latest IT project. The feedback may lack nuance, but so do consumer responses on Twitter.

Businesses have already learned how to use social media as a tool to attract and retain customers. IT has to follow suit as its monopoly is all but gone. The internet, mobile, and other technologies have considerably lowered the barrier of entry for thousands of external IT service providers who are looking for a slice of the IT budget pie. From a company's perspective, this is a good thing—as competition allows for better allocation of scarce resources, the business gets more for the same amount of money. It also means more exposure for the internal IT team to market forces, which was once the sole domain of the business portion of the company.

Besides the drive to realize more value from a given budget, market exposure also forces IT teams to invest in capabilities that are critical to the business. Think of serving customers consistently across multiple channels with a strong focus on user adoption and added value. The challenge is a golden opportunity for a proactive, business-savvy IT team while spelling the end for those that fail to make the transition. In the latter case, the business has no choice but to directly source from external IT service providers.

To build the capabilities that are required in order for businesses to grow in the markets of today and tomorrow, IT first has to understand them. For that reason, this chapter starts by describing several key properties of the heterogeneous, dynamic, and highly complex internal and external customer segments that are faced by IT and businesses, as it has to be a co-production. The second part provides the reader with several tools and pointers in the right direction, followed by two examples. The first one covers the digital transformation of Air New Zealand ten years ago, and the second involves a utility company that is embracing the *smart grid*. Table 3.1 provides three statements that cover the chapter as a whole.

Table 3.1   Statements to think about when reading this chapter

Statements
The customers and key partners of the business are the customers of IT.
The functional silos that most companies are organized in are a major inhibitor along the path to digital business models.
Success starts with the letter *P*—people, product, process, performance, price, place, and promotion.

3.1 WHY THIS PRINCIPLE MATTERS

Shifting customer behavior dramatically changed the definition of a branch in the banking sector. Instead of visiting a physical outlet, nine percent of the transactions by Bank of America customers in the fourth quarter of 2014 were conducted via a mobile device. In the bank's call with analysts, CEO Brian Moynihan noted that: "*We don't know exactly where this goes 'cause it will depend on customer behavior, but what we do know is that we have to dominate the physical side and the e-commerce online mobile side at the same time.*"[i] With that said, the transformation of analog value propositions and channels into hybrid or digital equivalents scratches only the surface.

Digitalization reshapes whole markets and industries. Business schools are threatened by massive open online courses, the blockchain technology underpinning Bitcoin is quickly turning into a major headache for banks, and the music industry is reluctantly getting used to companies like Spotify and Pandora. Instead of requiring every customer to incur an out-of-pocket expense, these business models tap into different revenue streams. Customers are offered a basic value proposition for free—paid by:

- Advertisements or cross-subsidization by complementary value propositions
- Offering the same customers value-adding features that they are willing to pay for (*freemium* or *premium*)—think of additional storage, quality of data (like photo resolution), or charging commercial companies

Customers love free goods, as free is even better than cheap. Introducing a business model that offers a free substitute for a product that customers currently have to pay for is therefore one of the most powerful ways to disrupt a market. As the future is unknown, companies have to regularly assess both the business model and the IT business model as the existing rules of the game, customer preferences, and revenue streams *can* be turned upside down any day. It's better to lead that shift than to lag behind.

Catering to the customers' desire for individuality is less disruptive than completely overturning the existing business model. Touched upon in the previous chapter, customers want more than a Ford Model T in any color as long as it is black. Companies like Netflix and Amazon mastered the skill of selling large numbers of unique items in relatively small quantities while still making a profit. Apple took this concept to the next level when it introduced the iPhone in 2007.

In July 2015, anyone owning an iPhone had access to 1.5 million apps and a music library of 30 million songs. Over the years, Apple has steadily added more functions (e.g., online payments and access to exclusive content, like bonus tracks and health and fitness tracking), creating a powerful barrier to entry for competitors and high switching costs for customers. Hence, many companies strive for a position similar to Apple as the alternative is obsolescence, or at best, joining the *invisible network*.

The latter represents the part of the ecosystem with no direct contact to customers. It affects banks, book publishers, app developers, and other companies and individuals that use one of the established customer-oriented ecosystems to sell their offerings.

In 2016, the battle to be *the* gateway to the customer was still undecided. BlackBerry and Nokia lost the race, while Microsoft and Sony were playing catch up. The players with the best cards seem to be Apple, Google, Facebook, Samsung, and Amazon. But one or two wrong moves, and the deck of cards may well look very different a few years down the road.

Another force disrupting business-to-customer (B2C) and business-to-business (B2B) markets is the miniaturization of hardware and smarter software. Soon, everybody and everything with a microchip will be networked to each other—a state better known as the Internet of Things (IoT). For consumers, the IoT combined with advanced analytics promises to provide highly relevant information (*show me only neighborhood restaurants at my current location*), more free time (e.g., a robot cleaning the house or the fridge ordering groceries), and new value-added services (e.g., predictive health monitoring or a digital personal assistant).

Take a leap into the future, and *the singularity* comes into view. The concept represents the ultimate fusion of humans and technology and was made popular by technology guru Ray Kurzweil in his 2005 book, *The Singularity Is Near*. He borrowed the term *singularity* from physics where it is used to describe the center of a cosmic black hole where all energy and mass is compressed to an infinite small point. The book indicates that the combination of Moore's law and the integration of IT, robotics, nanotechnology, and biology will eventually lead to conscious computers and humans living without a body. According to the *New York Times*, Kurzweil swallows some 150 pills daily to reduce the aging process in an effort to be there when that happens.

To be a business partner, IT has to sense and act on the fundamental shifts taking place in most B2C and B2B customer segments.

The fun does not stop there though. For IT, the key partners[1] of the business are also a customer segment. The world's leading provider of lithography systems[2] for the semiconductor industry, ASML collaborates with hundreds of external key partners. ASML focuses on the high value-added integration role, including product competence and manufacturing cycle times, relying on external partners for the design and manufacturing of specialized subsystems. With up to 90% of the total system cost sourced externally, key partners are deeply integrated into the value chain, having virtually unrestricted access to strategic information—such as technology and the product road map, R&D projects, and technological breakthroughs. As a result, key partners can tune both their investments into new innovations and manufacturing process to ASML. Obviously, it is the IT team that provides the platform to enable the world class collaboration and supply chain management (SCM) practices that are required by this complex, but very successful, interdependent network.

The collaboration between ASML and its key partners is nevertheless fairly traditional as it involves the delivery of physical components. Often enabled by recent advances in technology, other companies implemented more complex interdependent business models. Seed producer DuPont and farm equipment maker John Deere joined forces to improve the yield of seeds. Besides using GPS and other technologies to optimize the planting and fertilization of the seeds, yields are improved further by acting on data collected from soil tests, damage by pests, and weather services.

Nike and Apple also combined their strengths when creating the Nike+ fitness solution. The success of their synergy was demonstrated by reporting a user base of almost 30 million by the end of 2014.[ii] IBM integrated Facebook's ad-targeting technology into its retail suite. The combination allowed retailers to combine Facebook's user data with their own data, opening up the company for more personalized and effective customer relationships.

---

[1] See Chapter 6 for the difference between key partners and other external suppliers.

[2] Machines used to manufacture CPUs, GPUs, memory modules, and other types of microchips.

All mentioned relationships are based on the need of individual companies to specialize. In the year 1900, value chains were straightforward enough to be operated by one company. Over time, products steadily became more complex, creating a network of dozens or even thousands of interdependent entities (see Figure 3.1). Today, a B2C customer can also be a crowdsource supplier, using social platforms to both buy products and find work. There are also platforms reducing the *search stress* for B2B customers, and they too can have two roles. What all network entities share is a heavy reliance on IT.

The leading companies in such networks, like Ford's supply chain and Apple's ecosystem, have the most to gain from an uninterrupted, real-time flow of ideas, decisions, information, and data. They have to decide whether an electronic data interchange connection and access to the supply management system is adequate or more is needed. Suppliers considered by businesses to be of strategic

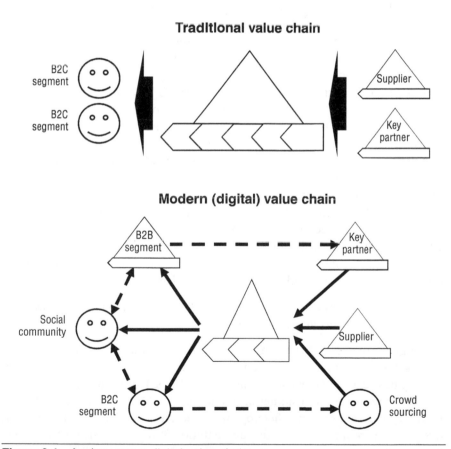

Figure 3.1   Analog versus digital value chain

importance should be flagged as such by IT teams. The companies' short- and long-term success may well depend on them.

To be a business partner, IT has to treat the key partners of the business as VIP customer segments.

Last, but certainly not least, are the internal customer segments besides that of external B2C customers, B2B customers, and key partners. The manufacturing department needs IT to facilitate the convergence of industrial IT and administrative IT. The latter being the traditional sweet spot of IT. Marrying *smart* machines with advanced analytics, SCM, and enterprise resource planning (ERP) opens the the door to dramatically improved financial performance. And every executive loves the sound of lower stock levels, less waste, and improved agility in the production process (e.g., smaller batches).

Simultaneously, the HR department wants a new, flashy intranet portal with all the relevant information for employees. CFOs want to cut cost by moving from an on-premise bookkeeping solution to software as a service (SaaS). It goes without saying that CFOs expect the current integration with the ERP system to be there after moving to the cloud; the same applies to regulatory compliance and security.

Business users expect an experience similar to the one on their phone or tablet. No more applications whereby interaction design was merely an afterthought or hurt your fingers due to the weird keyboard shortcut necessary to access certain functions. They expect to be treated as actual customers. When unhappy or disappointed with the solution provided by IT, they just step into the office of their manager and point her or him in the direction of an external IT service provider they found on the web.

It is neither fair nor the best decision for the company, but it does demonstrate a clear side effect of the technological maturity that we have reached. It allows for the democratization of IT decision making. New technologies and solutions enter a company both from the top down and bottom up. The rules of the game have changed, and IT teams have to adapt.

To be a business partner, IT has to treat the business users the same way the business treats its external customers.

The digital value chain has become at least as important as the value chain producing the actual service or product—both cross company boundaries, connecting upstream and downstream network entities. Due to their heavy reliance on IT, many represent customer segments for IT. They are neither static nor homogeneous, but dynamic, heterogeneous, and highly complex. The principle *less inside, more outside* is therefore an invitation to regularly answer the following questions.

Considering the impact of new technologies on a company's market position, strategy, and business model:

- Do we know the relevant trends in our external environment (e.g., the shift from analog to digital business model or deregulation)?
- Which external B2C or B2B customer segments are likely to be disrupted in the near future by a digital business model (e.g., based on freemium or crowdsourcing labor like Uber)? Better still, can we proactively introduce a disruptive business model ourselves?
- In case several B2C or B2B customer segments are under threat, which have the highest priority in the next six months? Which in twelve months?
- Which B2C, B2B, or key partner segments go to the next phase of their life cycle (e.g., introduction, growth, mature, or decline)?
- What are the key initiatives for our internal customer segments in the coming twelve months?

The next part of this chapter will provide at least some answers.

3.2 FROM INTERNAL FOCUS TO EXTERNAL FOCUS

Improving IT's capability to better serve external and internal customer segments starts with understanding the key differences between analog, hybrid, and digital business models. Each has its own barriers to entry from competitors and business challenges. Combined with the knowledge of market forces and trends that dominate digital markets, IT teams can position themselves as an equal partner when the business puts the digital strategy on the agenda.

3.2.1 Digital Business Strategy 101

New technologies don't change the basic laws of economics, but they do have the potential to change almost every other aspect of running a business. To prevent themselves from ending up on a burning platform,[3] executive teams should frequently reconsider the overall business strategy—like reframing the current dominant business model—and invest in scenario planning, such as the preparation for *what-if* situations. The higher the anticipated technology density of the market the company operates in, the higher the frequency and *aggressive* the scenarios should be.

---

[3] Former Nokia CEO Stephen Elop told his colleagues they were standing on a *burning platform* when former market leader Nokia was unable to effectively compete with Android and iOS.

A restaurant with a Michelin star can hardly benefit from IT. It is strictly an analog business model and will remain so for the years to come. When paying $150+ for a dinner, the customer expects to be served by a human being, not a robot. On the other hand, things are about to change in fast food restaurants. Both frying and serving will be automated to reduce cost and improve service consistency. While the business model of the restaurant with the Michelin star remains future-proof, the fast food industry is at risk of being disrupted by a competitor that completely reframes theirs.

Customer preference and competitors have ensured that most companies have already moved to at least a hybrid business model, as shown in Tables 3.2a and 3.2b. In some cases, shifts (like turning *dumb* lights and refrigerators into *smart* ones) had limited impact on business models. In other cases, they were more fundamentally disrupted—as Uber did with the taxi industry and Airbnb with the hotel business.

Table 3.2a   Technology density of the market drives strategy

	Analog	Hybrid	Digital
Key Properties	Analog value proposition (e.g., solution, content) and channels	(Partially) digital product and/or channels combined with analog products and/or channels	Digital value proposition (e.g., solution, content) and channels
Examples of Barriers to Entry Faced by New Entrants	• High investments in fixed assets and branding are required • Access to scarce resources (e.g., rare materials to make electronic components)	• Existing company can leverage on strong brand of analog business model to expand in digital markets • High investments in fixed assets a precondition for particular value proposition	• Lock-in through ecosystems or patents • Strong network effects favor first-movers/ fast-followers • Lack of exclusive content (e.g., music, TV series) or other IP rights
Examples of Business Challenges	• Access to cheap resources (e.g., steel, concrete, energy) or other sources • The need to stay ahead of copycat companies by differentiating products and/or services	• Creating a seamless cross-channel strategy (e.g., know the customer, individualized offerings, pricing) • Combining highly dynamic channels with more stable ones	• Catching the next disruptive wave at the right moment • Staying part of the *visible network* in B2C market • Abundance creates lack of attention and a need to differentiate from the rest • Lack of standards limit market adoption

Table 3.2b Technology density of the market drives strategy, continued

	Analog	Hybrid	Digital
Key Properties	Analog value proposition (e.g., solution, content) and channels	(Partially) digital product and/or channels combined with analog products and/or channels	Digital value proposition (e.g., solution, content) and channels
Examples of Business Models Prone to Disruption	• Home construction by advanced robotics and IoT • Logistics by autonomous cars, and later, by planes and ships • Dentists by advanced robotics in time • Hair salons by automation (admittedly, hair cutting is too complex and unlikely to be disrupted any time in the near future) • Expensive restaurants are unlikely to be disrupted due to the nature of the business	• Retail after Amazon • Cab rides after Uber • On the brink of being hybrid: cars, household appliances, clothes • Fast food industry (physical product, robots for cooking and serving)	• Anything that can be translated into 0s and 1s (e.g., video, music, magazines, information, communication, collaboration)
Business Trend	Shrinking, most companies with analog business models add at least digital channels and/or solutions	Growing fast due to: • Autonomous growth (e.g., Airbnb business model is a hybrid from day one) • Analog and digital business models turning hybrid	Fast growing, some companies with digital business models diversify by adding analog channels and solutions

It is not all bad news for established companies though. When they are able to overcome the organizational inertia, they have enough going for them to keep the competition at bay. While a start-up business may have a tantalizing vision and people with drive, it has no brand awareness or established customer relations. Combined with easy access to capital, deep domain expertise, and the fixed assets like physical warehouses and manufacturing equipment that are tied to the analog parts of the business model, established companies that are seeking success in the digital market are at an excellent starting position.

The current strengths, market position, differentiators, and core competences[4] are important inputs when defining, or even redefining, digital strategy. Digital strategy is a plan to realize a company's vision and key objectives in hybrid and digital markets. Depending on the importance of digital initiatives to the organization, digital strategy is either more operational in nature (e.g., the manner in which IT and customer-facing departments deliver a consistent cross-channel experience) or true to its name (e.g., transforming the analog business model in a disruptive digital equivalent). In the latter case, the following list from Laudon and Laudon may be of use, as it provides an overview of digital business models that companies can pick from:[iii]

- **Virtual storefront**—Tesla cuts out the middleman and sells directly to the consumer. Amazon aggregates the offerings of many producers, reducing the *search stress* for customers. Tesla benefits from lower cost, Amazon from customers paying for the convenience.
- **Information broker**—Information brokers aggregate useful information about certain topics (e.g., personal health) or product categories (e.g., electric energy) and presents it in an easily digestible way to the customer. Advertisement or a kickback from companies that have their information displayed generate the necessary revenue.
- **Transaction broker**—Mostly part of the invisible network, these companies save customers time and money by providing a seamless financial and/or logistical transaction. The revenue model is based on a fee per transaction.
- **Online marketplace**—From funding new ideas through Kickstarter to a parent selling used baby toys, both need a place where buyer and seller can meet. The companies providing these platforms earn revenue through advertising and transaction fees.
- **Content provider**—These companies own the right to sell or rent content (e.g., books, music, movies, or academic articles) or apps. Different payment structures exist, including flat monthly fees, and renting or buying per item.
- **Online service provider**—Think of access to online storage, but also SaaS providers like Salesfore.com. Revenue is generated through a freemium model or pay-per-use. With the explosive increase in SaaS offerings, this is the largest and most diverse category.

---

[4] Defined by Prahalad and Hamel as "*a harmonized combination of multiple resources and skills that distinguish a firm in the marketplace.*"

- **Virtual community**—Facebook, LinkedIn, WhatsApp, and forums are part of this category. These companies provide a platform for people with similar interests. Revenue is generated through advertisements and upselling (e.g., Facebook offering pay-to-play games).
- **Portal**—Largely surpassed by other business models, early entrants into the digital market, such as AOL and Yahoo, became billion-dollar companies by offering a versatile website with a wide variety of content (e.g., sports, news, finance, and weather) and functions (e.g., e-mail and chat). Advertisements are the main revenue source.

The preceding list should be considered as a starting point only, as the combination of human creativity and a constant stream of new technologies results in an almost limitless number of business opportunities and threats. Therefore, in hybrid and digital markets, the name of the game is business model innovation, both incremental and radical. And, in order to be more than just a mediocre player, it is important to appreciate the dominant forces at play in digital markets.

3.2.2 Dominant Market Forces and Trends

Overall, the internet and mobile access have a positive effect on the buying power of customers due to the level playing field forced upon companies. Pricing and other product information from dozens of sellers are available within a few clicks or swipes. Another positive for customers are the low switching costs for things like online storage and business models using advertisements and freemium to generate revenue.

To counter these effects, companies created value propositions with positive network effects and closed ecosystems. Google, Apple, and Microsoft control the operating system, apps, and content of their ecosystem, creating a convenient but walled garden for customers. All restrict both the export of existing apps and content to other ecosystems and the convenient access to non-approved apps and content. The result is a significant barrier against exiting the ecosystem, and thus, less buying power for the customer (see Figure 3.2).

Positive network effects occur when the value of the offering depends on the number of customers. Microsoft and Adobe used the effect to become the de facto standards for writing documents and Facebook used it to dominate social media. In two decades, Amazon became *the* global online retailer, reporting 244 million active users in 2014 and 54 million Amazon Prime customers in 2016. Here, too, the end game for these companies is less buying power for the customer.

At first sight, these companies may seem untouchable; however, Yahoo, Blackberry, Microsoft, Nokia, and Twitter demonstrate the thin line between

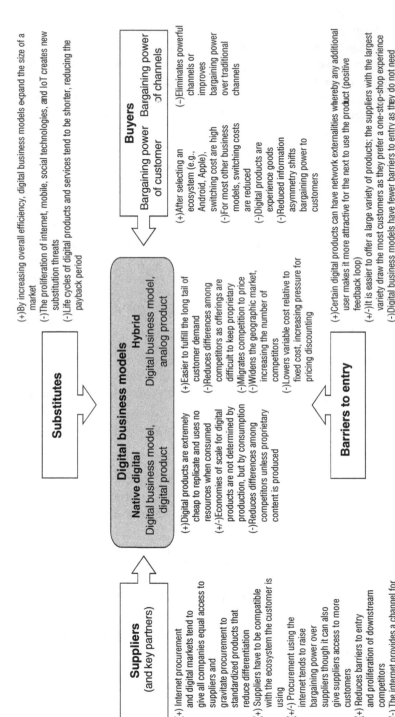

Figure 3.2   Five forces analysis in a digitalizing world (adapted from Porter, M. E., *The Strategic Potential of the Internet Strategy and the Internet*, 2003)

Substitutes

(+) By increasing overall efficiency, digital business models expand the size of a market
(-) The proliferation of internet, mobile, social technologies, and IoT creates new substitution threats
(-) Life cycles of digital products and services tend to be shorter, reducing the payback period

Buyers

Bargaining power of customer

Bargaining power of channels

(+) After selecting an ecosystem (e.g., Android, Apple), switching cost are high
(-) For most other business models, switching costs are reduced
(-) Digital products are experience goods
(-) Reduced information asymmetry shifts bargaining power to customers

(-) Eliminates powerful channels or improves bargaining power over traditional channels

Digital business models

Native digital
Digital business model, digital product

Hybrid
Digital business model, analog product

(+) Digital products are extremely cheap to replicate and uses no resources when consumed
(+/-) Economies of scale for digital products are not determined by production, but by consumption
(-) Reduces differences among competitors unless proprietary content is produced

(+) Easier to fulfill the long tail of customer demand
(-) Reduces differences among competitors as offerings are difficult to keep proprietary
(-) Migrates competition to price
(-) Widens the geographic market, increasing the number of competitors
(-) Lowers variable cost relative to fixed cost, increasing pressure for pricing discounting

Suppliers
(and key partners)

(+) Internet procurement and digital markets tend to give all companies equal access to suppliers and gravitate procurement to standardized products that reduce differentiation
(+) Suppliers have to be compatible with the ecosystem the customer is using
(+/-) Procurement using the internet tends to raise bargaining power over suppliers though it can also give suppliers access to more customers
(+) Reduces barriers to entry and proliferation of downstream competitors
(-) The internet provides a channel for suppliers to reach customers, reducing the leverage of intervening companies (cut out the middle man)

Barriers to entry

(+) Certain digital products can have network externalities whereby any additional user makes it more attractive for the next to use the product (positive feedback loop)
(+/-) It is easier to offer a large variety of products; the suppliers with the largest variety draw the most customers as they prefer a one-stop-shop experience
(-) Digital business models have fewer barriers to entry as they do not need physical channels, a sales force, or other high up-front investments
(-) The technology used to create digital business models is tough to protect, requiring difficult to copy combinations of business and IT capabilities to differentiate on anything else than price

success and failure. Wearable tech (e.g., glasses, watches, virtual reality, tech integrated into clothing, and sensors attached to the skin) is at the verge of re-shaping the mobile market. It is these periods of high flux in a market when existing players are at their most vulnerable (e.g., Microsoft missing the first mobile wave). Unfortunately, the solution is not as simple as being first; the fast followers are often the ones who reap most of the benefits.[iv]

Formulating an effective digital strategy is actually hard work.

The digital strategy also needs to formulate an answer to increasing up-front investments combined with shorter payback periods. With every product cycle, the customer expects a *wow* experience, requiring the company to invest in new, differentiating features. Used to an abundance of choice and desire for instant gratification, the same customer requires little incentive to move to a competitor. Personalization, service, unexpected additional value add features, and anticipating wants and needs are some of the tools available to companies to mitigate this risk.

The bargaining power of suppliers and key partners is a mixed picture. Apple, Microsoft, and Google have to negotiate with content owners on the conditions under which their music, movies, magazines, and books can be sold. For small app builders, the situation is the opposite, as most lack bargaining power. Over-all, digitalization had a positive effect on the bargaining power of companies, as the internet enables equal access to all suppliers, gravitating procurement to standardized products and competition on price. Suppliers can counter this effect either by offering differentiating products, such as a sapphire screen instead of a glass phone screen, or by using the internet to reach customers directly.

Nothing is carved in stone, though. In their book, *The Second Machine Age*, Brynjolfsson and McAfee point out that both human development and population were on a very gradual upward trajectory between 25,000 BCE and the late 18th century. The invention of writing, the rise of religions, and the discovery of new countries all contributed to progress. But it was the Industrial Revolution that pushed the human social development index into a steep upward trajectory. The invention of the computer and other technologies pushed the trajectory to an almost vertical incline as digitalization allows us to boost our *mental power* on top of the *physical power* that was enabled by the first revolution.

The following list is an overview of emerging technologies that are part of the second revolution. They allow companies to blow past previous limitations, develop new business models, and create new customer segments:

- **Automation of knowledge work**—IBM's Deep Blue and Watson are two prime examples of systems that are able to perform increasingly complex human tasks (e.g., involving unstructured commands and subtle judg-ments). Buyers will benefit from lower prices, even though some of the same buyers will lose their jobs in the process. The barrier to entry will be relatively high, due to the complexity and the head start that several existing companies have in this area.

- **The Internet of Things**—From the health of your dog[5] to the position of the blinds covering the windows, soon almost everything can be monitored or influenced by an app on your phone. Unlike the automation of knowledge work, the barrier of entry is low, as the cost and durability of sensors improve with every new generation. Private buyers have to consider the tradeoff between convenience and security, while companies can look forward to lower production costs and improved decision making.
- **Cloud technology**—The ability to start a company without having to invest in expensive software and hardware solutions lowers the entry barrier in most industries. Suppliers have the choice to join an existing ecosystem, challenge it, or create their own niche market.
- **Advanced robotics**—The impact of automated knowledge work on the service industry is similar to that of advanced robotics on industrial production and farming. While replacing a bookkeeper or dentist requires different business rules and data than automated crop harvesting and home construction, they leverage similar technological advances. For commodity products, cost will go down, while previously uneconomical long-tail offerings come within reach of customers.
- **Autonomous and near-autonomous vehicles**—In harbors and on factory floors, autonomous vehicles have been a familiar sight for years. Car manufacturers are now pointing toward 2020 as the year they will introduce autonomous passenger cars. Private buyers will enjoy the convenience of reading the newspaper while driving to work, while COOs can look forward to a lower bill for logistics. Taxi and truck drivers are among those who have to start looking for another line of profession.
- **Next-generation genomics**—High-speed DNA sequencing unlocks novel biological applications in farming (e.g., creating drought resistant crops) and healthcare (e.g., sequencing the genome of an unborn fetus using a drop of blood from the mother). Combined with synthetic biology (*writing* DNA), it opens the door to producing medicine that can target an individual patient.

---

[5] A Dutch start-up, Sparked, has already created a device that can monitor the health of cows. It sends notifications to the farmer if the cow needs medical care or even when it's giving birth. The sensor is attached to the ear, from where it reads the vital signs of the animal and wirelessly sends information to a back office for number crunching purposes.

- **Energy storage**—Advanced data analytics, *smart meters*, and energy storage solutions (e.g., molten salts, hydrogen, compressed air) turn the whole electricity grid into a large-scale energy storage system. The entry barrier for new suppliers is high due to the necessary up-front investment and domain expertise. Combined with certain materials, even a human body can produce enough electricity to power, for example, a hearing device, removing the need to wear it externally.
- **Advanced materials**—The ability to manipulate materials at the nanoscale enables the creation of materials with new properties (e.g., reduced electric resistance, strength, durability). Some nanomaterials have already found their way to buyers in things like toothpaste, sunscreens, window coatings, and high-end bicycles, but most are still waiting in laboratories for a cost-effective production method.
- **Advanced oil and gas exploration and recovery**—This is irrelevant to the average IT department, as the only touch point is the energy bill of data centers. Nevertheless, gas production through fracking and distilling oil from tar sands are two developments that benefit from technological advances like microseismic data analysis and predictive fracture modeling. Besides their impact on the profit for oil and gas companies, their impact is limited to the macro economy (e.g., such as energy independence).
- **Renewable energy**—Cooling requires so much energy that Canada and Scandinavia may become important destinations for future data centers. Pumping warm cooling water into deep earth layers during summer and retrieving it during winter is another method to optimize the energy bill and environmental impact. For data centers in sunny or windy places, solar panels and wind farms can be used to achieve a similar effect. Biofuels, geothermal power, and ocean energy are some of the other technologies being used to reduce the dependence on fossil fuels.

Understanding the specific context of hybrid and digital markets is an important precondition to create an effective digital strategy. The strategy itself has to be company-specific, however—starting with the customer segments that the company wants to serve with its value propositions.

3.2.3 Customer Segments in a Digital Market

The marketing department of a car lease company asked IT to realize a mobile platform in the form of an app for drivers. To improve driver adoption, the customer journey was based on the life cycle from the driver's perspective. The app therefore included modules that covered the selection of cars, contract signing, tracking of fuel consumption, scheduling of maintenance appointments, damage reporting, and the eventual handing in of the car at the end of the contract term. In the case where the lease and fuel bill were paid by the employer of the driver, the employer was treated as a separate customer segment. They received a dashboard with aggregated driver data and gamification functions to influence the behavior of the drivers (e.g., to achieve goals like reducing the fuel bill).

The main benefit of the app was to lower the operating cost for the lease company. Before the introduction of the app, the car had to be taken to a designated site at the end of the contract term to check the car for dents and scratches. With the *turn-in module* of the app, the driver takes a predefined set of pictures and sends them directly to the back office for analysis. The app also reduced the workload for the lease company. Hence, one app targeted three customer segments:

- One B2C segment (the drivers)
- One B2B segment (the drivers' employers)
- Multiple internal business segments (the lease company)

The three customer segments and the value propositions are depicted in Figure 3.3. It reflects the complexity that both the business and IT had to deal with when extending the company's digital value chain. The most important challenge turned out to be the mismatch between the customer journey of the driver and the organizational structure of the lease company.

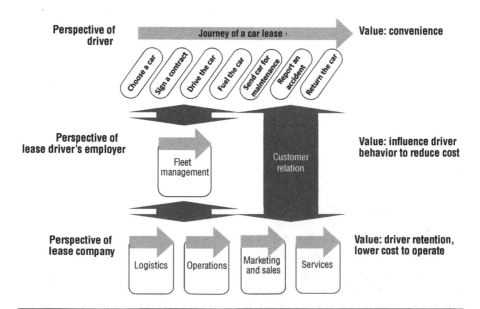

Figure 3.3   One solution, three customer segments

The business units were organized for operational excellence, each covering a part of the drivers' life cycle, which sometimes overlapped. The first cracks in the project emerged when the individual business managers started to push the interests of their own silo. With the marketing department unable to enforce its vision, the app soon became an unguided projectile. To complicate matters further, the app required access to business rules and data stored in a heteronomous, and often pre-web service and pre-application programming interface, application landscape. Some applications had a release cycle of once or twice a year, ending the speed-to-market that was envisioned by marketing.

The project taught the marketing department of the lease company that launching an app entails more than hiring a couple of developers. It requires strong business governance, unambiguous ownership, and an adequate technical impact analysis. The IT team learned that translating an end-to-end customer journey into an app is very different from automating an internal business process.

What went well in the project is the attention to customer segmentation. The driver and employer both have different needs and customer journeys. By dividing customers into groups with similar needs, it will be easier to give them what they want. From a managerial perspective, segmentation helps IT to focus and optimize the allocation of the available budget. When segmenting the business, IT can consider aspects like:

- Business domain (e.g., marketing or logistics)
- Business life-cycle phase (e.g., introduction, growth, mature, or decline)
- Technology density of the business model (e.g., channels or value proposition)
- The actual user (e.g., internal business, B2B customer, or B2C customer)

Customer segmentation is a form of differentiation and will therefore be discussed further in Chapter 4. Together with customer relationships, channels, and value propositions, customer segments also form the front-end of the IT business model covered in Chapter 6. Nothing surpasses *know thy customer* in importance.

3.2.4 Channeled Value Propositions

The value proposition is also very high when it comes to importance. The value proposition is a clearly defined statement that is designed to convince the buyer that one particular product or service will add more value or better solve a problem than doing nothing or choosing an alternative from an external vendor. More generally, a value proposition answers the following questions:

- What is the problem that needs solving?
- What is your solution or product?

- What is the value you provide?
- What makes your solution unique?

Ideally, a value proposition can be expressed in one sentence. If it takes half an hour to explain the benefits and the problem it solves, something is wrong. Another indication that a value proposition will hit its mark is that it solves a problem that is both blatant (instead of latent) and critical (instead of aspirational). These problems are acute—putting revenue, margin, and thus careers at risk. From an IT perspective, finding a solution is something that the business will be happy to pay for.

In the book *Value Proposition Design*, Osterwalder provides ten criteria that make a value proposition great:

1. Focus on the jobs, pains, and gains that matter most to customers
2. Focus on unsatisfied jobs, unresolved pains, and unrealized gains
3. Target few jobs, pains, and gains, but do so extremely well
4. Go beyond functional jobs and address emotional and social jobs
5. Align with how customers measure success
6. Focus on jobs, pains, and gains that a lot of people have or that some will pay a lot of money for
7. Differentiate from competition on jobs, pains, and gains that customers care about
8. Outperform competition substantially on at least one dimension
9. Difficult to copy
10. Embedded in great business models

The same book also emphasizes the interdependence between value proposition and customer segment. Only together do they create a *product-market fit*. Value propositions from IT that target internal customer segments achieve product-market fit when they are able to reduce transaction cost, processing time, better decision making, or the usual suspects mentioned in Table 3.3. There is some overlap on reasons to buy between B2B customers and B2C customers, but there are plenty of differences, too. B2B customers typically buy because they want to focus on their core activities, lower their risk profile, or access specific knowledge or capabilities. Reasons why B2C customers spend their money include aesthetics, status, and social inclusion, which is very different from the purely rational reasons of internal business executives and external B2B customers. Consequently, the business expects the solutions from IT to reflect these differences.[6]

---

[6] Value propositions for B2B and B2C segments are joint initiatives. Neither the business nor IT individually possess all the required capabilities. This important topic is covered in Chapter 7.

Table 3.3   IT's direct and indirect customer segments

	User, Internal	B2B Customer, External	B2C Customer, External
Compelling Reasons to Buy	• Save cost, time • Increase revenue, profitability • Enhance existing or enable new activity • Faster and better decision making • Increased agility, speed-to-market • Frictionless integration and collaboration with key partners	• Activity is not core • Lower risks (investment or otherwise) • Better cost-quality-scope ratio than make • Access to new capabilities or competencies • Increase speed-to-market	• Cost • Functionality, features • Newness • Status, social inclusion • Usability, aesthetics • Social responsibility, environment, ethics
Generic Value Proposition	• Lower cost • Enhance differentiating capabilities • Improve attractiveness as employer • Disruptive digital business model • Lower barrier for business to buy instead of make	• Differentiating or cheaper product or services • Proprietary capabilities (e.g., patents)	• Create new market space • For existing markets: lower cost than the competitors and differentiate features compared to competitors
Example Value Proposition in Terms of *What*, *Customer*, and *Value*	The new business intelligence solution allows executives to find relevant information quicker and easier, increasing production utilization by 10%	Our company has the only white label e-commerce platform that allows trading companies to scale their volume by 100% in one day	Our insurance company gives a 10% discount to customers using its self-service portal
Aspects Related to Buying Decision	Formal, rational, politics, (in)tangible value, policy related to sourcing	Formal, rational, tangible value	Emotional, mix of tangible and intangible or latent value
Center-of-Gravity Required Capabilities	Functional domain knowledge, technology capabilities, customer relationships	Value proposition, differentiating company capabilities, customer relationships (including collaboration)	Marketing, customer relationship management, customer segmentation value proposition, and channels

To get the value proposition to the customer, channels are needed. These too got disrupted by the internet and mobile apps, and are at the brink of another shift with the introduction of unmanned aerial vehicles, virtual reality, augmented reality, smart watches, and other wearable tech. To start with the first shift, for decades the showroom of the dealer was the only sales channel available to a car manufacturer. In 2009, Ford decided to supplement the traditional marketing approach by launching the Fiesta Movement on social media. More than one year before the Fiesta became available to buyers in the United States, Ford enticed 100 social media influencers to drive a Fiesta and share their experiences. The blogs, videos, and other content resulted in 50,000 requests for information about the car—and 10,000 cars sold in the first six days.

Digital channels hold many benefits over analog ones, including global customer reach, a shop that never closes, and the ability to collect more detailed customer data. However, digital channels are also more difficult to control. A shared post about a company's use of child labor, whether founded or not, can reach customers around the globe in a matter of seconds. Channels have five key objectives or phases and IT teams can add value to all of them. These objectives or phases are as follows:

- **Raise awareness**—The internet and social technologies enabled companies to reach potential customers regardless of their location and time zone. Anytime, anywhere, customers can easily find value propositions that companies offer and feedback from existing customers, reviewers, and the like.
- **Support decision making**—Published content like blogs and vlogs, websites, and apps differentiated via user experience and features, social media engagement, and a smooth multi-channel experience can all have a positive impact on the buy decision of a customer. There is also a downside. It is now easier than ever to compare value propositions from different companies. To reduce search-stress, information brokers or brand-agnostic retailers like Amazon, Walmart, and Sears aggregate information and present it in such a way that the customer can make an informed decision.
- **Fulfilling a need**—Day or night, rain or shine, urban or rural, customers can buy whatever they want, whenever they want; it is just a matter of a few clicks, swipes, or even a fingerprint scan.
- **Deliver the value proposition**—Cassette tapes and LPs have been replaced with either streaming services or mp3s, and the same applies to books and movies. Often, neither plane tickets nor dinner bookings require a printed copy; a QR code or bar code on the screen is enough.

- **Providing after-sales support**—Just about everyone has used an FAQ or forum for troubleshooting a problem or downloading a user manual. For more complex service requests, websites incorporate chat functions (whether it be video, audio, or just text) and the ability to exchange documents for situations like mortgage negotiations with a bank.

Due to their importance, channels are at the very heart of the business. Thinking in channels is not rocket science and most IT departments already provide a *multi-channel experience* to the business users without referring to it as such. Examples include e-mail functions via desktop clients, web client, and mobile app. It is but one of the three basic channel strategies available to a company, as listed here:

- **Single channel**—There is one channel available to customers that covers all the channel phases.
- **Multi-channel**—Multiple channels like websites, call centers, mobile apps, and physical shops are available to the customer. All channels operate independently, meaning a physical purchase by a customer is not linked to his or her online shopping profile. Similarly, quality levels and process will differ per channel.
- **Cross-channel**—The available digital and analog channels are fully integrated and customer information is shared across channels. Regardless of the channel and the activity, the customer receives a seamless and flexible experience.

Customer segments, value propositions, and channels—these are terms that not every IT professional is familiar with. They should be, however, as the relentless drive to automate increasingly complex activities results in IT teams that are small but highly skilled, creative, and flexible. One of those skills is relationship management. As long as business executives consider the tangible and intangible added value (including image and relationship) of the internal IT teams' value propositions is higher than the cost, she or he has a compelling reason to buy internally.[7] It is thereby important to use a broad interpretation of *cost*. The quality of the developed software code may be excellent, but if the business had to jump through too many hoops to get there, the business may still consider it a negative business case. Customer relationship management includes the practices and tools that are used to analyze and manage customer interactions throughout their life cycle in order to prevent this from happening by continuously sensing and acting on new wants and needs.

---

[7] Assuming the business is allowed freedom of choice—regardless of policy—in the long term, it is in the best interests of the internal IT team to adopt a competitive mindset.

3.2.5 Building Stong Relationships between IT and the Business

With the convergence of business and IT, the latter gets more exposed to marketing practices. This is a good thing, as marketing represents the art of building strong relationships with customers and creating value for both parties.[v] The business knows that a good relationship is not the same as saying *yes* all the time. IT has to strike a balance between customer satisfaction and the available budget. The relative success of IT to do so can be measured by observing the following four responses:[vi]

- **Consumer behavior responses**—A business executive contracting an external supplier to fulfill a specific need is a reaction that can be measured easily. More positive signals[8] include requesting higher-value projects, ordering new or different value propositions, and increases in volume.
- **Consumer intermediate responses**—The annual, or even biannual, user satisfaction survey is part of this category as much as the annual increase or cut to the budget.
- **Direct customer responses**—Think of business executives requesting a meeting to discuss a new joint initiative and users asking questions via the self-service portal or IT's Yammer channel.
- **Innovativeness responses**—The moment the business starts proactively approaching IT to participate in the development of new business models, value propositions, or channels, the positioning of a business partner is within sight. Proactive requests to enhance existing products or services can also be labeled under this category.

Depending on the outcomes, either incremental or radical change is required from IT. The following questions may help to pinpoint the strengths to focus on and weaknesses to avoid in the relationship and realized value. Is the outcome of the measurement coincidental or a trend, and if so, what are the reasons? Related to this question is finding out why IT *loses* in one situation and *wins* in another. Is there a recurring pattern that can be identified and addressed? Are there certain types of projects that are consistently escalated to the highest level of the company, or certain business needs that are always sourced externally by the business?

Anybody who ever studied marketing started with *product, price, place,* and *promotion* as the basic tools to attract and retain customers. For B2C and B2B segments served with value propositions that require limited interaction

---

[8] Assuming buying externally by the business is undesirable, which is not necessarily the case, it can be IT policy to allow the business to source certain niche demands directly from best-of-breed vendors.

between the company and the customer, these four Ps provide a solid starting point. Value propositions with a large customization or service component require extensive interaction between buyer and seller. Here, the following four Ps from Barnes are more suitable: *product, process, performance*, and *people*.[vii] Not only are internal and external B2C and B2B customer segments better off with the latter Ps, so too are key partners. They also need considerable bidirectional coordination and collaboration to be effective. Success in serving these customer segments, therefore, depends on the ability of IT to create a customer-centric culture. The team members have to be intrinsically motivated to deliver a good service, as the daily interactions between IT employees and colleagues from the business are outside of the direct circle of influence of management. Plan-do-check-act cycles and customer-centric performance metrics are also important. These are not meant as a disciplinary tool but as input for personal and team feedback, coaching, and learning.

Especially for entrepreneurial IT, a customer-centric culture is crucial, as the environment is often too dynamic to be captured by standard processes. In highly volatile and complex environments, responsibilities have to be distributed lower in the organization than is usual for foundation IT. Controls have to be relatively *soft*[9] and the strategy and policies *porous* to allow for the necessary wiggle room. In marketing terms, it is the majority of the channel phases that are handled at tactical and operational levels, with executive involvement limited to key go/no-go moments and strategic initiatives. The smaller the product portfolio, number of customer segments, and other aspects that have a positive effect on the complexity and uncertainty faced by the company, the easier it is to enforce strict top-down governance over the relationship.

As covered in Chapter 4, entrepreneurial IT may even result in the fusing of both the business and IT arms to remove any source of friction. Relationship management as an activity ceases to exist for that part of the portfolio. The last part of this chapter examines two practical situations.

3.3 BEGINNERS' COURSE: FROM OFFLINE TO ONLINE

When Ralph Norris became CEO of Air New Zealand in 2001, the airline was grounded and was depending on an $800 million bailout by the government for its survival. The 9/11 terrorist attacks had just taken place, dampening customer

---

[9] Soft controls are intangible and subjective in nature and focus on stimulating desired behavior by emphasizing tone at the top, integrity, trust, shared values, and morale. Hard controls are tangible and objective and include authorization mechanisms, formal approval, verifications, and performance reporting.

demand for flying, and a survey among the airline staff showed a complete lack of confidence in the leadership team. Morale was further depressed by the plan to reduce headcount in an attempt to reduce the imbalance between cash in and cash out. A reduced cost base was not enough however. Air New Zealand required a reevaluation of its whole business model.

Was Air New Zealand to follow low-budget carriers like Southwest and Ryanair and focus on regional flights, or become a global player like Lufthansa and Singapore Airlines? Due to the location of New Zealand, full-service long-haul connections to Asia, Europe, and the United States had to be part of their business portfolio. For regional flights, a low-cost approach was selected, requiring the airline to operate two business models simultaneously. The long-haul operator would be branded *Air New Zealand* and the regional player *Domestic Express*. To pull it off, technology was used as an enabler of the necessary flexibility and low-cost operating model.

The website would become *the* channel to create awareness among customers for the airline's offerings, evaluation, purchase, and after-sales. It allowed the company to cut out the fees of the travel agents and the administrative cost for processing the tickets sold by phone or other channels. Even before the turn-around, customers could buy tickets via the internet, but the site was too cumbersome to navigate and few opted to do so. An e-business specialist was hired to enhance the customer experience and workflow when progressing through the channel phases. As a result, the evaluation and purchase phases on the new websites for Air New Zealand and Domestic Express were reduced from ten to five steps. Other functions enabled customers to check in online, reducing operating costs of staffing and rentals for check-in desks.

For this airline, technology turned out to be more than a utility. It enabled the airline to abandon its analog channels in favor of two websites. These would be *the* entry points for the customer, regardless of whether the customer was looking for a full-service intercontinental flight or a cost-conscious short distance trip. In a matter of months, the IT team went from support function to strategic enabler, with external support from experts. In 2013, the government of New Zealand felt confident enough to reduce its share in Air New Zealand from 73 percent to 53 percent.

3.4. ADVANCED COURSE: DEMOCRATIZATION OF ELECTRICITY MARKET

Until the government deregulated the electricity market, the electric utility company enjoyed the perks that come with having a monopoly. The margins were abnormally high and the service poor and outdated. Three years after the deregulation, the market was buoyant with new value propositions from nimbler and more focused competitors. Still used to generous budgets, the business invested considerable amounts in new initiatives in an effort to retain market share. However, lacking a clear strategy to deal with the new competitive landscape, the initiatives lacked focus and attention for realized value. Customers were leaving in droves and the recently appointed CEO warned the top 100 senior executives that the current and next fiscal year's financial figures would be disappointing.

A side effect of this unconcerned diversification strategy of the business was a heterogeneous IT landscape. Every year, the share of the IT budget that was spent on integration and maintenance grew. The CEO, therefore, asked the CIO to make rationalizing the application portfolio one of his focal points for the next fiscal year. Basically, the CIO had to ask business questions like, *"Which one of the three existing ERP systems becomes the new target system for the whole company?"* Hence, contrary to what some may think, an application rationalization program is primarily a business challenge. IT provides the necessary qualitative and quantitative insights, formulates advice from a technological perspective, and executes the decisions that are made by the business.

Far more challenging for IT was enabling the business to recapture lost market share. Competitors used a variety of value propositions to capture market share. Some earned their money by positioning themselves as a broker between demand and supply, while others offered point solutions like *smart meters*. The utility company pursued a one-stop-shop strategy, requiring the CIO to define an answer to not only smart meters, but also a *smart grid*, bring-your-own-electricity (BYOE), and advanced analytics. Some were completely new, while others were built upon existing IT capabilities.

Data analysis was already widely used by the business to define prices, combining demographic data like income, location, and age; cost data that covered oil prices, production, and transportation costs; and usage data such as winter-summer patterns. The data models, however, were based on a one-way business model: the utility company produced all the electricity consumed by the customers. The commoditization of solar panels and wind turbines in combination with smart meters enabled a two-way model: a consumer as a source of both demand and supply. From an environmental and macro-economic perspective, this trend had several advantages:

- It reduced transport losses and allowed for better utilization of all assets within the network.
- Customers became active instead of passive players, enhancing their involvement in energy usage and saving.

- New energy generation and storage sources, both sustainable and not, could be hooked up by *plug-and-play*.
- The network was able to react more quickly to undesired events by diverting power and, therefore, improving its resilience.

Nevertheless, both the business and IT of the utility company initially treated BYOE as a strategic risk. Hence the investment spree by the business; they were panicked reactions of trying to protect the status quo. It was a natural reaction of a century-old business model that suddenly got disrupted. The employees felt at a loss and had to go through the motions accompanying radical change: paralysis, denial, anger, bargaining, depression, exploration, and eventually, acceptance.

The market does not wait for anyone, and the new CEO soon presented a new strategy of no longer building walls around existing customer segments and value propositions, but using the still considerable financial reserves, asset base, and deep domain expertise of the organization to get ahead of the pack again. They would embrace the new opportunities enabled by new technologies and changing customer preferences.

The impact of this move on IT was considerable, as it required the convergence of administrative and industrial IT. With a smart grid, the existing devices that were used to transport, smoothen, and change the voltage levels of electricity become *active* components while simultaneously adding new categories of devices (e.g., local storage, local production, smart meters). As a result, millions of formerly *passive* devices and houses became *active* network participants. Even electric cars will soon join this network. Marketing, operations, and billing were but a few of the functions affected by this transformation.

Before the introduction of the smart grid and BYOE, the operations department and its industrial IT systems had operated in relative isolation. They chose their own technologies, standards, policies, and processes and even had their own physical network. Suddenly, they had to be treated as a customer segment by IT, as the data generated by the smart grid had to be fed into the administrative IT systems and vice versa. At both the technical and organizational level, existing patterns had to be reviewed and adjusted by operations and IT. After living as estranged neighbors for years, they had to rekindle their relationship.

The employees of the planning department had another challenge. Regardless of the weather, customers always expect the lightbulb to work when flipping the switch. This is no problem when all electricity is produced by coal, gas, or nuclear power plants. With the introduction of solar panels and wind turbines, far more complex algorithms were needed to predict and match demand and supply. Hence, their question for IT: "*How can we leverage on different data sets coming from the smart grids, weather, oil prices, among others, to define opti-mal production and price points?"* They were not so much looking for a tool or technology, as they were looking for a partner who could turn large amounts of data into a relevant result. The new business model resulted in new internal customer segments for IT and a demand for different value propositions.

Equally challenging for IT was the impact of the smart grid on the external customer segments. The old single homogeneous customer segment was split into three new segments:

- Customers averse to change (e.g., due to privacy concerns) would stick to the old analog meter as long as possible
- Customers adopting a smart meter to optimize their electricity usage
- Customers adopting a smart meter to both produce and use electricity (*prosumers*)

The emphasis for IT regarding the first category consisted of supporting the marketing department in their efforts to persuade customers to adopt smart meters. By building a strong relationship with these customers, marketing cre-ated an environment whereby they could help the customers to use electricity more wisely and teach them how their behavior influenced the monthly bill. Leveraging on mutual trust, the customer would be more willing to learn the benefits and eventually replace their meters. Besides using analog channels that involve community presentations, face-to-face meetings, and publications in local magazines, the marketing department also deployed gamification, e-learn-ing, and online simulation tools to create a safe environment for customers to experiment and learn. These, combined with customer testimonials, blogs, vlogs, and a targeted presence on social media platforms, resulted in a solid digital portfolio to support the awareness and decision-making channel phases.

The two other customer segments did not have to be convinced anymore. They were interested, accepted the implications, and were willing to partici-pate in terms of sharing both data and electricity with the company. They were looking forward to the smart in-home displays, programmable communicat-ing thermostats, direct load controllers, and the web apps that come with all of these devices. Here, the primary challenges for IT included uniting with the operations team to integrate the houses of the customers into the smart grid, which is also called the advanced metering infrastructure. Next, the electricity consumption data that was collected by the smart meters in houses had to be regularly transmitted back to the utility company's back office systems—known as the meter data management system (MDMS)—for processing. The MDMS system, in turn, fed the customers' apps, billing processes, forecasting, and out-age management.

Just as our phones and TVs evolve, so too do smart meters and networks. Experiments with broadband internet via the electricity network have failed up until now, but ten years from now, things may well look very different. Just imagine the consequences and business opportunities—and their impact on the IT team.

REFERENCES

i. DeCambre, M. (January 2014). How iPhones Are Forcing Banks to Rethink Brick-and-Mortar Branches. Link: http://qz.com/167313/how-iphones-are-forcing-banks-to-rethink-brick-and-mortar-branches/.

ii. Business Wire. (2014). http://www.marketwatch.com/story/nike-fuel-lab-launches-in-san-francisco-2014-04-10?reflink=MW_news_stmp.

iii. Laudon, K. C. and Laudon, J. P. (2005). *Management Information Systems: Managing the Digital Firm* (9th edition).

iv. Anthony, S. (June 2012). *First Mover or Fast Follower?* Harvard Business Review. Link: http://blogs.hbr.org/anthony/2012/06/first_mover_or_fast_follower.html.

v. Kotler, P., Armstrong, G., Wong, V. and Saunders, J. (2009). *Marketing Defined: Principles of Marketing* (5th edition), p. 7.

vi. Ling-yee, L. (2010). Marketing Metrics' Usage: Its Predictors and Implications for Customer Relationship Management, Industrial Marketing Management.

vii. Barnes, J. (2001). *Secrets of Customer Relationship Management*. McGraw-Hill.

4

LESS UNIFORM, MORE DIFFERENTIATED

Less uniform, more differentiated represents the ability to deliver contextual IT solutions.

When searching for a restaurant on your mobile device, it yields those nearest to your current location. If your search history indicates that you like Chinese food, the results will highlight those establishments. To create this kind of personalized experience, Google Now, Cortana, and Siri have combined several data sources, such as location and past usage patterns, to deliver a personalized experience. The capability to show the restaurants in your current location instead of, say, Moscow reduces the *search stress* faced by customers, and the time saved is a source of customer benefits. Similarly, nobody is interested in car accidents or a derailed train with toxic chemicals a thousand miles away. Only those incidents close to you and the ones you care about are relevant. Here too, the context (e.g., location) is at least as important as the event itself.

A business has a similar expectation. When requesting a new application, the context, such as stable versus emerging market or having little or intense competition, is at least as relevant as the functional need. An application with a world-class user experience and feature set is a failure when launched after the competition has seized the market. At the solution level, the context has to be reflected by both the design and realization of the value proposition.[1] Nonfunctional requirements and DevOps are two of the tools available to do so. Hence, this could be a very short chapter; but it is not, as differentiation has more touch points than software development and operations.

The tradeoff between standardization and differentiation is, first and foremost, a strategic topic. A business model and IT landscape optimized for

---

[1] More generally known as content versus process. The first (content) captures the *what* (e.g., the solution or system) and the second (process) the *how* (e.g., development, operations processes).

customer intimacy is very different from one that is optimized for operational excellence. Strategic context is also embodied in the choice of the business to position itself as a prospector or a defender. Covered in the second part of this chapter, the model by Miles and Snow is introduced as one of the tools that IT can use to derive the relevant sources of contextual business value.[i]

The last part of this chapter describes an IT service provider struggling to combine foundation IT and entrepreneurial IT within one organization. Holding on to the standard structure, the chapter now continues with arguments supporting the relevance of the key principle *less uniform, more differentiated*. Table 4.1 provides three statements that cover the chapter as a whole.

Table 4.1   Statements to think about when reading this chapter

Statements
In hybrid and digital markets, IT has to mirror the external environment.
The context of the business need is at least as important as the need or want itself.
ITIL and COBIT can be sources of value in some situations and sources of waste in others.

4.1 WHY THIS PRINCIPLE MATTERS

The market crash of 1987 and the global economic meltdown in 2008 were macroeconomic events that companies could not avoid. Deregulation and disruptive innovations had a similar effect at the industry level. Suddenly, the rules of the game changed, and companies had no choice but to adapt. Oil was used for centuries to produce light until the invention of the electric lamp during the 1870s. Hundreds of companies that had been manufacturing oil and gas lamps saw their demand suddenly evaporate. The longer, more stable, and profitable the period before the sudden shift, the more difficult it will be to change existing business patterns and behavior.

A typical example in this category is the insurance industry. Until the invention of the internet, their business model had barely changed for several centuries. The internet and other so-called disruptive innovations suddenly created a situation whereby successful companies eventually failed, despite doing everything right.[ii] Suddenly, small start-ups started selling insurance at a considerably lower price point than had been possible with the existing business model.

According to Brown and Goolsbee, the internet reduced prices for life insurance by eight to 15 percent during the period between 1995 and 1997, thereby increasing consumer surplus by \$115–215 million.[iii] A similar effect was identified by Brown.[iv] He found that, relative to real prices in 1992, identical policies were about one percent lower in 1994, but almost 19 percent lower in 1996 and 27 percent lower in 1997. And then, of course, there was the impact that the internet had on intermediaries. Instead of calling an agent, customers started their search on Google or specialized information brokers.

In other markets, the impact of the internet may be less severe or at least take more time to disrupt existing business models. These markets have a different context as they may be subjected to different social trends (e.g., consumerization and sharing), economic trends (e.g., growth and decline), political trends (e.g., less strict intellectual property laws), demographic trends (e.g., aging population and improved education), and technological trends (e.g., entry barriers for certain technologies). The thinner the protective layer provided by the business, the more IT is exposed to these and other trends. It is a condition whereby there is not enough time for IT to wait for the business to spoon-feed them answers. Hence, in hybrid and digital markets, CIOs and IT teams should regularly analyze the context their company operates in and act accordingly. The answer to increased competition, economic downturn, or more powerful buyers is far more complex than designing a new application. These shifts require from IT—first and foremost—strong, strategic, out-of-the-box thinking.

The external environment continuously reshapes the context that the company, and consequently IT, operate in. Within the boundaries set by the external environment, every company has to forge its own path to success. Dell was founded in 1984 and was added to the Fortune 500 in 1992. Its key to success was building direct relationships with the customer via the internet. At the time, most competitors were targeting consumers via analog sales channels, such as brick-and-mortar shops. Selling directly to the customer also enabled Dell to build-to-order instead of the traditional build-to-stock model. It kept waste to a minimum and allowed the customer to choose from a wide selection of configuration options. Dell pursued a customer intimacy strategy, contrary to the operational excellence strategy of its competitors. For the latter, price was the main differentiator, while Dell targeted customers who were looking for choice and flexibility. Even though Dell changed its strategy around 2008, it is still a classic example of a customer-intimacy-focused business model.

The flexibility offered by Dell was not free, but its success showed the viability of the strategy. There was a considerable customer segment that was willing to pay a slightly higher price, as it valued customization. More specifically, a company cannot offer the cheapest and most customized or innovative product at the same time. A company has to choose one of the following three basic strategies as proposed by Treacy and Wiersema:[2] [v]

- **Operational excellence**—The key objective of the company is cost leadership. Revenue is generated by fulfilling the need of large and homogeneous customer segments with uniform value propositions by using standardized processes, strict governance policies, and mature technologies.
- **Customer intimacy**—Customers are offered personalized value propositions to fulfill their specific needs or wants. Success depends on the soft skills, domain expertise, and customer knowledge of the team.
- **Product leadership**—Customers are offered superior value propositions, incorporating the latest technologies and insights. This allows the company to charge a premium for its value propositions.

Regardless of the company or strategy, every marketing department wants a customer relationship management solution and an engaging website, while the production departments need enterprise resource planning (ERP) functions to manufacture products, and the logistics team needs a supply chain management solution. Even many of the functions may look similar at first sight, and therefore, some may think that the three strategies listed only affect the customer-facing part of the company. Production, logistics, and other downstream value chain activities would remain shielded.

Dell clearly demonstrates that this is not the case. Build-to-order has a profound impact on both production and logistics, let alone offering an optional service whereby a customer can change the configuration up to 24 hours after ordering it by paying an additional fee. Keeping the delivery date fixed—based on the expectation that only a very small percentage of the customers would use such a feature—would require some seriously complex planning software and company-wide flexibility.

Most law firms pursue a customer intimacy strategy, competing fiercely among each other to attract and retain customers. The accompanying high cost of customer acquisition results in a drive to quickly increase the share-of-the-wallet. To do so, it is crucial to adopt a strong customer-first mentality (see Table 4.2). The specific wants, needs, and journey of the customer is leading the business processes and, therefore, also the IT value propositions that follow. The strategic-context that IT has to operate in is shaped by the drive of the business

---

[2] While focus remains a key success factor, technological advances reduced both the cost of certain innovations (e.g., app-based business models) and cost of operations (e.g., leveraging the cloud), allowing companies more room to maneuver without the risk of getting *stuck in the middle*.

Table 4.2 Translating business strategy into IT positioning

	Product Leadership	Customer Intimacy	Operational Excellence
Business Economics	Early market entry enables charging premium prices and acquiring large market share; speed-to-market is key	High cost of customer acquisition results in focus on increasing share-of-the-wallet; economies of scope are key	High fixed cost makes large volumes essential to reduce cost; economies of scale are key
Culture	Battle for talent, low entry barriers, many large and small players thrive	Battle for scope, rapid consolidation; few big players dominate in a business-to-consumer (B2C) market; in a business-to-business (B2B) market, many large and small players thrive	Battle for scale; rapid consolidation; a few big players dominate
Competition	Employee centered, pampering the creative stars	Strong focus on service, customer comes first mentality	Cost focused; stressed standardization, predictability, and efficiency
Examples	High-end car manufacturers, pharmaceutical companies	Amazon, law firms, hospitals, private aircraft charter companies	Telecom and third-party logistics companies, budget airlines
Context of Business Demand	Most innovative and breathtaking features, speed-to-market, brand image	A seamless extension of customers' business process or journey through domain knowledge, customization, and flexibility	Cost, cost, and cost; supplemented by scalability, predictability, and reliability
Typical IT Positioning in Hybrid or Digital Market	Business partner, some prima donna behavior is accepted as it can lead to a disruptive innovation	Business partner for customer-facing value propositions; faithful servant sufficient for remainder of portfolio	Depending on the business maturity, a business partner or faithful servant

to offer a seamless extension of their customers' business processes or journeys through domain knowledge, customization, and flexibility.

The starting point for a company that is pursuing an operational excellence strategy is very different. Cost leadership requires a standardized product portfolio that is enabled by a relatively uniform set of business processes and IT solutions. The compelling reason for customers to buy is not customization, but price. The strong focus on cost and economies of scale affects every decision the business and IT make. Whereas the CIO who is employed by a law firm of a hospital may opt for a best-of-breed sourcing strategy, the CIO of a telecom, a budget airline, or a third-party logistics company will consider large-scale outsourcing to leverage on the scale of IT service providers. The business strategy is therefore IT's second key source of contextual information. More precisely, the continuously evolving business strategy as the external environment may force a company to change its direction to remain competitive (see Chapter 5). A company's business strategy and business model continuously reshape IT's positioning, strategy, and business model.

The third and final argument of why IT should be less uniform and more open to differentiation can be derived from a company's internal structure. The demand profile of a marketing department is very different from the department that is responsible for human resources. The marketers want to try new things on a daily basis, requiring a different type of relationship and value proposition. The chief marketing officer from OpenText, Kevin Cochrane, described it as follows: "*Marketing needs to own the entirety of the customer experience. I need new business capabilities, and I need to have complete control over system innovation. Let me have more control over the front-end experience. Let me run fast and expose new capabilities.*" [vi] The need of most HR managers is limited to an intranet to communicate with the employees and a standard commercial-off-the-shelf (COTS) solution to automate the back-office processes.

Even at the activity level, there is a need for differentiation, as shown in Figure 4.1. Enabling the marketing department to target social media-savvy early adopters in a B2C segment is very different from relationship management in a mature B2B segment. The first scores higher on properties related to entrepreneurial IT than the second. What applies to one department, however, is not necessarily true for the others. At the editorial office of a newspaper that I consulted for several years ago, e-mail was considered an absolutely business-critical channel to receive news and other content from both reporters and citizens. Yet, the HR department of the same publisher only started to make noise after several days of downtime. Hence, the same technical solution can be part of more than one IT value proposition (see Chapter 6).

Looking ahead to the next chapter and reflecting on the dynamics faced by business and IT, the position on the curves in Figure 4.1 is not static (nor exact science for that matter).

The business model of companies tends to shift down the slope. Start-ups with a native digital business model typically start on the top left, but move down the slope in time. This development is well illustrated by Facebook abandoning its unofficial motto "*move fast and break things*" in 2014, then replacing

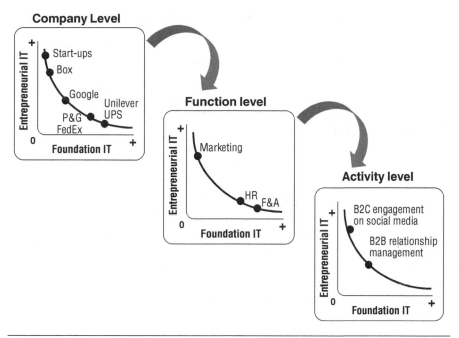

Figure 4.1   Differentiation at various levels

it with *"move fast with stable infrastructure."* The change signaled to its business partners, such as app developers, that it had moved to the next phase in its business life cycle. The influence of time is not restricted to the business model; every technology emerges, matures, and commoditizes (unless it fails prematurely).

The continually evolving wants and needs of the external and internal customer segments reshape IT's value propositions, channels, and relationship management. Nothing is absolute or immovable. Even the most uniform processes or standardized application portfolio may one day be disrupted by new legislation, a macroeconomic event, or changing customer preferences. To prevent being caught off-guard, IT should regularly analyze the context it operates in and act accordingly. The principle *less uniform, more differentiated* is therefore an invitation to regularly answer the following questions.

Considering the impact of new technologies on the companies' market position, strategy, and business model:

- Are we able to quickly sense and act on shifts in our external environment and business domain?
- Is the current relative importance and positioning of IT still optimal? What is the outlook in one, two, or more years from now?

- Are our current capabilities to differentiate adequate? What is the outlook in one, two, or more years?

The next part of this chapter will provide at least some answers.

4.2 HOW TO BECOME LESS UNIFORM, MORE DIFFERENTIATED

There are still companies out there that are judging the effectiveness of IT by the number of certifications (like ISO 27000), assurance reports (such as ISAE 3402), and implemented frameworks (e.g., COBIT). To be fair, these and others allowed IT to transform itself from a black art and/or a bottomless money pit into a civilized and predictable servant. According to Luftman and Kempaiah, of the 197 mainly Global 1000 companies analyzed in 2007, retail, transportation, and hotel/entertainment industries showed the largest improvement in business-IT alignment maturity after investing in COBIT, ITIL (Information Technology Infrastructure Library), or other frameworks related to IT governance.[vii]

While certifications, assurance reports, and frameworks are useful tools to measure and improve performance, they are no silver bullets. Their focus on structural elements, such as standard processes, function descriptions, and reporting templates, assumes a predictable and relatively uniform environment—an assumption that is reinforced by their continued expansion in both depth and breadth. From a modest 10 processes in Version 2, the ITIL Version 3 expanded into 26 processes, while COBIT Version 4.1 comes with an impressive 34 processes. The closeness to foundation IT is also reflected in the way these frameworks approach the interface between business and IT:

- The business strategy is input for the IT strategy
- The business is responsible for articulating its needs and wants

In fast-moving hybrid and digital markets, there is simply not enough time for IT to wait for the business to finish its strategy. Neither can the business be expected to dictate all requirements for a digital value proposition or multi-channel initiative in isolation. Initiatives launched in these markets are true co-productions, requiring close collaboration, mutual trust, and an iterative decision-making and realization process. Hence, one way to segment is foundation IT versus entrepreneurial IT.

The optimal segmentation in a large diversified corporation may look slightly different. When roughly half the business units pursue an operational excellence strategy while the other half serve their customer segments with the most innovative product, IT should seriously consider differentiating along these lines. Hence, there is no one-size-fits-all approach to differentiation. The only common demeanor is regularly checking the fit between external environment, business, and IT positioning.

4.2.1 Regular Strategic Fit-Gap Analysis

The optimal segmentation of the internal and external customers by IT starts with understanding its own raison d'être. For a company in a stable analog market this may be as simple as providing several standard utility services, such as office automation and several COTS business applications. Nevertheless, it remains good practice, even for these companies, to regularly analyze the external environment for emerging shifts. Of the 47 companies described in the best seller *In Search of Excellence* by Tom Peters, all but 14 suffered serious profit erosion within four years after the book was published. Even more telling is that General Electric was the only company listed at the Dow Jones in both 1896 and 1996—all others either went bankrupt or were delisted due to mergers or acquisitions.

The higher the technology density of the current or expected markets the company operates in, the more relevant are the steps depicted in Figures 4.2a and 4.2b to IT executives. Contrary to markets with a low technology density, IT has to be on top of both relevant technology and business trends to ensure that IT positioning and investment orientation remain in tune with the external environment and business strategy. Business and IT have an interdependent relationship. Individually, they are unable to be successful. Hence, the more IT knows about relevant customer trends and competitor behavior, the better it can team as an equal partner with the business and vice versa.

For business models with low technology density, IT can follow the classic business IT alignment paradigm whereby the business provides IT with a clear-cut set of objectives and initiatives. Here, the scope for IT is limited to identifying and analyzing relevant technology trends, including potentially disruptive ones. The IT strategy follows the business strategy, instead of one shared digital business strategy.

Both the importance of market segmentation and the five forces model from Porter in Figure 3.2 were covered in Chapter 3. Regardless of the models used, it is the shared insight in the opportunities and threats that counts. Combined with insight in the pace that the external environment changes, the team can either opt for a well-structured and planned *wave* of change or a more radical approach to deal with unexpected *storms*.

The positioning or raison d'être of the company as a whole is embodied by the mission, vision, and strategy of the business. In addition to Treacy and

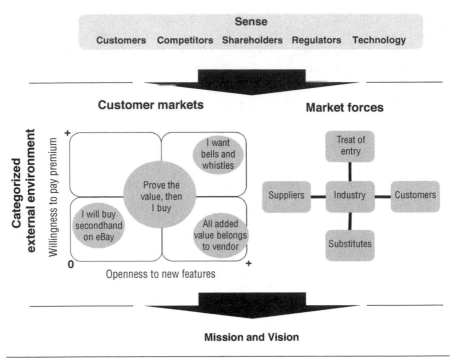

Figure 4.2a   Deriving the positioning of IT

Weiersema's value discipline model, there are two other useful models. One allows IT to identify the so-called value configuration of the business. Stabell and Fjeldstad pointed out that Porter's value chain model had a perfect fit with manufacturing companies, but less so for professional service firms, as found in law, engineering, and medicine.[viii] These solve customer-specific or one-off problems—the *value shop* configuration. Telecom providers and retail banks are part of the *value network* category, as they create value by facilitating exchanges among customers.

The differentiation is reflected in the wants and needs of the business (see Table 4.3). A telecom provider earns money in a fundamentally different way as compared to a law firm, resulting in considerable waste if IT should fail to translate the specific context into their IT business model and value propositions. Taking value shops as an example, they solve problems for external or internal customer segments. According to Coombs, there are two major articulations of core competencies related to R&D-related activities.[ix] The first covers the ability of the investment process to optimize the technology and product portfolio in such a manner that it strengthens the core differentiators of the company. The second reflects the harvesting mode, whereby the value shop joins other

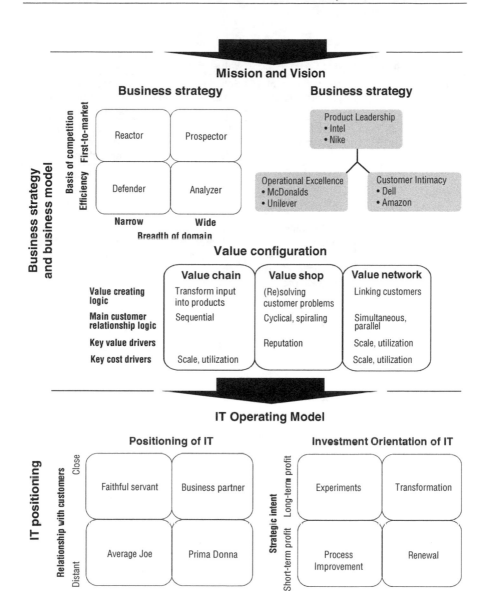

Figure 4.2b   Deriving the positioning of IT, continued

Table 4.3   From value configuration to added value of IT

Characteristics	Value Chain	Value Shop	Value Network
Value creation	Transformation of input into output	Solving clients and customer problems	Connecting clients and customers to each other
Work form	Sequential production	Integrated and cyclical problem solving	Monitored and simultaneous connections
Added value of IT	• Decrease cost per product • Enable better ways to produce or distribute the product • Include value-add IT functionalities to product, process innovation	• Facilitate collaboration • Knowledge management and enrichment • Diversify into new services, integration existing services	• IT infrastructure as enabler • Increase efficiency, utilization • Include value-add IT functionalities to service
Example	Paper factory	Law firm Crowdsourced R&D	Telecom company Social media companies

company functions in the market-driven exploitation of core competencies to produce specific value propositions for customers.

The better that IT understands these and other differences between the value configurations (and other sources of contextual information), the better it can target and serve the business and the customers of the business.

Due to the topic of this book, the value network is of particular interest. Facebook, Twitter, eBay, Yahoo, and Amazon are all part of this category—connecting those who want to exchange content, goods, or data. These established names will soon be joined by newcomers that leverage on the proliferation of increasingly small and powerful sensors in the age of the Internet of Things. These sensors take the data generated by customers to the next level, enabling new value propositions and even more precise targeting of advertisement. Hence, where the value of a new Facebook user ranged from 50 cents to several dollars in 2013, this number is likely to multiply in the coming years. Even Microsoft and Apple can be considered value networks, as they provide a technology platform connecting developers of (web) applications, content providers, and customers.

Depending on the ambition level of the business—like using Apple, Facebook, or Amazon as gateways to reach customers versus investing in an innovative custom-built platform to reach customers directly—the challenges faced by the IT team could vary from being fairly easy to requiring serious thought. When opting for launching a company-specific platform, the guiding economic principles of its value configuration have to be reflected by IT's value proposi-tions. Like telecom operators, digital platforms have high up-front cost followed by very low variable cost. Regardless of whether Facebook has two hundred us-ers or two hundred million, a platform needs to be developed and maintained. Utilization, economies of scale, and a value proposition enjoying positive net-work effects are, therefore, key benefit drivers for the business.

Hence, when the CEO lists digitalization of the existing analog business model as one of the strategic objectives for the coming years, it is especially the context that is related to the value network configuration that the CIO and his or her team should take a closer look at.

The model from Miles and Snow in Figure 4.2 is helpful in order to mini-mize the gap between the optimal and current IT positioning and investment decisions.[x] The model identifies four categories of business strategies, three of whom are sources of superior performance (prospector, defender, and analyzer) and one of average or less-than-average performance (reactor).

Prospectors are highly innovative, continually seeking new markets and opportunities. Defenders attempt to seal off a narrow product-market combi-nation and excel in retaining their existing customers. The analyzer is some-where in between, cautiously following the prospectors' every move and quickly adopting successful introductions. In parallel, the analyzer protects and serves its existing markets. Reactors don't have a consistent and proactive market ap-proach, nor do they try to actively influence their external environment—they drift along with the current.

In Table 4.4, the defender strategy is split into low-cost defender and dif-ferentiated defender, as both require a different IT business model (see Chapter 6). The context of the low-cost defender shares similarities with an operational excellence strategy, while a differentiated defender has product innovation and customer intimacy to choose from. Included in the table is also the typical positioning of IT for each business strategy category. That leaves translating the information gathered from the external environment and business to the positioning and investment orientation of IT.

The two axes of the model used to reflect the positioning of IT depict the sophistication of value propositions and relative distance between business and technology domains.[xi] The least mentally stimulating working environment for an IT professional is the Average Joe quadrant. Here, IT is considered a mere utility, resulting in large-scale outsourcing to optimize cost. The retained IT team is small and most team members will be dedicated to sourcing and contract management. The faithful servant is the reliable butler who is always willing to help, no questions asked. The business is the senior partner and IT the junior, focusing on execution. It is, therefore, also the quadrant with the highest risk of budget overruns, as the business just keeps adding items to the product backlog.

Table 4.4   From business strategy to IT positioning

	Prospector	Low-Cost Defender	Differentiated Defender	Analyzer	Reactor
Business Economics	Early market entry enables charging premium prices, very successful hits and costly misses; focus on product innovation	Lowering prices requires high volumes to reduce cost; focus on economies of scale, process innovation	Focus on product enhancements to differentiate and demand some price premium	Mixed Use cash flow from stable markets to fund new initiatives Compete on features, quality, service, or price	Follow the flow
Product-Market Scope	Dynamic market segments, both broad and narrow New or not well-established markets	Mature, stable, and well-established markets	Mature, stable, and well-established markets	Mixed portfolio of prospector and defender market segments	Lack of clear focus and direction
Agility	Very high, also high speed-to-market	Low	Medium	Mixed	Low
Center of Gravity IT Positioning for Hybrid or Digital Market	Business partner, some prima donna behavior is accepted as it can lead to a disruptive proposition	Faithful servant, business partner behavior expected for strategic initiatives	Faithful servant, business partner, or even prima donna behavior for strategic initiatives	Mixed Prospector part: business partner or even prima donna Defender part: faithful servant	Average Joe or faithful servant

While the faithful servant will hardly ever say *no*, the business partner is less shy. The business partner has matured from a dependent parent-child relationship to an interdependent adult-adult relationship. He or she earned this position by demonstrating the ability to co-create the complex and dynamic value propositions required to be successful in technology-rich markets. The prima donna is also able to think out of the box, innovate, and crack complex problems. Due to the distance between the business and IT, there is, however, a considerable chance of hit-and-miss initiatives. It is an ivory tower with the potential of brewing up the next big thing for the company; thus, if managed incorrectly, a prima donna can be a waste of valuable resources.

The needs and wants of the business are rarely homogeneous enough to fit in one quadrant. The model should therefore be used to determine the center of gravity for the IT department (e.g., faithful servant when ninety percent straightforward foundation IT and ten percent moderately complex entrepreneurial IT). As pointed out in the case in the following paragraphs, optimizing the IT business model for the dominant demand type tends to have a negative effect on the exceptions. A management team that is optimized to deliver foundation IT tends to struggle when confronted with entrepreneurial IT, or defender IT teams receiving requests from the prospector business unit. *Less uniform, more differentiated* is therefore primarily related to critical thinking instead of pushing a square peg into a round hole.

The last model to tickle the mind focuses on the investment orientation of IT. Closely related to IT positioning, the framework by Ross and Beath provides generic investment strategies for clusters of value propositions and is depicted at the bottom right of Figure 4.2c.[xii] One axis reflects the time horizon of the investment (short term versus long term) and the other reflects the difference between shared and business unit specific value propositions.

The investments with the highest risk profile are transformations. Their objective is redesigning the business model of the company (e.g., from offline retailer to all-in online retailer), implementing a company-wide ERP system, or realizing an ambitious technology-driven business process management initiative. Transformations require radical change and are therefore a source of both considerable future benefits and risk. Experiments share the long-term view of transformations, but their scope is more limited. Both Fujifilm and Kodak realized in the 1980s that photography would be going digital, but reacted differently to the challenge. Fujifilm decided to invest in new markets and business models, while Kodak thought its brand, combined with buying its way into new markets would be enough to be successful. A combination of long-term strategy and high-quality execution of the experiments ensured that Fujifilm would prosper in the wake of digital photography, while Kodak filed for Chapter 11 bankruptcy protection in 2012.

Renewals are investments that are focused on quickly enhancing shared capabilities. Think about things like deploying new technologies to lower transaction cost through cheaper and more powerful hardware, adding new functions to the shared corporate applications (e.g., responsive web front end on top of legacy back office application), or to address security concerns (e.g., Microsoft ceasing to patch Windows Server 2003). Where transformations try to ignite a new growth market or launch a business life cycle, renewals aim to optimize the performance of existing ones. Process improvements and renewals share the focus on the short term, but focus on business unit specific markets, products, and business models.

Deriving and regularly reevaluating the context under which the company and business operates not only results in a better positioned IT function and better targeted value propositions, but also in better operational decision making. Think of using an agile Scrum or waterfall development approach, or making the decision to build a custom application or buy a COTS solution.

4.2.2 When Iterative, When Sequential

Samsung introduced its wearable Gear, and even the Gear 2, before Apple introduced its Apple Watch. The reviews of especially the first-generation Gear Smartwatch were mixed at best, and consumers had a similar view considering a 30% return rate in Best Buy locations.[xiii] For Samsung, being first was more important than offering the best experience. To mitigate the risks associated with this go-to-market strategy, Samsung uses a relatively high release frequency for its products. Apple follows a different strategy. Products are tested and refined within the company walls until considered mature enough to appeal to the customer segments targeted by Apple. Both companies use iterations, but their implementations differ.

The business and IT teams of companies with a hybrid or digital business model face a similar challenge: deploy a new version of a popular app to all users out there and incorporate their feedback into the next release or keep the iterations restricted to a small joint team, deploying only the polished versions. The next, and inevitable step, is external customers driving the product backlog. When it became widespread knowledge in 2014 that the Chrome web browser drained more energy than necessary, public voting on Google's forum ensured that the bug's priority got elevated, forcing Google to take notice.[xiv]

The potential effects of using internal business users or even external customers as guinea pigs is one of the topics that has to be discussed when considering agile methods. It is one of the trade-offs when choosing between agile and waterfall software development. Agile's iterative development *sprints* of two or three weeks is a reaction to more heavily regulated waterfall models that develop the whole system in several sequential phases based on a complete set of business requirements. Subsequently, the sweet spots of waterfall development are situations where the requirements:[xv]

- Are known completely at the beginning of the project and are not likely to change significantly.
- Are understood completely before the beginning of the project.

According to the same author, the waterfall[3] approach also facilitates a more efficient staffing and resource allocation—reducing the direct IT cost of an epic, user story, or function point. The relatively long duration of the various realization phases like design and testing also creates more room for more time-intensive tasks like documenting user cases and drafting manuals for the operations and support team. Combined with a more thorough testing and acceptance approach, the waterfall model is a safe bet in a risk averse and/or efficiency driven environment with relatively static and well-defined requirements. Think of a one-on-one conversion of a Delhi or other legacy application to a modern language or the software development for a nuclear plant or F35 jet fighter. The 8 million lines on board the F35 Lightning II are embedded in thousands of components, such as the radar, engine, and cockpit, that are manufactured by hundreds of suppliers. To ensure that they function in perfect harmony, there is no freedom to deviate from the predetermined principles, frameworks, and requirements.

Besides the agile Scrum method as the obvious case to realize entrepreneurial IT and the waterfall model as a suitable candidate for the most stable part of the foundation IT portfolio, there is also a third way. Less known, but nevertheless worth mentioning, is the spiral model, as seen in Table 4.5. It is a risk-driven development methodology that was first described by Barry Boehm in 1986. Depending on the risk profile, the team can use any appropriate mix of simulations, prototyping, or specification-oriented development to reach the desired end result. If Samsung were to use the spiral model for the development of its products, both a lack of appealing features and time-to-market would be considered risks that have to be mitigated until the business considers the residual risk acceptable.

As the spiral model does not prescribe a specific development approach, it can be used for initiatives that score both low and high on uncertainty and complexity. In case of a high-risk profile, the team can opt to start with several simulations or small prototypes to root out the biggest uncertainties—eventually followed by one or more waterfall spirals to develop the requirements that are

---

[3] Including the V-model (validation and verification model) as it's also sequential but not completely linear like waterfall. The stages turn back upward after the coding phase is done.

Table 4.5 Software development and their sweet spots

	Waterfall (Including V-Model)	Spiral Model	Agile
Goals	Defined at executive level, intended	Flexible; goals can be either intended or emergent	General vision and direction, but detailed goals not known and partially emergent
Business Context	• Known markets, business models, and products and processes in combination with known customer reactions • Known external environmental parameters (e.g., price elasticity, regulation) • Low risk appetite	Flexible; most for projects with a high initial risk profile	• New markets, business models, products and processes, and unknown customer reactions • Fast moving competitors, dynamic customer behavior • Vision or ambition as starting point
Typical Starting Point of the Project	All requirements are collected through interviews, workshops, and other means before any coding is done; all requirements in scope are equally important	Flexible; risk profile of project determines the optimal approach	Customer cannot articulate requirements up front, only key concepts, generic user stories, and a vision. The requirements are defined and reprioritized throughout the duration of the project
What Is Fixed?	Requirements are fixed, in case of issues: more budget, delayed deployment. Very little to no room for requirement changes during realization process	• The so-called *six invariants* of the spiral model[1]	Requirements are developed, tested, and deployed using iterative cycles: • For a predefined number of sprints (so budget is fixed) • Until a minimum viable product is available • Until the business is satisfied with the end-product (budget is variable)

Project Approach	Sequential, original model consists of seven steps: requirements specification, design, construction, integration, testing and debugging, installation, and maintenance	Every iteration is aimed at systematically reducing the risk profile of the initiative, using a mix of various development approaches	Iterative, with each sprint going through these steps: planning, requirements analysis, design, coding, and technical and functional testing
Examples	• One-on-one refactoring of legacy code • Adjusting legacy applications (e.g., add hard-coded interface) • Creating very complex and mission critical solutions (e.g., nuclear, defense)	• Several unproven functional concepts in combination with known requirements • Known functionalities, but user resistance against change	• Solutions requiring high and constant involvement of business users • Solution with considerable speed-to-market benefits (e.g., first to market or fast follower)

[1] See https://en.wikipedia.org/wiki/Spiral_model for more information.

certain. The spiral model is, therefore, even suitable for situations too uncertain (or even wasteful) for the agile Scrum method. Simulations, virtual reality, mock-ups, and other tools allow the team to validate highly uncertain assumptions without writing a single line of code.

The spiral model may also be an answer for companies with a strong risk-averse culture and *hard* control environment. The latter challenge is reflected in the *State of Agile Development Survey 2009*, where *management control* was stated as one of the main concerns regarding adoption of the agile method. When trying to implement agile in a company founded in a *rule-based* society and active in a risk-averse industry, the required organizational paradigm shift is considerable (see the case that was described in Chapter 2). The spiral model may be just the right thing, as it explicitly focuses on reducing risk and can be used in combination with multiple development approaches. If there is one thing managers like, it is having more than one option to choose from.

Another, less hotly debated topic than the waterfall model versus the agile development, is the choice between custom software and COTS software. Ask a developer to choose and the answer is predictable—"Custom development allows for a perfect fit!"—as is the answer of the average purchase officer—"Buying COTS is cheaper!" Hence, here too, it pays off to agree on a certain set of guiding principles to ensure the decision is based on the relevant context instead of personal preferences.

4.2.3 Custom, Configuration, or Standard

There are millions of companies out there, all looking for solutions to automate their business processes. The majority of the business processes are mature, not unique (contrary to, for example, the central government), and not distinctive (e.g., enables an unfair cost or differentiating advantage in combination with business capabilities). It is the sweet spot targeted by suppliers of standard software-as-a-service (SaaS) applications and configurable platforms, which includes content management systems and document management systems. It represents the largest share of the estimated $620 billion spend on software by companies in 2015.[xvi]

Custom-built software is far from dead, however, with a share of $136 billion. Even more impressive is the compound annual rate of growth (CARG) of 33 percent in the period between 2011 and 2015—considerably higher than the 10 percent CARG of the overall software market. There are several reasons why this part of the market is flourishing:

- New technologies emerge both faster and in greater numbers compared to the past. As there are no standard solutions available during the early life-cycle phases, companies have no choice but to invest in custom-built solutions if they want to leverage on emerging technologies (see Chapter 5).
- All companies with the exception of reactors seek *distinctive* capabilities as they are a source of competitive advantage. For companies that are active in hybrid or digital markets, this translates into investing in both business and IT capabilities that are difficult to imitate or substitute, and are rare, immobile, or very costly to create. Standard software can only score high on cost.
- Mobile phones, smart watches, smart glasses, virtual reality headsets, and smart TVs are but a few of the digital channels available to companies. When the business wants to add one or more of them to their business model, IT has to build an app or other solution that stands out from the crowd.
- SaaS suppliers offer standardized functional silos, including application programming interfaces (APIs) to communicate with other SaaS applications and on-premise applications. When buying solutions from multiple suppliers, the client company has to invest in tracking, exchanging, and governing master and reference data.

With the exception of integrating SaaS applications, there is a high correlation between the growth drivers of custom-built software and entrepreneurial IT, as seen in Figure 4.3. Foundation IT covers the other side of the spectrum, with configurable platforms holding the middle ground. When the HR department

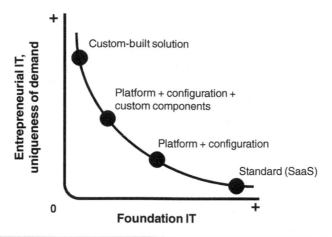

Figure 4.3   The solution continuum

wants an attractive intranet to publish content that is relevant to employees, it wants to customize the look and feel, integrate certain content feeds, and add simple workflows. To fulfill this need, SharePoint, Jive, or other content management platforms provide the necessary flexibility and foundation for things like database, interfaces, and segregation of duties.

Even *custom-built* does not necessarily require coding in Java, C#, Ruby, or other programming language anymore. Prototypes, proof of concepts, and even moderately complex mature business applications can be built using development platforms[4] from OutSystems, Google, CloudBees, Salesforce.com, or Mendix. Increasingly, the developer is replaced by a business analyst who will generate an application by creating a visual model of user stories and functions (e.g., calculation). While these platforms tend to be less suitable for complex business critical applications, their low up-front investment and positive effect on time-to-market makes them interesting candidates for IT customer segments that want to experiment a lot via R&D and marketing or regularly request moderately complex applications.

Last, but not least, it is important to take note that the choice for custom, platform of standard depends on more than context alone. The available budget and skills sets, contractual obligations, existing technology landscape, and politics are all generic constraints that influence the final decision. The same applies to the waterfall model versus the agile method. If a senior executive has had a

---

[4] Also known as an *enterprise application platform as a service* solution.

bad past experience with agile, that option may be out of the question, even though the context strongly points in that direction.

Besides attention for generic constrains, it is also worth investing some time in determining the specific pros and cons of the topic at hand. The context of a business demand may point toward custom built; but, if the company lacks the capabilities to develop internally and is too immature to source externally, whether it be to fulfill a product owner role or to avoid signing an unbalanced contract, a standard solution may be the better choice. The advantages of a standard solution include:

- Limited capital investment; however, the yearly recurring operational expenses may be higher due to license fees.
- Every new release adds new functions that may be of value to the business users.
- Better speed-to-market; since only the testing and implementation phases remain, there is no need to design and develop.
- Less time required from the business and IT. The fees of consultants from proprietary software suppliers may, however, be substantially higher than fees charged by suppliers for custom-built software.

Unless willing to pay for a customization project, the other side of the coin includes inflexibility, slower response to changing customer or industry needs, forced upgrade cycles, and intellectual property rights owned by the supplier.

The principle *less uniform, more differentiated* has more touch points than development approaches and custom versus standard. As covered in Chapter 6, all building blocks of the IT business model should reflect both the positioning of IT as a whole and the context of individual business needs. Only then is waste minimized and value creation maximized.

Also, not covered yet is the relation between time and differentiation. Until now, the assumption was entrepreneurial IT today is also entrepreneurial IT tomorrow. This is not necessarily true. Everything changes, or in other words, goes through a life cycle. Before explaining the principle of *less static, more flow* in Chapter 5, let's take a look at another case study of, once again, an IT service provider.

4.3 FROM LOW TO HIGH GEAR

Over a period of several decades, a medium-sized IT service provider had built a broad portfolio of standard software solutions that targeted both horizontal markets like finance, accounting, and HR, and vertical markets like banking and central government. Conservative financial policies, several high-margin solutions, and a strong focus on cost leadership allowed the company to regularly acquire small best-of-breed competitors, further strengthening its portfolio. During its existence, the company had never reported a yearly loss—in short, it was rock solid.

Of the 1,800 employees, some 1,700 worked for one of the twelve market-oriented business units. The remaining 100 employees were tasked with providing shared services like HR, IT, and accounting. The company did not pay the highest salaries in the market, but neither had it ever had to lay off large groups of employees. In some markets, the company had a near monopoly, theoretically ensuring that the employees could look forward to a stable future. Yet, trouble was brewing in paradise.

The last acquisition took place more than a decade ago and the application landscape started to show it. The employees of acquired companies had been properly integrated into the IT service provider, but the applications were merely copied from one server to another. Some had been built in Cobol, others in Delphi, Progress, Oracle, C++, or VB6. None had a web-interface and many had hardcoded interfaces. One application was still running on a Windows NT 4.0 server (virtualized on top of Windows 2016), as upgrading had been considered too cumbersome by the developers.

As none of the solutions offered by the IT service provider targeted entrepreneurial IT, it took a long time before the existing customers started to complain about the lack of an attractive interaction design, support of mobile devices, web services, and APIs. Competitors took notice and started to push their solutions that were outwardly superior looking but functionally inferior. Senior managers quickly recognized the threat and scrambled into action. They allocated several million dollars to modernize and rationalize the application portfolio.

The results—after spending the first two million—were limited to frustration and an unusable product. The existing managers, product owner, project manager, and developers had collectively underestimated the complexity of the initiative. They tried to realize a huge functional backlog with, for them, new technologies like the C# development language, new architecture standards (e.g., component based APIs), new nonfunctional requirements such as being OWASP compliant, and a new development approach like that of the agile Scrum method.

Summary: after more than two decades of realizing small incremental application changes using the same technology-stack, the team had lost the capability to realize something completely new.

A product manager does not necessarily possess the skills required to be an effective product owner. Neither does a good project manager, by definition, make a good Scrum Master. Furthermore, a two-day training in agile can barely cover all the theory, let alone the practical dos and don'ts. For a project surpassing 15,000 development hours, this approach is a recipe for disaster.

Three months after the initial failure, a new project was reinitiated to give it a second try. The big difference was the composition of the team. They came to the realization that the project required skills that were closely related to building custom software instead of enhancing and optimizing an existing product. The new team, therefore, consisted of members with deep domain expertise and insight in the expectations of the customers and members who excelled in custom-built software.

Summary: even though the application itself fulfilled a business demand that was related to foundation IT, radical modernization required skills that were more closely related to entrepreneurial IT.

The chain is only as strong as its weakest link. Besides providing office automation functions and supporting shared business applications (like invoicing and time tracking), the shared IT function was also responsible for deploying development, test, and production environments (deploying a virtual server could take up to two months so even the most patient and forgiving internal business users and indirect external customers can get frustrated). Yet, many deadlines turned out to be too ambitious on several occasions, resulting in a call or e-mail two days before the deadline that they were not going to make it. External infrastructure-as-a-service cloud providers were initially a no-go due to the existing security policy. After several missed deadlines and escalations reaching the board, the CEO decided to adjust the policies and start an initiative to improve the performance of the internal IT function.

Summary: to minimize waste, the whole end-to-end realization process (i.e., the IT business model) has to be optimized for a specific customer segment or value proposition category.

There were even more sources of waste, however. For the first modernization project, another IT service provider was contracted to supply developers who were experienced in developing custom software using agile Scrum. This approach was not only more expensive than using internal resources, hiring externals also meant that valuable experience and knowledge would leave the company when the project came to a close. It was therefore neither scalable nor sustainable. The only choice left to the board was abandoning its defensive harvesting strategy and modernizing the company as a whole. At that time, the average age of the employees was around 50 and they were used to stability and predictability. Until then, most people who entered the company with an entrepreneurial IT profile had left after a year or so.

To address this unsustainable situation, hiring and retaining young talent and activating the existing population became strategic key objectives. As mid- and higher management levels can be both crucial activators and inhibitors of cultural change, the existing team was infused with young talent at all levels of the organization. Besides a long-term HR development program, the board also decided to invest in a separate business unit that was dedicated to custom-built software. The new business unit would act as a *modernization factory* for the other business units, leveraging on an offshore captive center to execute a large part of the actual coding.

Instead of closing the business unit after the modernization program, the board intended to retain it and position the business unit as an incubator for the rest of the company. Entrepreneurial IT and foundation IT don't mix that well, but they were both needed to create a sustainable business model. The new business unit was therefore tasked with developing prototypes and proof of concepts for other business units, experimenting with new technologies, and building shared application components for the other business units, such as user authorization and payment components.

After five difficult years and several lost customers—albeit, still without incurring a loss—the IT service provider slowly became more competitive and agile again. The majority of the applications were web-based, had a responsive design, and were pleasant to work with. The cultural change was still a work in progress though. There was a vision, plan, and budget for coaching and training, but it was difficult for many employees at the operational and mid-level to let go of the past. Changing the mindset, behavior, and skill set of the existing population would remain a clear and present struggle.

Summary: companies that move slower than the external environment create a debt. One day, payment will be due, including accumulated interest.

REFERENCES

i. Miles, R. and Snow, C. (1978). *Organizational Strategy, Structure, and Process*. New York: McGraw-Hill.
ii. Christensen, C. (1997). *The Innovator's Dilemma*. Harvard Business Review Press.
iii. Brown, J. R. and Goolsbee, A. (October 2000). Does the Internet Make Markets More Competitive? Evidence from the Life Insurance Industry.
iv. Brown, J. (2001). The Internet Makes Life Insurance Markets More Competetive. Working Paper Series of The Geneva Association, International Association for the Study of Insurance Economics.

   v. Treacy, M. and Wiersema, F. (January–February 1993). Customer Intimacy and Other Value Disciplines. Harvard Business Review.

  vi. Pratt, M. K. (February 2014). 7 Things Marketing Wants to Say to IT. CIO.com. Link: http://www.cio.com/article/747797/7 Things_Marketing_Wants_to_Say_to_IT?page=1&taxonomyId=3148.

 vii. Luftman, J. and Kempaiah, R. (September 2007). An Update on Business-IT Alignment: "A Line" Has Been Drawn, MIS Quarterly Executive.

viii. Stabell, C. B. and Fjeldstad, Ø. D. (1998). Configuring Value for Competitive Advantage: On Chains, Shops, and Networks, Strategic Management Journal.

  ix. Coombs, R. (1996). Core Competencies and the Strategic Management of R&D.

   x. Miles, R. and Snow, C. (1978). *Organizational Strategy, Structure, and Process.* New York: McGraw-Hill.

  xi. Van Der Zee, H. T. M. (2001). Measuring the Value of Information Technology.

 xii. Ross, J. W. and Beath, C. M. (Winter 2002). Beyond the Business Case: New Approaches to IT Investment. MIT Sloan Management Review.

xiii. Grant, R. (October 2013). Samsung Galaxy Gear Smartwatches Have Embarrassing 30% Return Rate. Venturebeat.com. Link: http://venturebeat.com/2013/10/28/samsung-galaxy-gear-smartwatches-have-embarrassing-30-return-rate/.

xiv. Amadeo, R. (July 2014). Why Google Took Years to Address a Battery-Draining "Bug" in Chrome. Arstechnica.com. Link: http://arstechnica.com/gadgets/2014/07/why-google-took-years-to-address-a-battery-draining-bug-in-chrome/.

 xv. Gibbs, R. D. (2006). *Project Management with the IBM Rational Unified Process: Lessons from the Trenches.* Harvard Business School Publishing.

xvi. Poulos, N. (2015). Why Custom Apps Grew $100B in the Last 5 Years. Link: http://www.bowerycap.com/blog/themes/custom-apps-grew-100b-last-5-years/.

5

LESS STATIC, MORE FLOW

Less static, more flow represents the ability to integrate multiple, interdependent, life cycles.

More precisely, the topic of this chapter emphasizes the importance of time. We use it to order events from the past through the present and into the future. As this is not a philosophy book, I translated it into something more practical: the life cycle. It is nevertheless worthwhile to spend a couple of sentences on time itself.

In the science fiction series *Star Trek*, the tricorder was named after three scan functions: GEO (geological), BIO (biological), and MET (meteorological). Today's wearables are quickly catching up on the last two functions, turning science function into something anybody can add to their Christmas list. Robots, autonomous cars, and rockets are other examples whereby real science had to play catch-up with human imagination. The internet followed the opposite path. It started to show up in science fiction books only after it was created as part of the ARPANET initiative funded by the U.S. Department of Defense.

Some disruptions just happen. Time is a source of surprises.

Time can be both fixed and fluid. There are sixty minutes in an hour, no more, no less. Nevertheless, in some markets, time seems to move faster than others. Employees of Samsung or other smart phone manufacturers are active in a market that is shaped by the fear of falling behind the next time there is a shift in customer technology preferences. They closely follow each other's moves and constantly seek that new differentiating feature that will make the next product launch a success. Compare that to the dynamics faced by government workers of a small county.

Time can be monetized as this: a dollar today is worth more than the same dollar tomorrow. Even the ability to postpone a decision can be monetized using *real options* (see Chapter 7). One thing that is not possible is stopping time.

Even the largest and most robust corporations—the ones that think of themselves as impervious to the impact of time—will eventually be disrupted. Companies, markets, value propositions, channels, and technologies are born, grow, mature, become old, and inevitably get replaced by something new—restarting the cycle.

Only one escape route is available to a company to avoid obsolescence—Darwin's theory implies: *It is not the strongest of the species that survives, nor the most intelligent that survives. It is the one that is the most adaptable to change.*

The structure of this chapter is similar to that of the previous three; first the why, followed by the how, and then a case study. Also, similar to previous chapters, Table 5.1 provides three statements that cover the chapter as a whole.

Table 5.1   Statements to think about when reading this chapter

Statements
IT has to be able to mirror the different shapes and durations of business life cycles.
The standard IT strategy process is too slow and sequential to be effective in many markets.
The entrepreneurial IT of today is the foundation IT of tomorrow.

5.1 WHY THIS PRINCIPLE MATTERS

For decades, fashion brands introduced two collections per year. Then, Zara developed the capability to have clothes in its store 30 days from the moment it identified a new trend. Moving from a cycle of six months to a fraction of that period gave Zara a strategic advantage over the competition, however temporary it was. To shorten the life cycle without ending up with warehouses full of unsold clothes, Zara invested in sophisticated forecasting, planning, and other supply-chain related technologies.

Despite the pivotal role of IT during the business transformation, it remained relatively isolated from the business. Even adopting a software release cadence tuned to the business cycle had a limited impact on the IT team. This is about to change though. The miniaturization of sensors, LED lights, processors, and other technology related to the shift toward the Internet of Things (IoT), enable clothes that measure your health, change color using miniaturized LEDs, store your music, and have sleeves with an embedded screen allowing you to make calls and navigate. A decade from now, the phone as a physical product will come under threat of becoming an endangered species.

At that point, Zara's business and technology life cycles have to operate in complete sync, requiring the fusion of business and technological capabilities to remove any source of friction. At a certain point, the new features and services enabled by the embedded technology may even become more valuable than the basic purpose clothes provide today. The Zara of today may be the Apple of tomorrow. The hiring of the former CEO of Burberry, Angela Ahrendts, by Apple may well be partially instigated by the desire to prevent that from happening. As the dissolving of industry boundaries can be observed in many markets, the C-suite, and especially the CIO, had better take notice. It is not every day that such a strategic opportunity presents itself to reposition the IT team, in part or in whole.

With the progression of time, technology as a supporting capability is increasingly being replaced by technology as a core business capability.

IT professionals who are working for companies with an analog or hybrid business model don't have to look far to find practices that will help them to prepare for the upcoming transformation. The technology sector is a constantly shifting landscape that is used to sync business and technology life cycles. Emerging technologies trigger the business cycle, like how the invention of high-density laptop screens created a new category of laptops, instead of the other way around—such as Zara's business ambition triggering the need for a new supply chain management platform. Tech companies also know that a new technology, revolutionary or not, needs a clear or compelling relevance to the customer's life. A large marketing budget cannot compensate for the lack of need. The focus should be on the people, not the product. And last but not least, the IT professionals need to learn to think faster.

Like smart clothes, milk cartons with sensors that measure both the quality and quantity of the milk are still years away from us. Hence, combine proactive planning for these long-term strategic changes with short term initiatives that are focused on increasing the *digital maturity* of IT teams. One of the first steps on that maturity ladder is the capability to tune the IT business model (discussed more later on) to the business life cycle. Simply stated, an IT business model optimized for foundation IT will struggle to support the business that is introducing a new, technology-rich product in the market.

The translation of a technology-rich business product to the IT business model is depicted in Table 5.2. Its applicability is limited to hybrid models, as analog business models require less convergence to function effectively while the fusion of capabilities is required for native digital models. The top part of the table provides several key business aspects per life-cycle phase, followed by a translation to foundation IT and entrepreneurial IT.

The business life cycle starts with the translation of a vision or opportunity into a value proposition that customers are likely to buy. This means the business

Table 5.2   From business life cycle to IT life cycle

Business Perspective				
Business Life-Cycle Phase	**Introduction**	**Growth**	**Mature**	**Decline**
Market Growth	Low to high	High	Low to steady	Decline
Level of Uncertainty	High	Medium	Low	Low
Price Point	High	Steady to decline	Decline	Low (recover variable cost plus margin)
Number of Customers	Small (early adaptors)	Growing quickly, break through	Large, mass market	Declining
Investment in Fixed Assets	Low	(Very) high	High, moving to low	Asset recovery
Profit	Negative	Average	High	Medium to nil
IT Perspective				
	Entrepreneurial IT		**Foundation IT**	
Business-IT Cooperation	Focus on convergence (e.g., close collaboration, joint team, iterative)	From close informal collaboration to formalized and planned	IT business alignment	IT business alignment
Importance of Speed-to-Market	High	High to medium	Medium to low	Low
Importance of Reliability and Predictability	Low to medium	Medium to high	High	High
Innovation Orientation	Joint product innovation	Joint product enhancements	Enable business and IT process optimizations	None. IT asset recovery. If required, conversion of legacy software
IT Management Orientation	Strong leader, creative stars	Organizer plus mix of creative stars and practical practitioners	Manager plus administrators and operators	Manager plus administrators and operators
IT Sourcing Orientation	Access to differentiating features and innovations. Improve speed-to-market, volume flexibility; Minimize investment risk	Build key capabilities internally, volume and quality augmentation through partners	Sourcing decisions based on drive for efficiency and reliability	Extend business life cycle through efficiency-oriented IT outsourcing

is not looking for a team of risk-averse IT administrators, but colleagues who are proactive, business savvy, and creative. As success is still uncertain during this phase, investment in fixed assets should be kept to a minimum. Resources should be dedicated to acquiring customers, as they have a key attribute that is crucial to every new introduction: word of mouth. Those same initial customers are also a valuable source of feedback, feeding the backlog of the iterative development team.

In case the value proposition indeed appeals to a strong customer need, it moves toward the growth phase. Here, the experimental nature is replaced by the need to scale and become profitable. Investments in fixed assets and a more permanent team structure become a safe bet. While moving through the growth phase, entrepreneurial IT increasingly turns into foundation IT as the emphasis on planning, forecasting, reliability, and efficiency continue to grow. The boundary between entrepreneurial IT and foundation IT is, therefore, not as black and white as depicted in Table 5.2. To enable a smoother transition between both, this book leverages on the four-quadrant portfolio model from Ward and Peppard (see below).[i]

With the progression of time, entrepreneurial IT becomes foundation IT.

Table 5.2 also reflects the importance of foundation IT for the company as a whole. The profit margin is at its highest during the mature phase, providing the necessary funding for new value propositions. The teams responsible for entrepreneurial IT and foundation IT are, therefore, of equal importance to the company. With that said, as markets become more complex and uncertain, foundation IT has to become more nimble than it was twenty years ago.

Also more diverse than 20 years ago are the shapes of the business life cycle. Base products like bread and butter still go through the phases of the traditional life cycle, as does the solution required by the HR department to pay the salaries as seen in Figure 5.1. Fads are another timeless phenomenon; value propositions that don't make it beyond the introduction phase. More recent are shapes introduced by companies like Zara and the big bang market adoption. The first shape shares many similarities with the introduction of a hyped game. Demand very quickly picks up after the introduction, requiring a supply chain that can scale quickly.[1] Depending on customer demand, the remainder of the life cycle either qualifies as a fad or enjoys short growth and maturity phases (e.g., by adding new levels for games or introducing the same jacket design with a new material). Big bang introductions have an even more *aggressive* shape.

---

[1] Software and data are cheap and easy to scale. However, when hardware components (e.g., sensors, cloth fabric) are involved, a more complex supply chain is required.

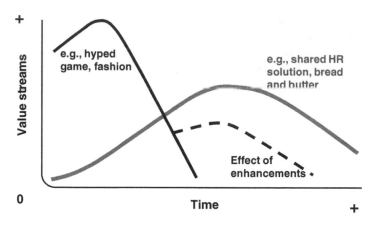

Figure 5.1   Heterogeneous life cycles

Uber and Airbnb completely ignored the existing business models and market players. They were not interested in lowering the price by a few percent or offering a slightly better service. Instead of investing in cars or hotels respectively, they launched platform-based business models using apps as their primary channel to serve their customers. It is a channel that can both scale infinitely cheaper and faster than the existing hard-asset-based business models. Everybody with a smartphone can be a customer or supplier in a matter of minutes, allowing these companies to capture a huge market share in a matter of months. These business models enter the market with a bang.

With the progression of time, the shape of the life cycle may change dramatically as the accompanying business model gets disrupted.

The last argument as to why this principle deserves specific attention is captured by the hype cycle for emerging technologies from Gartner.[ii] Like business products, new technologies can be a fad or take longer than expected to realize the projected business benefits. Depending on the required convergence of business and technology life cycles, the information in Figure 5.2 is either of strategic importance or merely informational. IBM had bet the company when deciding to heavily invest in the personal computer. For IBM, the return on investment (ROI) was considerable. But for every success story, there is at least one first mover whose dreams ended with disillusionment. One reason is captured by the Dutch *Law of the handicap of a head start.*[2] Around 1812, London launched an

---

[2] There is a theory that suggests that an initial (technology) head start in a certain area may result in a handicap in the long term as more robust and scalable substitutes emerge. More information can be found at: http://en.wikipedia.org/wiki/Law_of_the_handicap_of_a_head_start.

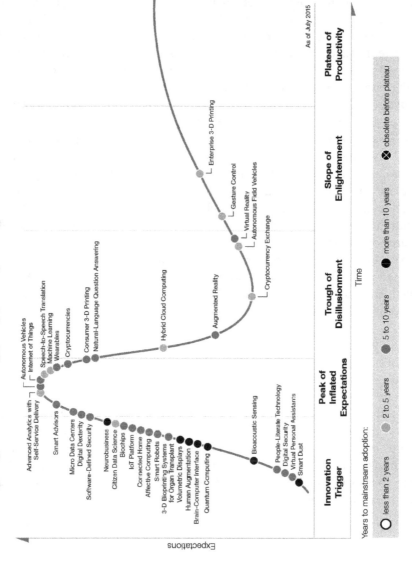

Figure 5.2   Gartner Hype Cycle for emerging technologies 2015 (Gartner)

initiative to improve public safety by installing streetlights using the best technology available at the time—natural gas lamps. After spending years and large sums to realize the required infrastructure, the technology suddenly became obsolete; Thomas Edison invented a reliable way to produce electricity in 1879. As a result, while most European cities used electricity for public lights for most of the 19th century, London still relied on gas.

Besides the introduction of a superior technology, the lack of standardization presents another key risk related to the first life-cycle phases. Just think of the battle between VHS, Video 2000, and Betamax or Blu-ray versus HD DVD. To mitigate these strategic risks, companies can either wait and see which technology and standard will prevail, invest small amounts in multiple candidates, or shift part of the investment risk to external partners. At the operational level, most challenges will be related to creating the capabilities that are required to translate the emerging technology into a viable business model or value proposition.

Neither the benefits nor the risks of a new emergent technology are fixed for businesses. They change while moving through the life-cycle phases. Both the potential upside and downside are highest at the start—slowly declining when the technology, value propositions, and processes mature (as can be seen in Table 5.3). The strategic risk profile shows an uptick at the end, however, as many companies get too comfortable with the existing technology portfolio. Microsoft initially underestimated the impact of mobile technology on its business model, while SAP and Oracle struggle to counter the threat posed by nimbler software-as-a-service (SaaS) providers.

Complacency and/or active inertia inhibits the experimentation and incremental change required to ensure that companies move in time, such as in the case of mainframe to server-client to web-based applications. If the value of a technology is 100 today, it is 100–n tomorrow. Few things are therefore as dangerous as extrapolating past success to predict the future. Future success requires critical thinking and regular reassessment of past decisions.

> *With the progression of time, both the benefits and risks of a technology change.*

Building thicker walls can only slow down the impact of time. A company has to be in tune with its environment, or even better, one step ahead. The same applies to the IT team. It has to organize itself according to the different speeds that the business is moving in. As time moves faster in new native digital markets when compared to mature analog markets, the principle *less static, more flow* may seem less relevant to the latter. Don't worry; it is only a matter of time before that assumption is disrupted by a start-up that ignores the once-winning rules of the game. The principle *less static, more flow* is, therefore, an invitation

Table 5.3 A risk profile is not static, it evolves over time

	Technology Trigger	Peak of Inflated Expectations	Trough of Disillusionment	Slope of Enlightenment	Plateau of Productivity
Strategic Risk	Early adaptor is exposed to both potential high return and high losses. Considerable investment risk.	Inflated return expectation combined with underestimated risk.	Underestimating consequences of cancellation. Inability to recover assets.	Overestimating differentiating aspects of technology.	Underestimating technology lock-in. Ignore potentially disruptive substitutes.
Operational Risk	Lack of experience by both business and IT with new processes, systems, and skills.	Unexpected losses due to immaturity of processes, systems, and skills (e.g., high return rates from customers).	Dealing with operational consequences of cancellation (e.g., nobody thought about Plan B).	Underestimating residual operational risk.	Minor topic due to high maturity at this stage.

to regularly answer the following questions once we consider the existing speeds that the markets move in, along with their technology density and maturity:

- Which of the current business life cycles are expected to speed up or slow down? What is the expected increase or decrease (e.g., 50% in two years)? What is the impact of these changes on IT?
- Which existing beliefs underpinning the business model and business life cycle are most likely to be disrupted in the near future? What is the expected impact on underpinning IT value propositions and technology?
- Which emerging technology can dramatically change the flow of existing business life cycles? What are the key opportunities and threats for both business and IT?

The next part of this chapter will provide some of the answers.

5.2 HOW TO BECOME LESS STATIC AND FOLLOW THE FLOW

In his article, *IT Doesn't Matter*, Nicholas Carr argued that the wide availability of IT prevents it from providing companies with a sustainable strategic advantage.[iii] As an example, he referred to the reservation system of American Airlines. It provided American Airlines with a strategic advantage until the competition caught up. Eventually, American Airlines even spun off its reservation system, as it had become a commodity within the industry.

To remain ahead of the pack, American Airlines and every other company can, therefore, never stop seeking new sources of strategic differentiation. Depending on the strategy (e.g., prospector versus defender) and market (e.g., many or few competitors), the topic is either constantly top-of-mind or of secondary importance. Google is a prime example of the first category, introducing and discontinuing dozens of products every year. Another technology-driven company that is well-known for its innovative and constantly updated product portfolio is 3M. Nevertheless, from an IT perspective, 3M can be considered part of the same category as Zara. The interdependence between the business and IT life cycles are limited—for now.

When new sources of strategic differentiation require fused business and IT capabilities, things have to be organized differently, starting with the strategic process. Assuming speed is *the* key factor for success in the markets that the company is targeting,[3] the traditional paradigm whereby the IT strategy follows

---

[3] Compared to, for example, differentiation based on geographical location (e.g., success depends on using locally produced farm products) or strategy (e.g., half the market requires customer intimacy, the other half, operational excellence). See also Chapter 4.

the business strategy is too slow. For the fast markets and/or first phases of the business life cycle, a pass-through (see the following section) is required.

5.2.1 Pass-Through Strategy

The starting point for the approach depicted in Figure 5.3 is the external environment because it contains the customers with the needs and wants. For start-ups, only the left part is relevant, as none of their value propositions had time to move beyond the first life-cycle stages. Incumbent companies have both new and mature value propositions, necessitating differentiation—they need a gear box.

When faced with unforeseen opportunities and threats that require quick and decisive action, even the business does not have time for its standard business strategy process. It can take weeks or even months to go through the workshops, scenario planning sessions, and other meetings that are required in order to define a multi-year strategy and program. In markets where the operationally responsible business executives get ecstatic when they are able to predict what

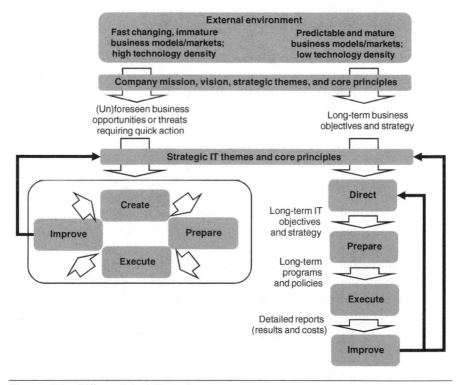

Figure 5.3   Differentiated IT strategy process

will occur in the next six to twelve months, the standard time-consuming process simply does not pay off. Hence, the suggestion to define a strategic *checklist* containing companies' mission, vision and strategic themes, and core principles.

To realize a strategy, the traditional approach dictates the definition of one or more programs (e.g., get a foothold in *market A* by the end of this year), each with their own responsible executive. Besides several advantages, this approach also has an important downside: unmanaged interdependencies and synergistic effects between the individual initiatives are likely to get lost since those who are responsible focus only on their own scope, planning, and budget. Changing priorities and other relevant information may not reach other important stakeholders. By defining one or more strategic themes, business and IT base their decisions on a portfolio of interrelated initiatives. It allows them to slow down or speed up a coherent set of programs and projects instead of focusing on realizing point objectives.

Core principles balance flexibility and speed with the desire to prevent strategic accidents,[4] such as taking on too much risk or doing business with blacklisted countries. Like strategic themes, their level of detail is limited, relying on the quality of the hiring process to ensure that the decisions made are in the best interest of the company and its customers. Furthermore, as it is impossible to foresee all opportunities and threats, they should be open for discussion (*comply or explain*).

After passing through the business filter, the business opportunities (both foreseen and unforeseen) or threats requiring quick action are promptly allocated to one or more operational joint business IT teams to define either a real-time strategy, for example, a considerable long-term revenue potential, or a tactical plan to manage things like an unforeseen operational risk. To prevent *strategic* IT accidents (e.g., large investment in emerging proprietary technology), IT should also invest in their own strategic checklist. It has to prevent ending up with an unmanageable and unfundable mash up of technologies, security policies, and external suppliers. Moreover, an entrepreneurial IT value proposition today may well become a business-critical foundation IT value proposition in a couple of years—further emphasizing the need to create a shared strategic IT baseline.

The right side of Figure 5.3 depicts the traditional sequential process based on the strategic alignment model from Henderson and Venkatraman.[iv] It is relevant for value propositions with long lifespans as they have enough time to stabilize, warranting multi-year business and IT strategies. When reaching this part of the life cycle, the technology has commoditized, removing any first or

---

[4] Contrary to more operational *creative accidents*—which are an important source of both learning and bottom-up emerging strategies.

early mover advantage the company may have enjoyed earlier on. As a result, new IT investments are primarily driven by market pull (e.g., initiative to reduce manufacturing cost) and technology refresh (e.g., upgrade operating systems [OSs]). The strategic option available to the business during the introduction phase to push a new emerging technology to the market (*technology push*) is no longer a valid option as the needs and wants of the customers are known (hence, *market pull*).

From an organizational perspective, it is important to take into account that a technology push is proactive in nature, while business or market pulls tend to position IT as the faithful servant. A technology push is identified with creative breakthroughs and destruction, while market pull is driven by the desire to introduce a replacement or substitute.[v] Translated to the Miles and Snow model, the IT strategy of prospectors and analyzers in technology- and data-rich markets likely gravitate to a technology push, while CIOs of defenders will pursue a business pull approach. Neither is better, but they require a different skill set and culture from the IT team to be executed effectively. The difference between technology push and market pull can also be observed by looking in more detail at the interaction between the relevant life cycles.

5.2.2 Loosely and Tightly Coupled Life Cycles

Life cycles can be observed in science (e.g., biology, psychosocial development), business (e.g., product life cycle), IT (e.g., software release life cycle), and systems engineering. Relevant to operationalize the principle of *less static, more flow* are two business life cycles consisting of the market life cycle and product life cycle, and two IT life cycles consisting of the IT value proposition life cycle and technology life cycle. Depending on the technology density of the market, these life cycles are either loosely or tightly coupled:

- **The market life cycle**—These cycles tend to have the longest duration. The market for cars with combustion engines is already more than a century old, and only now are electric cars slowly but thoroughly disrupting this market. Another example is the replacement of landline telephones by mobile phones. The latter was introduced in the 19th century, surpassing even the car.
- **The product life cycle**[5]—Every five years or so, car manufacturers launch an updated version of existing models or introduce a completely new model. With a life cycle of six to 12 months, manufacturers of mobile phones have considerably less time to earn their ROI and prepare the next product.

---

[5] Also known as the *business life cycle* in this book as it is referenced to from an IT perspective.

- **IT value proposition life cycle**—A product life cycle may need one or more enabling IT value propositions over its lifespan. Reasons to invest in multiple IT value propositions include entering new markets (e.g., different legislation), adding enhancements (e.g., additional after sales service channel), scalability (e.g., demand far outstripped expectations), and efficiency (e.g., business starts competing on price). In digital markets, the product life cycle and IT value proposition life cycle may be one and the same.
- **The technology life cycle**—Similar to the business life cycle, technologies are introduced, then followed by an eventual maturing into a commodity. Virtual reality and wearables are still in the early stages of their respective life cycles, while online storage is already considered a commodity even though Box was founded in 2005 and Dropbox in 2007.

For many tech companies, the technology life cycle is an important constraint. LG introduced the first organic light-emitting diode (OLED) screens in 2010, and even though Apple would love to incorporate them in its iPhones and iPads due to their superior properties, their only product in 2016 with an OLED screen was the Apple Watch. Apple's subcontractors were unable to produce the number of screens at the stringent quality standards prescribed by Apple. The bakery around the corner is at the other extreme. Bread and bagels don't need any IT to taste good. The IT team's responsibility is limited to automating the secondary business processes, whether it be inbound and outbound logistics or accounting. Besides being very loosely coupled, the life cycles of analog-based products also tend to be long. The bread market is not known for its innovations nor for its introduction of disrupting substitutes by entrepreneurs. Hence, the life cycle of the accompanying IT value propositions tends to be dictated by the mandatory upgrade cycle of the software vendors, such as the obsolesce of Windows XP. The IT-related wants and needs of the baker barely change over time.

A hybrid business model may actually be the most challenging because it combines elements from both extremes. The physical store and warehouses of a hybrid retailer have lifespans of three decades or more. Its online store and mobile app have a lifespan of three years or less. The customers, nevertheless, enjoy a smooth multi-channel experience whereby every channel plays a clear, and often distinct, role. Some retailers, such as IKEA, use their website primarily to inform potential customers about their products, and in doing so, draw them to their physical stores for the actual sell. Many companies use Twitter to provide after-sales service, and Facebook to create interest for new or planned products.

Besides effectively guiding customers through their decision-making journey spanning multiple channels, a hybrid also includes the digitalization of the products or value propositions themselves. Smart lights, fridges, thermostats, and dog collars further converge the analog and digital worlds. Companies considering the partial digitalization of their products face several challenges, including:

- **Shorter product life cycles**—A dog collar or 60-watt light bulb can be sold for more than a decade without any upgrade. Add sensors and hook it up to the internet and suddenly the customer expects the company to introduce a new version every year, as it is now perceived as a *tech product*. The product is now considered part of the same category that our phones and other gadgets are in; they need to have the latest and greatest feature sets to sell.
- **Shorter and longer IT value proposition life cycle**—Assuming the IT team enables the product digitalization, in part or as a whole, the shorter life cycle faced by the business also affects the time available to design, develop, test, and deploy the necessary software and infrastructure. At the same time, when buying an internet-enabled receiver or amplifier, the customer expects the accompanying mobile app to work for at least the next five years. With Google and Apple regularly introducing new versions for their mobile OSs, this translates into a yearly test and update cycle for products that are out of both production and warranty.
- **Tighter coupling between business and technology life cycles**—For analog products, the prices of raw materials and energy are important constraints, combined with the capabilities of manufacturing equipment. With the rise of increasingly sophisticated robots and 3-D printing, in combination with the digitalization of the products themselves, the business and technology life cycles move from loosely to tightly coupled.

The challenge faced by teams that are responsible for hybrid business models is reflected in Table 5.4. The team has to enable the analog parts of the business model, like business process automation, to create or provide access to digital channels, realize digital product features, and integrate the analog and digital parts of the business model into one harmonious and effective source of revenue and profit streams. To do so, the business and IT teams have to decide on topics including:

- What does our business product road map look like? What is the role of technology in the face of challenges and opportunities?
- Which capabilities, product features, and channels should be made internally, and which should be purchased?
- When deciding to create capabilities, should they be part of the business or IT domain? When do they share the responsibility?
- How to govern and manage the differentiated product and channel portfolios effectively and efficiently?

Table 5.4 Technology density drives the IT operating model

	Analog	Hybrid	Digital
Life-cycle Coupling	Loose; barely any dependency between business and IT life cycles.	Digital part of business model (e.g., channels and value proposition) tightly coupled. Analog parts loosely coupled.	Tightly coupled; business life cycles may even depend on the availability of a new technology.
Typical Role of IT	Supporting, enabling.	Source of channels and differentiating product features; supporting, enabling; integration.	Potential source of strategic advantage at the start of the life cycle; technology is integral part of business model.
IT Strategy and Governance	IT strategy follows business strategy (sequential). Stable, finely-grained governance. Focus on *hard* controls.	Differentiated approach (e.g., tactics and iterative, long-term oriented, and sequential). Overall (cross-channel) integration strategy and governance framework.	Early life-cycle phases: • Clear joint vision complemented with lean strategic checklists and iterative tactics. • Dynamic, moderately formalized governance. Focus on *soft* controls. In case the later life-cycle stages stabilize, a more sequential and standardized approach can be adopted.
IT Structure	• Traditional matrix organization (functional silos with processes to provide end-to-end service). • Business domain and IT domain are separated.	• Hybrid, a mix of horizontal, market-oriented teams (e.g., for new digital value propositions) and vertical, efficiency-oriented teams (e.g., for mature cash cows). • Hybrid, fusion for digital product/channel combinations, separated domains for more traditional part of business model (e.g., sell analog product via digital channel).	• Horizontal, market-oriented teams. Back office teams (e.g., transaction processing) can be organized as verticals. • Business domain and (part of) IT domain have fused.

- For which product market combinations do we need to create horizontal (fused) teams, and when should we allocate people to vertical *stove pipes*?

In contrast, IT teams that are responsible for analog business models have a relatively easy job. That is, until their world gets disrupted. Until then, they can derive their strategy and investment programs from the business strategy and remain a fertile ground for *finely grained* Control Objectives for Information and Related Technology (COBIT) and Information Technology Infrastructure Library (ITIL) implementations. There is no need for business and IT convergence beyond the business IT alignment paradigm (see Chapter 6), and teams can be organized in efficiency-focused stove pipes using processes to deliver end-to-end IT value propositions to the business.

When business and IT capabilities fuse to maximize the effectiveness in digital markets, the business strategy becomes the IT strategy. They merge into one integral digital strategy as do the teams. The retained IT team becomes responsible for the foundation IT value propositions that are supporting the secondary business processes and infrastructure used by the business for their digital business products—both of which could be outsourced.

In Ward and Peppard's model, the foundation IT value propositions supporting the secondary business processes are part of the support quadrant since they are neither business critical nor of strategic importance. They have a barely identifiable life cycle as they have already commoditized before they entered the company. Far more interesting are the other three quadrants because they turn out to be a useful tool to translate the business product life cycle into one or more underpinning IT value propositions.

5.2.3 Four Quadrants to Rule Time

The application portfolio matrix by Ward and Peppard provides a proxy of the business life cycle by combining the relative daily business criticality and strategic importance of the IT value proposition, as shown in Figure 5.4.[vi] Referring back to the article *IT Doesn't Matter*, a company can only have IT value propositions in all four quadrants when it has a hybrid or digital business model and both new and mature business life cycles. For analog business models, IT value propositions can only reside with the key operational and support quadrants, as all strategic differentiators reside in the business domain. Things change when the board decides to invest in digitalizing the analog business model.

At that point, the business and IT have to invest in one or more so-called high-potential initiatives. These are IT value propositions with the promise of becoming future super stars, but for now, require the company to invest. They are entrepreneurial IT in nature and are tied to the introduction phase of the

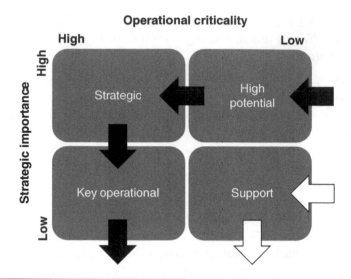

Figure 5.4 Time translated into portfolio quadrants (adapted from Ward and Peppard [2000])

business life cycle. These initiatives are not business critical yet, as in the case of pilot programs, and key success factors include creativity, speed-to-market, limiting investment risk, and combining business and IT capabilities. Due to the high level of uncertainty, this quadrant requires very active management (e.g., quickly invest more, exit).

When the business product turns out to be a success, it moves from the introduction phase to the growth phase and the accompanying IT value proposition moves from the high potential quadrant to the strategic quadrant. The combination apparently was successful in fulfilling a customer need and is difficult to copy by competitors. Apple introduced its MacBook Air in 2009, but it took the competition years to create a Windows substitute. During that period, Apple enjoyed a competitive advantage—allowing the company to demand a price premium. With the business product entering the growth phase, the relative importance of reliability, availability, and scalability also changes. The IT value proposition becomes business critical and this has to be reflected by the IT business model. The market and product are still very much in flux, however, so the skill sets related to entrepreneurial IT remain important.

A strategic advantage is temporary and, sooner or later, the competition will catch up. The market will become saturated and the competition will move on to pricing. The mature life-cycle phase can, nevertheless, be very profitable—as it is during the growth phase that the company has to invest most. When entering the mature phase, it is time to harvest and postpone the decline phase as long as possible. In the IT domain, the accompanying IT value proposition migrates from the strategic quadrant to the key operational quadrant. With it, the focus on product innovation, such as new features, shifts to process innovation like lower manufacturing cost. A similar shift can be observed for the IT value proposition; the key operational quadrant is about increasing efficiency and decreasing any source of risk.

After the key operational quadrant, the IT value proposition is put out to pasture. The functional life cycle[6] has come to an end. That leaves the support quadrant. It contains the IT value propositions that are neither of strategic importance, nor business critical. Workarounds, both automated and manual, are considered adequate when the system underpinning a support value proposition is down. It is the sweet spot for commoditized (SaaS) solutions to automate HR, facility management, or bookkeeping processes.

5.2.4 From Entrepreneurial IT to Foundation IT

Moving an initiative from the high potential quadrant via the strategic quadrant to the key operational quadrant can be very costly when not managed properly. For the high potential quadrant, the two key risks are underestimating the impact of success and the downstream impact of the technology used to realize the IT value proposition. Starting with the latter, a key operational team specialized in Microsoft technology is not looking forward to receiving an application based on stored procedures in Oracle. It sounds logical, but I have witnessed several occasions where businesses contract external suppliers to build a proof of concept application without prescribing nonfunctional requirements like development language and OWASP compliance. These businesses only begin to communicate with IT once the proof of concept has turned out to be a success and has already been labeled as *strategic*. At that point, IT either had to continue working with the external supplier, retrain or hire new software engineers, or invest in a reengineering project. In many cases, they choose the latter option, as the architecture and code quality of a proof of concept rarely scales well, both functionally and volume wise.[7]

Underestimating the impact of *success* is demonstrated by an institutional trading application developed by Morgan Stanley. It was a desktop application for large institutional customers that provided real-time access to market data along with the ability to trade. The initiative turned out to be a success and in an effort to further enhance the value, the customers were offered private

---

[6] Before that, an IT value proposition may be at its end-of-life from a technological perspective (e.g., Cobol program language), requiring IT to invest in a reengineering or conversion project.

[7] The previously mentioned strategic IT checklist can mitigate this risk by enforcing the *comply or explain* principle.

connections, as opposed to web Secure Sockets Layer. Many customers transitioned, but shortly thereafter, it started raining complaints. Success had turned into system crashes, leaving customers with millions invested in positions with no other choice but to call their broker to trade. The investigation into the root cause of the problems resulted in a long list of issues, from improperly managed configuration changes to undersized hardware components. To be able to deliver the quality promised to the customers, the network architecture had to be completely overhauled, including the communication protocols. According to ex-Morgan Stanley employee and current Google CIO Ben Fried, scaling required an integral approach:[vii] *"Without even thinking about it, the way we scaled up was through specialization. We added people to specialized teams, each operating within a functional boundary. We never said understanding how everything works is important."*

Managing the transition from one quadrant to another starts with defining *smart* criteria for each quadrant. Oil company Royal Dutch Shell interprets the term *operational criticality* very differently than, for instance, a law firm. The same applies to the term *strategic*. Both need to be operationalized and tailored to the company-specific context. Furthermore, an unambiguous description of the criteria prevents *noise* between business and IT when discussing the migration of a value proposition from one quadrant to another. Only when a regular *health check* points out that a value proposition is about to exceed predefined thresholds, is it tabled at the joint business IT steering committee that is being used to manage the portfolio.

The same criteria are also used to determine which changes are required in the application (and its architecture), support structure, security and risk framework, sourcing approach, and so on. In the high potential quadrant, operations and support activities are embedded in the DevOps team[8] and typically based on best effort, as seen in Figure 5.5. When moving to the strategic quadrant, the business, at least, expects the introduction of service levels even at its most basic, along with more attention to change, release, deploy, and incident management processes. Market success also increases the chance of unwanted attention from the darker parts of the internet, translating into additional security requirements like more sophisticated encryption technologies. The business expects IT to take care of these and other topics proactively, especially when an IT value proposition moves from one quadrant to another.

---

[8] To increase customer value, the high-frequency product flow from the developers has to be absorbed by the operations and support team. This concept provides the necessary principles, values, methods, key activities, and tools. More information can be found at: http://en.wikipedia.org/wiki/DevOps.

From	To
Speed-to-market, innovation, concept realization	Scaling, increasing robustness, adding features
Best-effort support and operations	Basic service levels, permanent operations, and support organization
Creative *stars*, visionary leader	Introduction of generalists and more influence of architects, security officers, and other guardians of robustness and scalability
Multidisciplinary teams, close involvement of business; business benefits first	Multidisciplinary teams, balance need of business with availability, integrity and confidentiality
Trust, open communication and (in)formal control	Stricter control requirements to mitigate increased risk profile (e.g., architecture, support processes)
Key partners deliver innovations, speed, and reduction of investment risk	Key partners deliver scalability of platform, differentiating features

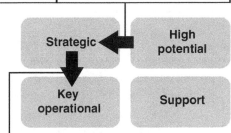

From	To
Scaling, increasing robustness, adding features	Reduce business and IT cost through process optimizations, *sweat assets* rationalizations, and economies of scale
Basic service levels, permanent operations and support organization, strive for ±80% process compliance	Strictly enforced standard service levels, standard service management, and operations processes
Introduction of generalists and more influence of architects, security officers, and other guardians of robustness and scalability	Strong drive to reduce cost while maintaining the agreed service levels
Multidisciplinary teams, balance need of business with availability, integrity, and confidentiality	Standardized matrix organization with functional silos and process coordinators ensuring delivery complies with agreed service levels
Stricter control requirements to mitigate increased risk profile (e.g., architecture, support processes)	Formal governance and control environment, aimed at optimizing cost and risk
Key partners deliver scalability of platform, differentiating features	Key partners deliver cost reductions (e.g., offshoring) and economies of scale

Figure 5.5   In and out of the strategic quadrant

During the stay in the strategic quadrant, the IT value proposition transitions from being an adolescent to being a young adult. With the coming of age, the IT value proposition gets ready to become part of the company's IT foundation. When entering the key operational quadrant, the emphasis on scaling and value-added features is replaced by efficiency and predictability. The business product has become a cash cow and the business wants to milk it without any disruptions. Hence, the business is looking for assurance that IT can minimize the likelihood and impact of undesired events. Frameworks like COBIT, ITIL, and ISO 27000 are some of the tools that IT can use to implement the desired *governance, risk management, and compliance* umbrella to manage both the benefits and risks of the IT value proposition.

When the sun finally sets on the business product, IT teams cannot simply remove the accompanying IT value proposition from their portfolio. Over time, other business products, processes, or applications may, unwittingly for the responsible Ops team, start to rely on them. Again, a health check can be used to determine the next transition, whether it be to retain, remove, or resize, among other things.

Managing these transitions, performing health checks, and portfolio management are all cost drivers. Only when businesses regularly want to invest in high potential initiatives, is it worthwhile to invest in a comprehensive life-cycle management process. In other cases, a leaner approach should do just fine.

5.2.5 One-Off Project or Permanent Team

In the short term, the cost associated with a permanent entrepreneurial IT team may drive a company to reject the idea. In the long term, this may, however, turn out to be a costly mistake, as entrepreneurial IT differs too much from foundation IT to expect the latter team to fulfill that type of need. Furthermore, when 90% of the team is allocated to foundation IT and the remaining 10% to entrepreneurial IT, the majority will slowly but surely push their culture and operating model upon the whole team. Innovation and speed-to-market require explicit management attention.

One of the first tasks of the responsible executive is to discuss the topic of entrepreneurial IT versus foundation IT with the business, including its implications, such as how high speed-to-market means less time for testing for bugs and thus, likely lower availability levels. Depending on the expected number and complexity of high potential initiatives, the business and IT can decide on how to best organize their realization.

When the business wants to invest once every two or three years in a highly complex initiative, using the latest and greatest emerging technologies and business capabilities, the team members may sometimes feel like the builders of the first atomic bomb during The Manhattan Project. In his book, General Leslie

Groves describes the project:[viii] "*The whole endeavor was founded on possibilities rather than probabilities. Of theory, there was a great deal. Of proven knowledge, not much. Basic research had not progressed to the point where work on even the most general design criteria could be started.*"

At the start of these novel projects only a general vision and direction is available. The team has to find out everything else along the way.

Compared to all other quadrants, these case-by-case teams are least likely to learn from past mistakes because there is no permanent organizational structure to retain lessons learned and best practices. It is, therefore, this quadrant that is most exposed to *strategic accidents*. Imagine a creative business executive with a strong vision, but limited experience with IT. They are likely to underestimate the importance of a managed transition from the high potential quadrant to the strategic quadrant.

Code quality, architecture, scalability, and security will all be of secondary importance—increasing the likelihood of serious security breaches or a large-scale outage. Hence, the break-even point for investing in a more permanent team and governance structure should lie well below a volume of 50%.

The *cheapest* permanent option is the one whereby both volume and complexity are low, such as in Figure 5.6. Here, the gap, in terms of technology, required skills, and level of uncertainty between the foundation IT portfolio and the need of the business for entrepreneurial IT, is relatively small. Hence, it should suffice to stretch the existing organizational structure, using external suppliers to fill in specific capability or skill gaps, like an agile Scrum development team or access to cloud-based app development tools. Instead of rigidly enforcing the standard architecture and security policies, these teams should be allowed to use a lean set of guidelines to keep the speed-to-market high and level of required investment low.[9] Combined with a similar approach for the standard process framework (e.g., a change management process with ten approval gates is not going to work), teams should be able to realize the need for entrepreneurial IT in the business.

Because the existing foundation IT team is used as a starting point, lessons learned can be retained and used when initiating the next project. Another advantage of this approach is the relative ease in which the IT value proposition can be migrated from the high potential quadrant to the key operational quadrant, eventually—it is more or less the same team that is responsible for both. However, using the same team is, at the same time, also the biggest disadvantage of this quadrant since foundation IT is their comfort zone. Unmanaged, the lean and mean change-management process designed for entrepreneurial IT

---

[9] Analogous to the previously mentioned *strategic checklists*, these checklists ensure the high potential initiative complies to a *minimal* set of nonfunctional requirements (e.g., always encrypt personal data).

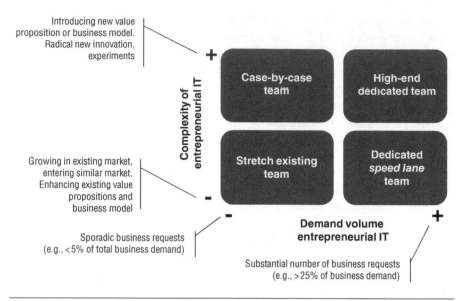

Introducing new value proposition or business model. Radical new innovation, experiments

Growing in existing market, entering similar market. Enhancing existing value propositions and business model

Complexity of entrepreneurial IT

Case-by-case team

High-end dedicated team

Stretch existing team

Dedicated *speed lane* team

Demand volume entrepreneurial IT

Sporadic business requests (e.g., <5% of total business demand)

Substantial number of business requests (e.g., >25% of business demand)

Figure 5.6   Temporary or permanent structure?

will quickly be replaced by the much more risk-averse version that is used to manage the rest of the portfolio.

The third quadrant, the dedicated *speed lane* team, covers the combination of high volume and low complexity. Think of businesses that request an almost continuing flow of product features and enhancements or relatively simple proof of concepts and pilots. Incorporating the fulfillment of these business requests into the existing exploitation processes would create too much strain, warranting a permanent team that would be focused on flow. Demand management and forecasting can be used to prevent unnecessary up or down scaling of the team.

The fourth quadrant, the high-end dedicated team, is the most challenging one. It requires teams to find solutions for a large volume of complex and time-critical business problems. Depending on the size of a company, there may be multiple teams operating at the same time, and deep domain expertise will be a key success factor. Due to these characteristics, these teams can most likely be found in companies with a technology-rich prospector strategy (e.g., 3M). Defenders will most likely stretch their existing teams to add the features they hope will keep the customers happy enough to stay.

The quadrants are not mutually exclusive. When a company launches its first IoT initiative, it will be very difficult to fit into the existing IT business model. For the third and fourth launches, things will go much smoother. Hence, a case-by-case team can evolve into a dedicated *speed lane* team when the need for radical change evolves into a need for continuous incremental change. As both agile and DevOps pursue flow efficiency, these frameworks are ideally suited for the speed lane.

5.3 TRADING FLOWERS AND PLANTS 2.0

The flowers and plants produced by farmers somehow have to reach the customers. Before the arrival of the internet, a one-on-one relationship between farmer and customer was impossible. It required two intermediaries: a trading company and a retailer. This case covers the digital transformation of the former, a company auctioning plants and flowers on behalf of the farmers.

The flowers and plants came from farmers located in over a dozen countries. For decades, the business model was based on transporting the product to one of four physical auction locations. The product was loaded into trolleys, pushed onto the floor, and sold to the highest bidder against the clock. The buyers, usually retailers, were responsible for the outbound logistics; again, using a combination of air transportation and trucks to transport them. It was not unusual for flowers and plants to be transported back and forth to the same country in this manner.

With several billion in yearly revenue, the company had grown into a multi-national giant, with huge amounts invested in *hard* assets. On a typical day, more than a hundred trucks would either deliver or pick up flowers and plants, requiring large docking areas—not to mention the floor space needed to process the thousands of auction trolleys packed with flowers and plants. Employees either used their car or a bicycle to move from one part of the site to the other.

The board members were all in their fifties or early sixties, and all had worked their way up over the years. They knew all there was to know about auctioning flowers and plants against the clock. They knew less about IT. The latter was considered of secondary importance, reflected by the lack of a CIO. The executive responsible for IT reported to the CFO.

Then, two things happened that disrupted their business model: both farmers and retailers began seeking economies of scale and the internet. To start with the first, price is an important competitive driver in many industries, including farming and retail. When a retailer is sourcing for red roses, it is difficult for a farmer to compete on anything other than price. The retailer faces the same pressure from its customers. When we want a dozen red roses, an important criterion is price. The quality of the rose is a mere dissatisfier. Most of us expect the freshest and highest-quality product before even considering buying them.

Fewer but larger farming operations and retailers meant that the traditional power balance was about to shift. When dealing with small farms and retailers, the trading company was needed to unite demand and supply. Retailers buying a million or more flowers have purchasing departments capable enough to source flowers directly from large farms. They don't need a middleman.

Without the internet, only the largest farming operations and retailers would have been able to engage in one-on-one relationships. With its introduction, the whole business model was suddenly at risk of becoming obsolete.

Late, but not too late, the board scrambled into action. The existing strategic belief set, value propositions, unique selling points, and business model all had to be reframed. IT could no longer be considered a mere utility, but had to be elevated in importance. The business strategy and IT strategy were merged into one company-wide digital business strategy, including a comprehensive transformation program. The existing asset base and deep domain knowledge would be used to transform the analog business model into a future-proof hybrid model, as seen in Table 5.5. Inevitably, there were some strategic accidents before things eventually smoothed out.

Used to one or two application releases per year along with months of preparation before starting a new project, the IT team was unable to respond adequately to the sudden demand from the business for proof-of-concepts and pilot projects that were expected to be delivered overnight. Until then, entrepreneurial IT was alien territory for IT, and they lacked the mindset, skill sets, and tools to react proficiently. During the summer period, it was common that projects were put on hold for three to four weeks as whole development teams

Table 5.5 Organizational impact of digitalization on flower trader

	Analog Flower and Plant Trading	Digital Flower and Plant Trading
Economic Model	High fixed cost in hard assets requires high volumes to recover them. Economies of scale.	The more suppliers and buyers the system uses, the more attractive it becomes (positive feedback loop). Economies of scale.
Strategy	Long-term planning horizon. Defender.	Medium-term planning horizon. In general, should be prospector or at least analyzer. *The actual company still had the luxury to act as a defender due to the extensive business network and deep domain knowledge. These universal core assets kept the barrier of entry high.*
Composition of Workforce	Large, as most jobs require very limited education.	Small, as most jobs require highly educated employees with excellent social skills.
Primary Role of IT	Supporting operations.	Strategic enabler.

went on vacation at the same time. Frustrated, the business engaged external suppliers to build several e-trading solutions. The good news was that most solutions turned out to be a success. They leveraged, for example, on the ability to trade flowers and plants around the clock, instead of just for a few hours. Every working day, the traders could bid against the clock. Video and picture functionalities allowed potential buyers to view the product while it was still at the farm location, eliminating the need to transport them between the farm and the physical trading location. Combined with an end-to-end financial transaction system, the trader was moving toward a new digital platform that would be useful for all but the largest farming operations and retailers. The latter category would continue to use long-term volume contracts at pre-agreed-upon prices as a means to reduce supply chain risk.

What the business had forgotten about was managing the transition from the high potential quadrant to the strategic quadrant. Some solutions were conceived in six weeks by cutting several corners. After a successful initial pilot period with a limited number of suppliers and buyers, the solution was considered ready for prime time. An application that is able to process 1,000 pictures, videos, and transactions per day is, however, not necessarily able to process 500,000+ pictures, videos, and transactions per day. Soon, several solutions started to crash every other day, and the business had to look to the internal IT team for help.

The business argued that too much revenue was depending on the e-trading solutions to continue the strategy to source them from external suppliers. Furthermore, to elevate them functionally to the next level, they had to be better integrated with the foundation IT solutions that were managed by the internal IT team. It would allow the business to turn the physical assets, existing foundation IT solutions, and the new e-trading solutions into a flexible portfolio of end-to-end service components. Regardless of the customer segment, whether they are small, specialized niche farming operations or larger ones focused on commodity flowers and needs—such as customers that only purchase flowers on physical trading floors or those who only require pictures or videos—by combining one or more service components, the business could offer a tailor-made value proposition.

Both business and IT agreed it was indeed best for the company to insource most of the e-trading solutions. With some solutions being built with PHP, Java, Oracle-stored procedures, or exotic niche tools—insourcing meant reengineering them. The internal IT team was too small to support a heterogeneous application portfolio.

In an effort to shed their reputation of being slow and reactive, the internal IT team decided to abandon the waterfall method and adopt the agile method to reengineer and improve the applications. Similar to the case of the IT service provider in Chapter 2, the initial implementation was flawed. Productivity fell off the cliff as developers spent most of their time chatting with business users.

When voicing her concern, the manager who was responsible for application development was rebuked by the team. In hindsight, the team's reaction was easy to explain. After years of development that was based on detailed functional and technical specifications, the developers and project manager-appointed Scrum Master were suddenly responsible for the whole development cycle instead of solely writing code. In other words, their scope changed from executing only to directing, controlling, and executing.

The standard agile training and certification programs only cover the theory, not the accompanying soft skills, professionalism, and mindset. The latter aspects are crucial for a successful implementation of agile, however, as the team has to be willing and able to combine freedom with responsibilities. Agile development requires a team with mature soft skills, using extensive coaching and master-apprentice relationships to educate junior members. Hence, those involved forgot that agile is based on a completely different paradigm than waterfall. This, too, is a transition that has to be explicitly managed—like high potential to strategic.

Also, other observations are similar to the IT service provider of Chapter 2. The more profitable and stable the business model, the less likely executives will proactively question its belief set. It required a near crisis to initiate the needed change of direction and the termination of a large group of employees—many of whom were hired only one or two years before. Therefore, sense and regularly reframe.

REFERENCES

i. Ward, J. and Peppard, J. (2002). *Strategic Planning for Information Systems*. Third edition.
ii. More information on the Gartner Hype Cycle methodology can be found at: www.gartner.com/technology/research/methodologies/hype-cycle.jsp
iii. Carr, N. G. (May 2003). *IT Doesn't Matter*. Harvard Business Review.
iv. Henderson, J. C. and Venkatraman, N. (1993). Strategic Alignment: Leveraging Information Technology for Transforming Organizations. IBM Systems Journal, 32(1), 4–16.
v. Walsh, S. T., Kirchhoff, B. A. and Newbert, S. (2002). Differentiating Market Strategies for Disruptive Technologies.
vi. Ward, J. and Peppard, J. (2002). Strategic Planning for Information Systems. Third edition.
vii. Gallagher, S. (2011). Google CIO and others talk DevOps and "Disaster Porn" at Surge Sean. Link: http://arstechnica.com/business/2011/09/google-devops-and-disaster-porn/.
viii. Groves, L. (1962). *Now It Can Be Told: The Story of the Manhattan Project*. New York: Harper.

6

LESS ISOLATION, MORE COHESION

Less isolation, more cohesion reflects the ability to operate multiple IT business models simultaneously.

Third-party logistics provider United Cargo uses United Airlines flights to deliver same-day packages. Flowers and transplant organs need to arrive within hours from shipping, and the capability to provide this service to customers differentiates United Cargo from many competitors. With speed being *the* core value of United Cargo, it is relatively easy to prioritize new IT initiatives.

One of the initiatives at the top of the list aimed to speed up the order entry process. Previously, the customer had to wait for the service representative of United Cargo on the other end of the phone call to access the different applications required to upload packaging information, verify billing and tracking data, and check on TSA compliancy. After executing the project, all information was a few mouse clicks away, considerably strengthening United Cargo's core value of speed in the customers' mind.

Generally, the better the company's strategic objectives are translated into the organizational building blocks that define a company, the more effective and efficient[1] its execution will be. Combined, the building blocks constitute the company's business model, answering questions like:

- Who is your customer?
- What customer need are you going to fulfill?
- How do you differ from your competitors?
- How will you generate more revenue than cost? and
- Which activities should we perform internally and which can be sourced from external partners?

---

[1] As stated in Chapter 1, effectiveness and efficiency cover two different managerial aspects. The first focuses on doing the right things (e.g., invest in project a or b) and the second focuses on doing them the right way (e.g., realize project deliverables using as little resources as possible).

With the digitalization of most business models, these questions become as relevant for IT as they are already for the business. Quoting Richard Boocock, CIO of Air Products and Chemicals: *"We live or die on creating customer value and shareholder value. There is only business value."* For this reason, this chapter introduces the *IT business model.* It is derived from Ostenwalders' business model canvas, adapting it to the technology domain by applying some minor adjustments.[i] This is only half of the story, however.

The IT business model for the high potential quadrant looks very different from the key operational quadrant (recall Figure 5.4). And what about the strategic quadrant? Does it warrant a separate business model or can the other two stretch themselves to bridge the gap? In other situations, the optimal design of the IT business model may be based on customer intimacy versus product leadership. Table 6.1 again provides three statements that cover the chapter as a whole.

Table 6.1   Statements to think about when reading this chapter

Statements
Thinking in business models is as important for IT as it is for the business.
Only when all of the organizational building blocks act in sync, can IT expect to satisfy or even delight the customer.
Dynamic and complex markets require managers that dare to let go of traditional management and control practices.

6.1 WHY THIS PRINCIPLE MATTERS

The term *business model* is covered by numerous books and articles, indicating both its importance and broad scope. Depending on the author, some or all of the following elements can be considered part of a business model: value proposition, positioning, strategy, capabilities, organizational structure, business partners, and operational processes. What they all agree on is its essence—a high-level drawing of the way the company earns money. While a broad scope may seem cumbersome in certain situations, a too narrow view is, according to Porter,[ii] one of the reasons why the internet bubble could become so big before it eventually burst. In his article *Strategy and the Internet*, he argues that the internet tends to weaken industry profitability without proving sustainable advantages in return, emphasizing the need for a solid strategy and competitive analysis to distinguish the company in the market. Both were often overlooked in the bonanza between 1995 and 2000, resulting in a cold shower for many stakeholders. Since the turn of the century, the internet has been joined by several other technologies (some of which were disruptive) and business models—but the same basic economic principles and business rules still apply.

Sustainable success as a company requires a coherent strategy and organizational design.

In the old days, a company's business model was of little concern to IT due to the shield provided by the business. The unpredictable and cold winds surrounding a company's activity in highly competitive markets rarely reached those in IT. With the digitalization of value propositions, distribution channels, and customer relationships, this is no longer the case. The rise of *platform* business models like Facebook, eBay, Kickstarter, iTunes, Nike Fuel, and providers of Smart Grids elevated the impact of IT on a company's business model to the next level. Contrary to the more traditional *pipe* business model, platforms *"do not just create and push stuff out. They allow users to create and consume value."*[iii] More generally, companies with a platform business model facilitate transactions across a network, removing supply chain inefficiencies and reducing search stress.

Due to strong network effects, these IT-enabled business models can be very profitable and enjoy a considerable barrier of entry. Advanced robotics, automation of complex knowledge work, and the convergence of biology and technology are likely to spawn yet another generation of disruptive business models, each more technology-rich than the previous. As a result, the next Facebook, Uber, or Box may well need only a few dozen employees to surpass a billion in revenue. The rest is taken care of by extremely capable software and hardware.

Consequently, a large part of the traditional CIO responsibilities will be taken over by the business. IT has become too important to treat as a separate domain. Unless the CIO and his or her team is able to tune its IT operating model to the companies' competitive advantages, core capabilities, value configuration, and business model. In that case, parts of IT may still be fused with the business domain, but with the CIO taking the lead instead of being led.

Sustainable success as an IT team requires running it as a business.

A growing number of business managers are familiar with service level agreements (SLAs), requests for change, and the difference between an incident and a problem due to widespread adoption of the Information Technology Infrastructure Library (ITIL), Control Objectives for Information and Related Technologies (COBIT), and other frameworks by IT. They are not part of the natural vocabulary of the business manager, however. A business manager thinks in customer segments, value propositions, customer relations, and channels. Due to the relentless convergence, or even fusion, of both domains, the two *languages* will inevitably result in waste and negatively affect the speed-to-market.

As it is the business, and not IT, that generates the company's revenue and profit, it is logical that the latter *molds* its operating model around the business. A concept universally adopted by business executives to guide its strategic decisions is the business model. A business model describes the rationale of how an organization creates, delivers, and captures value—economic, social, or other forms of value.[iv] While a business model and strategy may look the same at first glance, there are important differences. A business model explains how the different pieces of a business fit together. It ensures that everyone in the organization is focused on the kind of value the company wants to create. Only when the business model is clear, can strategies be developed to articulate how the company will deliver that value in a unique way that others cannot easily imitate.[v]

Rumor has it that the raison d'être of the IT team is also creating, delivering, and capturing value. IT also has value propositions, channels, resources, and a network of external partners, but they are known by other names. Hence, the conceptual gap between the business model used by the business and a business model used by IT should be fairly easy to bridge. The benefits of such an *IT business model* include:

- An explicit design that describes how the resources and mechanisms that are available to IT are deployed in a *coherent* manner to create, deliver, and capture value
- A means to communicate to the business and other stakeholders in a language both parties understand
- A framework to incorporate the services and products delivered by the external business partners into an integral service that represents value for one or more internal customer segments or external customer segments, business-to-business (B2B), and business-to-consumer (B2C)
- A structure that links decisions and activities to its monetary consequences

Of the many business model canvases introduced by scholars and practitioners, Osterwalders' model has developed itself into the de facto standard. One reason for its popularity is the simplification of a business model into nine elements, which lends itself well to the interactive and intuitive generation of new business models. *"The Business Model Canvas is a strategic management and entrepreneurial tool. It allows you to describe, design, challenge, invent, and pivot your business model."*[vi] In technology-rich markets, these activities are as relevant for IT as they are for the business. Both need to operate side by side using, wherever possible, the same management tools to minimize friction.

Sustainable success in hybrid or digital markets necessitates IT's adoption of an IT business model.

The principle *less isolation, more cohesion* is, therefore, an invitation to regularly answer the following questions. Considering the existing speeds that markets move in, their technology density, and their maturity:

- How much are the business' business model and IT's business model in sync?
- How much are the nine building blocks that make up the IT business model in sync?
- What is the optimal level of forward integration with the business?
- At what point should an IT team consider implementing more than one IT business model?

The next part of this chapter will provide at least some of the answers.

6.2 HOW TO BECOME LESS ISOLATED AND MORE COHESIVE

It will come as no surprise that the IT business model introduced in this book is based on the business model canvas by Osterwalder. To fit the specific context of IT, several adjustments have been made. First of all, when the company pursues a hybrid or digital business model, IT has to deal with both internal and external customer segments. The external B2C or B2B customer segments and their impact on IT's value streams are depicted in Figure 6.1 by dotted lines. Also, different from the standard canvas is the explicit inclusion of architecture as part of the building block key resources. Another adjustment is the replacment of

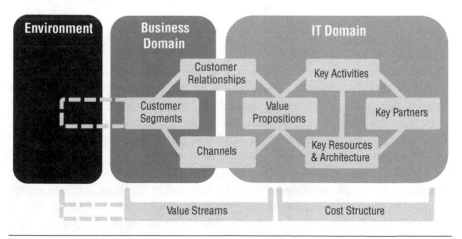

Figure 6.1   The IT business model

revenue streams by value streams and splitting the customer domain into two—internal business customers and external B2B or B2C customer of the business, as previously discussed. The reason to opt for value streams is the fact that revenue and profit are generated by the business. IT is an increasingly important partner, but is not responsible for profit and loss, unless business and IT have already fused together (like in tech companies).

The building blocks of the IT business model can be divided into three groups. The first group consists of the blocks that face the internal and external customers: customer segments, customer relationships, channels, and value propositions. Together these four identify, manage, and fulfill an often continuously evolving need or want of an internal or external customer. The second group contains blocks that focus on the actual delivery: key activities, key partners, key resources, and architecture. The linchpin between both groups is the value proposition. The third group captures the resulting value streams, such as an increase in business benefits and reduction in business risk, and the financial resources required to *fuel* the first two groups of building blocks. The cost structure itself can be divided in two types: recurring operating cost (operating expenditure) and one-off investments (capital expenditure).

Depending on the technology density of the company's business model, the building blocks of the IT business model push themselves more or less into the business domain and even the external environment. The internal business demand for foundation IT solutions is fulfilled with an *IT value proposition*, using the building blocks' customer relationships and channels to interface, as shown in Figure 6.2. When targeting an external customer segment with a new digital value proposition, the business and IT *team up* and create a *joint value proposition*. The responsibility for the value proposition is shared, using the (digitalized) building block channels and customer relationships of the business' business model to deliver them to the customer.

There is a third archetype. When business and IT domains fuse, the IT business model ceases to exist. It loses its relevance, and only the business model of the business remains. Whether to align, converge, or fuse is a topic covered later on in this chapter, as are several other organizational implications, such as centralization versus decentralization and formal versus informal governance.

Besides the ability to direct and manage differentiated value propositions, like high potential and support, the IT business model also fulfills the need for coherence. Introducing agile development within the key activities building block to boost speed-to-market and flexibility is doomed to fail without an investment in the accompanying skill sets and technology, which are represented by the key resources and architecture building block. Coherence is a critical precondition to reduce value leakage, both within the IT domain itself and when collaborating with the business to create a new joint, or even IT value proposition.

External-oriented Entrepreneurial IT initiatives

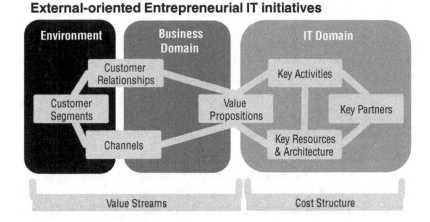

Internal-oriented Foundation IT initiatives

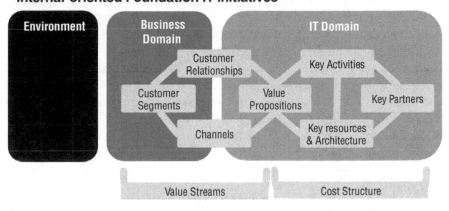

Figure 6.2 The two archetypes of the IT business model

As mentioned, convergence and *especially* fusion require frictionless communication between business and IT professionals. The business model for either the business or IT domain provides a shared canvas to discuss, prepare, and realize a new technology-rich business product. The business articulates its vision, the market opportunity and expectations regarding the value proposition, channels, and customer relationships, while IT advises from other angles on the potential of existing and emerging technologies to realize or even surpass the value envisioned by the business. In other words, the IT business model can be used to operationalize both the positioning of IT, like that of a faithful servant or business partner, and operationalize individual joint initiatives, such as a sports jacket with integrated sensors.

The IT business model is not a silver bullet; however, like ITIL, COBIT, ISO 27000, Scrum, and lean IT, it is a tool that can generate value when in the hands of the right person. Especially in highly dynamic technology-rich markets, the IT business model should enable especially IT to operate more effectively. But as stated in Chapter 2, before everything else, success requires vision, leadership, courage, drive, and a specific set of soft and hard skills.

6.2.1 Two Levels and Two Canvases

The IT business model can be applied at the organizational level and for individual initiatives. At the organizational level, the content of the building blocks is defined at a fairly high level of abstraction, such as the sourcing strategy for the key partner building block, compared to a detailed description for an individual initiative, like the naming of an external partner for the same building block. Depending on the volume and contextual variation (e.g., high potential versus key operational, or defender versus prospector strategy), there will be one or more canvases required at the organizational level.

When a company allocates 60 percent of its IT investment budget for experiments and the remaining percentage on process improvements and renewal, investing in two IT business models is the logical choice. The context of the two investment types lay too far apart to be realized effectively and efficiently by one homogeneous team. Another company spending only ten percent of its IT investment budget on bi-yearly transformation initiatives and the rest on process improvements and renewal, requires only one IT business model. Here, the transformation initiatives are realized through case-by-case projects (see Chapter 5).

The IT business model is equally valuable when IT, together with the business, want to realize individual initiatives. In that case, the business model is used as a canvas to articulate the building blocks for a specific initiative (see Figure 6.3 for an example). To prevent waste (e.g., defining a reference architecture for entrepreneurial IT twice), the canvases at the organizational level should be used as a reference. They set the boundaries (*comply or explain*).

Besides multiple levels, it is also relevant to note that the IT business model is not the only derivative of the original model. In an effort to create a business model canvas that is more suitable for entrepreneurs, Maurya created the lean business model.[vii] It focuses on the product and market aspects, assuming the more internally oriented activities, such as key resources and key activities, can be derived from the solution or unfair advantage. With these adjustments, the lean business model canvas wants to facilitate its users to be highly focused, think in actionable terms, and operate under conditions of extreme uncertainty.

The main differences between the standard and the lean model are captured in Figure 6.4 and Table 6.2. One of the core topics for any entrepreneurial

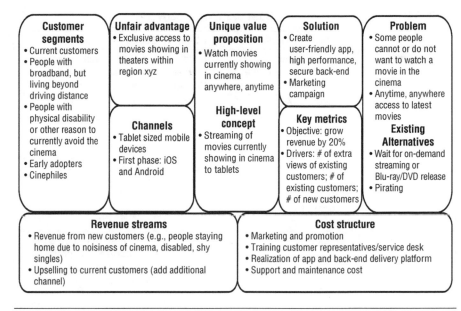

Figure 6.3   Example of lean business model canvas (adapted from Maurya [2012])

Standard Business Model Canvas

Lean Business Model Canvas

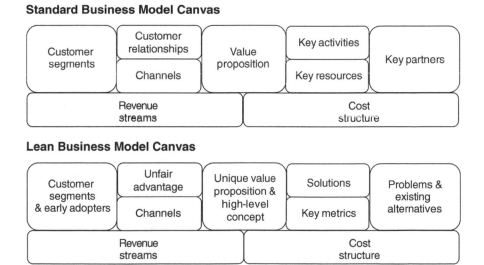

Figure 6.4   The business model canvases (Osterwalder [2010], Maurya [2012])

Table 6.2   Comparison of two IT business model canvases

Aspect	IT Business Model	Lean IT Business Model
Key Objective	Provide business model canvas for generic use	Provide business model canvas for initiatives operating under extreme uncertainty
Target Audience	Company executives, managers, consultants, and entrepreneurs	Entrepreneurs
Orientation	Outside-in	Inside-out
Key Features	Provide a shared language to describe a business model—include all elements important to describe and think it through	Enforce focus, highly actionable, focus on market and product
Additional in Lean Model	Not applicable	• The *problem* that has to be solved • The core *solution* to the problem • The *key metrics* that really matter • Any *unfair advantage* over the competition
Left out in Lean Model	Not applicable	• Key activities • Key resources • Customer relationships • Key partners
Type of Value Propositions	• Joint value propositions • IT value propositions	• Joint value propositions
Demand Type	Foundation IT, some entrepreneurial IT	Entrepreneurial IT

initiative is the problem or need that the solution and value proposition will fulfill. Solving the identified problem is the starting point when filling an empty canvas, ensuring focus and reducing the risk of wasting resources. The solution is what entrepreneurs can be most passionate about, at the risk of exaggerating the need or inability to look beyond the initial solution concept. The block key metrics facilitates the necessity to focus and measure success by means of a few core metrics, which we will discuss in Chapter 7. It is easy to create reports with dozens of objectives, drivers, and other performance indicators. It is hard to find the one or two metrics that represent the difference between success and failure. Equally important for entrepreneurial initiatives is leveraging on any unfair advantage, such as how the first mover enjoys strong positive network effects, as it provides a head start, temporary or otherwise.

In order to keep the business model canvas lean and as close to its foundation as possible, the addition of blocks resulted in removing others. The reasons to omit key activities and key resources are their internal orientation and notion that they can be derived from the solution. The customer relationships block has been integrated in channels while key partners will become, in most cases, only really key when the initiative has to scale-up while gaining traction in the market.

To make the IT business model concept more tangible, Figure 6.3 depicts a lean canvas for the problem of some people who cannot or are not willing to watch a movie in the cinema. Some people are physically incapable to travel or are embarrassed to be seen alone, while others don't go due to the distractions created by other movie-goers, such as talking during the movie or the ringing of cell phones. Hence, there is a demand for streaming movies while they are still being shown in the cinemas.[2] Imagine the situation whereby movie studios grant the three largest cinema operators in the United States the rights to stream first-run movies to mobile devices, starting the same day they appear in theaters. By charging at least the same price as a cinema ticket, it would still be a premium offering and not cannibalize the existing revenue streams of the operators. Even better, it would be a source of both growth, such as singles as a new customer segment, and profit, as streaming is cheaper. Companies like Netflix and Hulu would still be able to attract the more price-conscious customers who don't mind waiting, while offering a broader portfolio including exclusive content like TV series.

To launch it, the business and IT would have to join forces, with the business focusing on marketing the value proposition and IT on realizing the technology platform. The latter is easier said than done as IT's traditional role in cinema operators is limited to supporting front office and back office processes. Their positioning used to be Average Joe or faithful servant since the advanced digital projectors and sound systems are considered part of the business domain.

The good news is that IT is busy shedding its traditional positioning as customers want to buy their tickets online or use QR-codes to print preordered tickets at automated ticket dispensers. For the value proposition depicted in Figure 6.3, business and IT, nevertheless, have to take their relationship to the next level, as the digital streaming channel has to cover all the channel phases[3] and generate revenue. Since it disrupts the existing business model, some may want to merely pay it lip service. Hence, the IT business model covers a lot of angles, but not all. The accompanying organizational change has to be managed.

---

[2] While writing this chapter, Napster's cofounder Sean Parker was trying to launch this concept in the United States under the name *The Screening Room*. In South Korea, movie studios Disney and Sony battle piracy by streaming movies to devices while they are still in theaters.

[3] (1) Raise awareness, (2) support decision making, (3) fulfill the need, (4) deliver the value proposition, and (5) provide after-sales support. See Chapter 2.

For value propositions that don't have to operate early in the business life cycle, the logical starting point remains the standard business model canvas. My suggestion is to also use the latter canvas when shaping the organizational entity responsible for delivering entrepreneurial IT. Due to the omission of the key activities, key resources, customer relationships, and key partners building blocks, the lean business model canvas likely results in a hodgepodge of development languages, tools, project approaches, and other such things at the organizational level, wasting scarce resources. Even entrepreneurial IT needs to be run as efficiently as possible.

6.2.2 IT Business Model Meets the Business

When Jeff Keisling became CIO of Pfizer in 2009, he found a company under pressure. Several high margin drug patents were about to expire, while the R&D expenses required to create a new blockbuster drug kept going up. Pfizer had to adjust its business model—and IT would play an important role in it.

To allow the company to engage doctors, pharmacists, and other customers through new channels and markets, Keisling had to bring business and IT closer together. He used the integration program that followed the acquisition of Wyeth by Pfizer as a catalyst to execute his vision. Cooperation at the business unit level was improved by appointing hybrid IT business managers and decentralizing those IT capabilities required by the business to successfully create joint value propositions. Other topics, like technology standards, shared data, applications, and infrastructure assets remained part of the corporate IT agenda.

The tangible results included an open innovation platform connecting more than 500 external (key) partners and a cloud-based patient management system for doctors. Hence, even some pharmaceutical companies are transitioning, or at least supplementing, their pipe-oriented value chain business model with a platform business model.

Decentralization of IT capabilities is a popular way to reduce the distance between business and IT. By itself, it is no guarantee for success, however. Just as important are the right mindset and an IT business model tuned to the specific needs and wants of that particular division or business unit. In case the business operates in a technology-rich market, the business' business model and IT's business model have to converge beyond the traditional business IT alignment model from Henderson and Venkatraman.[viii] Here, frameworks like COBIT/ ValIT, ISO 27001, and ITIL come up short, as they are built upon the assumption that the IT strategy is derived from the business strategy and IT processes and architecture follow those of the business.

Digitalization requires a cooperative model focused on convergence "*as companies strive to link technology and business in light of dynamic business strategies and continuously evolving technologies.*" [ix] In his paper, Luftman also emphasizes that business and IT shouldn't wait for the other to make the first step, but should proactively approach each other. The discussion should not be business IT alignment or IT business alignment. Only a coherent and harmonious relationship is able to couple IT investments to organizational redesign and business process reengineering, initiatives that are sources of substantial productivity improvements, and even competitive advantage.[x]

The third archetype that IT and business can use to collaborate is fusion (see Table 6.3). When launching a new digital value proposition via digital channels or disrupting an analog business model with a digital model, any source of friction should be avoided. The efficiency gains of organizing (key) resources into stove pipes are less than its negative effects on speed-to-market and agility. As even new digital value propositions that are introduced by the business eventually mature, the collaboration paradigm may well transition from fusion to convergence over time—like when moving from the strategic to key operation quadrant, as it allows for better economies of scale. Here, too, does *less static, more flow* apply.

Table 6.3   Business IT collaboration paradigms

	Paradigms to Collaborate with the Business		
	Alignment	**Convergence**	**Fusion**
	Environment / Business Domain / IT Domain	Environment / IT Domain / Business Domain	Environment / Business Domain (fused with IT)
Business Model	Analog and key operational part of hybrid business models	Hybrid and key operational part of digital business models	Dynamic digital business models, channels, and value propositions
Dependence on Technology	• Low to medium • Non-daily business critical to business critical	• Medium to high • Business critical, particularly when digital is considered strategic by business	Strategic business asset, vital for future success of company
Key Properties of Business Demand	Relatively stable, business requirements are known	From dynamic and uncertain business requirements to stable requirements	Dynamic and uncertain B2C or B2B requirements
Projected Image of IT	A professional and reliable butler	A business savvy technology leader	An integral part of the business

Several pointers to operationalize the three collaboration paradigms are provided in Table 6.4. It shows the emphasis on control, predictability, and efficiency when alignment is the optimal collaborative model versus the emphasis on creative problem solving, speed-to-market, and go-getter mentality for convergence and fusion. The latter two rely on highly skilled and motivated team members and a limited set of key metrics and controls to realize the objectives

Table 6.4 Operationalization of collaboration paradigms

	Paradigm to Collaborate with the Business		
	Alignment	**Convergence**	**Fusion**
IT Relationship Management	• Collecting and realizing requirements • Highly standardized • Sequential • Focus on process compliance and operational excellence	• Advising and leading, followed by realizing • Somewhat standardized, focus on enabling flow • Iterative • Focus on realizing a vision, capitalizing on a business opportunity, or mitigating a threat	Not applicable, only B2C or B2B relations remains
Organization Level Properties	• Highly structured • Risk averse and compliance oriented • Improve what exists • Managers • Reactive • Strive for predictability and control • Team members with either business or technology background	• When result requires it, cross pre-set boundaries • Speed, creativity, and customer value first • Think outside the box • Leaders • Proactive • Get energy from uncertainty • Team members with both business and technology background	Merged business and IT capabilities Business with strong technology acumen and vice versa See also Convergence
Typical Structure Elements	• Product portfolio and detailed road map • Functional and technical designs • Service catalog • Service level agreement • Release planning	• Product portfolio and high-level road map • Vision and concepts • Epics, user stories, backlogs, burn down charts • Deployment pipeline	Mix of business and IT elements which change according to the life-cycle phase of the value proposition

(*soft control environment*), in contrast to the hard control environment that the business IT alignment paradigm is known for. As mentioned before, neither is better than the other. Both have proven their value, and still do. It is just a matter of the right context.

Besides understanding the opportunities embedded in fusing technology and business capabilities, it is also important to understand the limitations. For the production of the 787 Dreamliner, Boeing decided to source 60% of the parts from more than 50 suppliers, 28 of them outside of the United States. This allowed Boeing to shift investments in tooling and inventory to suppliers, reducing its risk profile at first glance. IT was an important enabler since all parties had to integrate and synchronize their design, manufacturing, and supply chain processes.

By January 2012, the 787 program faced a delay of three years because several operational risks had materialized. Some issues, like Alcoa not being able to supply fasteners quickly enough, were directly related to business risk, but others were of a shared nature. In one case, the wing joints failed in a real-life test, after being cleared in virtual simulations. Boeing and many of its suppliers used a shared virtual model to design and integrate the various aircraft parts, based on software from Dassault Systèmes. The software itself worked, but the two groups of experts—aircraft engineering and simulation software—apparently missed the mark when translating the airplane parts into a virtual world. Solving the weak spots in the wing joints eventually required fixes applied to 18 locations on the airplane model.

In other instances, delays occurred because Boeing missed insight into the problems that overseas suppliers were struggling with. The extensive use of composites and innovative airplane design resulted in many unforeseen issues. Instead of sharing them by using the available collaboration tools, the suppliers decided to keep the information to themselves. By the time the information reached Boeing, delays were inevitable. This shows that an IT-enabled framework to collaborate can only do so much. In the end, it depends on culture and communication practices to achieve the desired result. Hence, the journey always starts with Chapter 2—*Less Defensive, More Offensive*.

6.2.3 Organizing for (Un)Certainty

The customer relationships building block is the one driven by the desire to acquire customers, retain customers, and to upsell. For analog business models, IT only has to worry about retention[4] and upselling, as only internal customer segments are served. For hybrid and digital markets, the business and IT share

---

[4] In other words, prevent the business from buying from external vendors and/or outsourcing IT.

the responsibility to realize all three objectives (for IT's responsibility to fulfill the needs of its internal customer segments, see Chapter 3). This pivotal role translates into two key activities:

- Deeply influence the customer behavior (*active*)
- Sense changing needs and context (*passive*)

In order to do so effectively and efficiently, the customer relationships building block needs a seamless fit with all of the other building blocks. Key activities, key partners, key resources, and architecture that are optimized for foundation IT cannot effectively support a business unit that is active in an unstable and complex environment. The impact of context related to foundation IT versus entrepreneurial IT at the organization level is captured by the model of Duncan.[xi] It maps several organizational aspects to the relative stability and complexity of the environment, as can be seen in Figure 6.5.

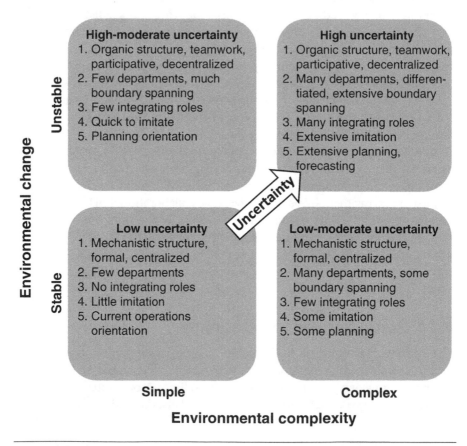

Figure 6.5 Organizational structure as a function of complexity and uncertainty (Duncan [1972])

- **Simple and stable**—The external environment and the customer segments are relatively homogeneous and change slowly. The relationships with external network entities are limited in number and predictable. It is the sweet spot of foundation IT and the accompanying organizational design (e.g., formal, structured, standardized, functional silos). Their IT demand of bakeries, cattle farmers, and brick manufacturers are part of this category.
- **Simple and unstable**—The number of external network entities (e.g., customer segments, suppliers) remains limited, but the product and its life cycle are highly dynamic. To address the frequent and unpredictable change of the product portfolio, the departments and external network entities have to work closely together (*boundary spanning*[5]). Tasks and responsibilities are typically delegated to the operational units, relying on a relatively soft control framework. Fashion brands (pre-Internet of Things) and manufacturers of low-cost gadgets are part of this category. The business demand qualifies as entrepreneurial IT due to the emphasis on agility and speed-to-market.
- **Complex and stable**—The external environment consists of many heterogeneous elements. Apart from the occasional disruption (e.g., universities and massive open online courses), the environment and value propositions change slowly. It is a quadrant that requires many internal and external stakeholders to cooperate, using sophisticated governance, collaboration, and communication mechanisms. There is a clear-cut business case for COBIT, ITIL, and elaborate service management tools. Car manufacturers (cars can stay more than five years in production), airplane manufacturers, and manufacturers of high-tech chemicals are companies that qualify for this category. Almost every centralized IT team of a large corporation also falls in this category.
- **Complex and unstable**—This is the most challenging quadrant and the apex of entrepreneurial IT. The external environment, product life cycles, and customer segments are all complex and highly dynamic. Manufacturers of mobile devices, wearables, and other high-tech B2C products are part of this category, as are most of their IT teams. The specialization inherent to these value propositions translates into a considerable need for both integration and boundary-spanning roles. The governance

---

[5] Companies (and IT) used to deal with uncertainty by adding stock and overstaffing. Just-in-time and lean manufacturing are two efficiency-enhancing concepts that reduce the need to buffer. In more complex and dynamic situations, the removal of slack has to be compensated by boundary-spanning roles that ensure that all stakeholders (e.g., business, IT, key partners) remain connected adequately.

structure is based on soft controls that are supplemented with a few key input metrics, such as budgets and objectives, and output metrics, like effects and results.

Regardless of whether the IT business model has to be optimized for entrepreneurial IT, customer intimacy, or a prospector strategy, eventually the building blocks have to be translated into departments, positions, and decision rights. Generally speaking, the more complex and uncertain the activities or objective, the more decentralized the distribution of decision rights[6] and the smaller the team size. Regardless of the size, all require some sort of vertical (e.g., direct, control, execute) and horizontal (e.g., inbound logistics, operations, outbound logistics) orchestration to collaborate effectively.

When mixing small, highly skilled and specialized internal teams with extensive outsourcing to best-of-breed partners, it is primarily the horizontal axis that matters. The need for horizontal boundary spanning and integration is not new, and within the business domain, the person responsible for a horizontal end-to-end chain is sometimes called the *process steward*. Within IT, the service manager has a similar role—being responsible for the integral service performance from an end-user perspective. Regardless of using waterfall, s-model, or agile Scrum, somebody has to manage the end-to-end flow from customer to development to operations, including any key partners.

The need to supplement the more vertically oriented standard IT governance and management practices was also identified by Peterson.[xii] He identified the following horizontal integration capabilities to coordinate and integrate formal and informal authority across business and IT domains:

- **Structural capability (connection)**—This capability is closely related to standard governance practices since they include the formal positions, decision rights, (boundary spanning and integrator) roles, steering committees, and other *power* related aspects. The decision to converge or even fuse is part of this category because it redefines the way business and IT connect and cooperate.
- **Process capability (coordination)**—This capability captures the flow from business strategy to IT strategy and the accompanying monitoring and investment activities. Sensing and acting quickly on unforeseen situations is also part of this category. A *definition of done* from the

---

[6] Advances in technology (e.g., real-time reporting, video conferencing) allow senior executives an increasingly large span of control, reducing the need to decentralize decision rights. According to Neilson and Wulf (2012), the CEO's average span of control doubled between the mid-1980s to the mid-2000s (from five to almost ten). Source: *How Many Direct Reports?* Gary L. Neilson and Julie Wulf, Harvard Business Review, April 2012.

developers in a Scrum team, an SLA, business case, and balance score-card are some of the possible tangible outputs.

- **Relational capability (collaboration)**—Of the three categories, this one is the most informal and intangible in nature. The previous two can be written down and enforced using hard controls, but team and one-on-one interaction and communication is more culturally determined. The tone-at-the-top, joint goal and incentive structures, convergence, and explicit attention to skill sets are some of the controls that are available to drive the collaboration in the desired direction.

When outsourcing part of the IT team, several responsibilities and decision rights are transitioned to a key partner, retaining the responsibilities related to control and direction setting. The same decision has a similar effect on the process capabilities, as several will shift out of the direct line of sight, while new monitoring and performance processes have to be implemented to supervise the performance of the key partner. Last, but not least, the new collaboration model will become more formal, especially if the contract is fixed price and based on an SLA. (With local staff augmentation, it is easier to maintain informal cultural elements.) Hence, consider the impact on all three capabilities when planning an organizational change.

The same applies when deciding to decentralize the application teams to the business units. Here, the responsibility for the infrastructure typically remains under corporate stewardship due to the benefit from economies of scale. However, when a central team that is emphasizing standardization, low cost, and robustness has to collaborate with multiple teams focused on speed-to-market, innovation, and flexibility, the inevitable result is tension on the boundary between both types of teams. The centralized team will implement comprehensive policies, procedures, and other structure-related elements, while decentralized teams tend to emphasis the relation (*the customer is waiting!*).[7]

Generally, the more dynamic and complex the task or objective, the lower the return on comprehensive structural and process capabilities. These situations require organizations and teams that score high on relational capabilities.

6.3 THE TELCO THAT LOVED TO REORGANIZE

This telco had a long and rich history. Before the government regulated the market, it was the only company in the country that customers could turn to for a telephone connection. The government still used its services as did many

---

[7] See also Chapter 2, as it involves a team with a role culture (Apollo) that has to collaborate with a task-oriented team (Athena).

large corporations. Overall, the telco faced a sliding market share due to more aggressive and nimbler competitors. By repositioning itself and shedding organizational and technological legacy, the telco had been able to slow the decline, but they were not out of the woods yet. In an effort to improve competitiveness and capitalize on potential areas of growth, executives launched an almost continuous stream of reorganizations. The following describes two of them.

The first case describes a reorganization whereby two directors explored the possibilities of optimizing their teams. One director was responsible for teams A–C, specialized in realizing and supporting IT solutions, while the second director took care of all the telecom solutions with teams 1–4. Neither interfaced directly with external customers, but provided their services to multiple internal business units. Both directors and their teams already collaborated on a day-to-day basis because the line between telecom technology and IT was very thin. The overlap between both domains and general lack of maturity resulted in considerable waste:

- The business was unsure where to go with their demand due to the vague boundary between IT and telecom
- New demands were handled inconsistently (e.g., different ways to initiate a new project), further adding to the confusion in the business domain
- Solutions offered to the business were technology oriented instead of service- or business-process oriented
- Most projects required extensive coordination and alignment between the IT and telecom teams, but both teams used their own frameworks (e.g., eTOM by telecom teams and ITIL by IT teams)

To address them, a small change team was tasked with defining and evaluating the available scenarios. The scenarios had to contribute to the overall objectives of the telco, such as the desire to become a *smart operator* and decrease time-to-market of innovations, and concede to key constrains like the scarceness of deep telecom expertise. Combined with the strategic key principles of both telecom and IT teams (e.g., use whenever possible off-the-shelf solutions and a standardized operating model), the change team had the inputs required to start. First on the to-do list was designing a new high-level operating model and accompanying team structure. As the portfolio was neither completely dedicated to *foundation IT* nor *entrepreneurial IT*, the new structure would be somewhere in between the horizontal or vertical stove pipes depicted in Figure 6.6.

By scoring the solutions in the IT and telecom portfolios on criteria like maturity of value proposition and technology, number of *target architectures*, uncertainty of business forecast, and required amount of specific domain expertise, the new operating model and organizational structure started to emerge. The business demand for innovation turned out to be limited and always required

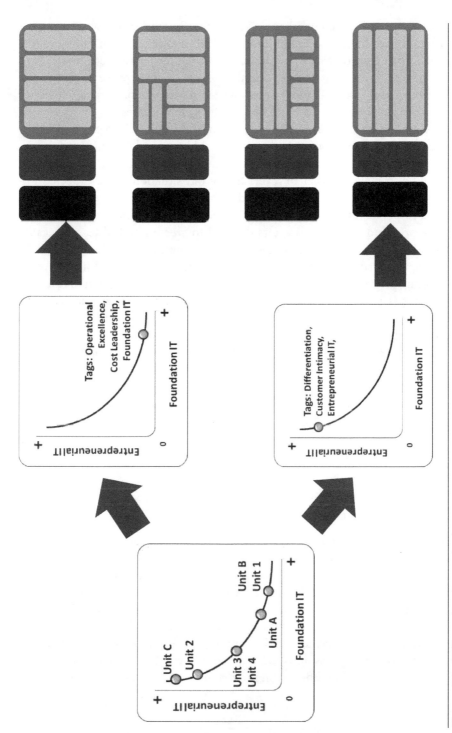

Figure 6.6 Differentiated organization structures

both telecom and IT components. One of the first decisions was, therefore, merging teams C and 2 which improved speed-to-market, team collaboration, and the utilization of scarce resources. Several other teams were reorganized into horizontal, business-process-oriented teams to achieve the required customer intimacy. Teams B and 1 were merged to yield considerable efficiency gains, such as better utilization of capital-intensive resources.

The next decision involved the translation of the design into physical or virtual teams. The creation of virtual teams would be easiest to achieve as the existing reporting lines and departmental structure would remain largely intact. It would also make it easier to revert to the old situation if the expected improvements failed to materialize. The disadvantages of virtual teams included unclear responsibilities and spending more hours on coordination. After weighing the pros and cons, the directors decided to create physical teams because it would send an unambiguous message to all employees involved. Other advantages included a reduction in coordination mechanisms and likelihood of conflicting priorities, and faster realization of the desired reduction in full-time equivalent (FTE) employees. Uncertainty among employees and focusing on internal team affairs instead of the internal customer were identified as the main disadvantages.

The FTE reduction succeeded, but a little more than nine months later, another reorganization was initiated by the board. Again, the teams were reshuffled in order to reduce head count. By this time, many employees barely knew why or for whom they were working. They just did what they were told to do by their line managers, who themselves also struggled to align their decisions with short-term and long-term customer value. As a result, the employees stopped caring. When delivering a service in a competitive market, this is the beginning of the end.

Less isolation, more cohesion includes the need for a connection between the company and its employees.

Another part of the telco was struggling with a similar challenge. Here, a director who was responsible for five external customer-facing business units noticed a lack of collaboration and communication, causing unnecessary delays, rework, and other sources of waste. The units were to remain intact as physical entities, but the emphasis would shift from performance as a business unit to the end-to-end experience of the external customer. Lean techniques in combination with business process management tools were to be used to optimize the business processes. As the business units relied on several complex and business critical applications, IT was identified as an important track of the change program.

Until then, every business unit had enjoyed considerable freedom regarding investments in IT. Apart from several shared core applications, each unit had their own portfolio with business unit-specific applications, service levels, and technologies. For the transformation to have any chance of success, the existing feudal governance approach had to be abandoned and replaced by a more federalized approach. With the latter, executives from both business and IT collaborate with each other at different levels. The strategic direction and principles are set at the C-level, with business units making decisions within these parameters. Hence, in parallel to designing the new end-to-end operating model, several members of the change team were tasked with rationalizing the existing heterogeneous IT landscape and governance structure.

After outlining the target end-to-end process design, governance structure, and IT landscape, the change team moved to the second phase—implementation. To reduce the risk profile of this phase, the director decided to start with a pilot. One set of business value propositions and its end-to-end business process were selected to learn and create a *template* for the rest of the portfolio. The pilot was split in three parts—business domain, IT domain, and joint domain. A joint steering committee was created to discuss progress, align priorities, and decide on any conflicts of interests. A simplified overview of the joint pilot track is depicted in Figures 6.7a, 6.7b, and 6.7c. It started with identifying the physical IT components (such as datasets, applications, and infrastructure), underpinning the envisioned end-to-end business process. The second step consisted of defining the most important end-to-end service requirement from a business perspective. For the pilot business process, it turned out to be the ability to confirm whether a customer was eligible for a fixed wireless broadband internet access contract, within two hours. The marketing department considered this *the* key driver due to feedback from customers and because the competition was lagging in this area. It would take central stage in the upcoming marketing campaign and expected to boost sales by 20% in the coming twelve months.

Further analysis found that order processing was the most critical discrete business activity in the end-to-end chain. If something were to go wrong with this activity, it would have a major ripple effect, preventing the business from delivering on its key driver. Based on this critical input from the business, IT started to design its virtual end-to-end IT value chain. To reduce complexity, the IT project team identified and bundled the dozens (or more) physical IT components that were required by a coherent set of business activities into a virtual *service component* (see Step 3 in Figure 6.7b). For every virtual service component, a set of key IT drivers (such as response times, release frequency, and availability level) was defined that applied to all of the underpinning physical IT components.

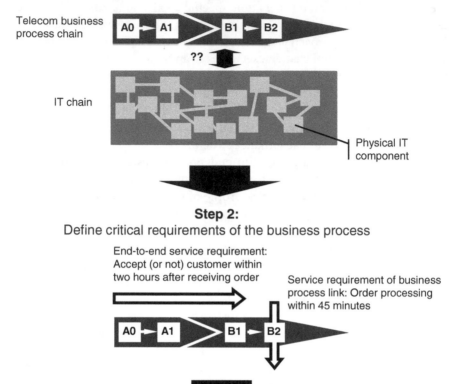

Step 1:
Identify IT components used by business process

Telecom business process chain

AO ← A1 > B1 ← B2

??

IT chain

Physical IT component

Step 2:
Define critical requirements of the business process

End-to-end service requirement: Accept (or not) customer within two hours after receiving order

Service requirement of business process link: Order processing within 45 minutes

AO ← A1 > B1 ← B2

Figure 6.7a   Integral end-to-end management (adapted from: Zielemans, F. and Meijers, J., Integraal SLM bij een groothandelsketen: Bedrijfsproces en IT pragmatisch koppelen, 2002)

By creating this layer of virtual service components, it became much easier to map the end-to-end business process to the underpinning technology. Hundreds of SLAs and reports were reduced to a fraction of that number as the complexity was pushed back into the IT domain. The virtual service components also shaped the new governance and service management framework (Step 4a). For every business process steward responsible for an end-to-end business process, IT appointed a process steward responsible for the accompanying virtual IT chain. Both the SLA and performance reports were revamped to reflect the new operating model. The IT process steward, in turn, networked with

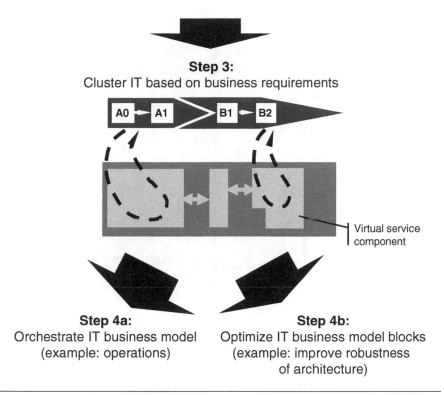

Figure 6.7b   Continuation of Figure 6.7—Integral end-to-end management, continued

IT service coordinators who were responsible for an individual virtual service component, using operational level agreements to formalize the expectations.

Last but not least, there was Step 4b. The virtual service components merely shielded the business from the complexity of turning a heterogeneous IT landscape into multiple interdependent IT value chains. For starters, one physical IT component could be used by multiple virtual service components. The solution for this one was fairly easy: the most stringent performance indicators were leading. A more daunting challenge turned out to be the dependencies between datasets, applications, and infrastructure components, both horizontally (e.g., applications exchanging data) and vertically (e.g., application depending on virtual server). When availability is critical, the service component should possess enough redundancy to continue functioning after one component fails (unavailability = both components 1 *and* 2 fail). However, analysis turned up several scenarios whereby the business process would come to a standstill if a single component failed (unavailability = components 1 *or* 2 fails).

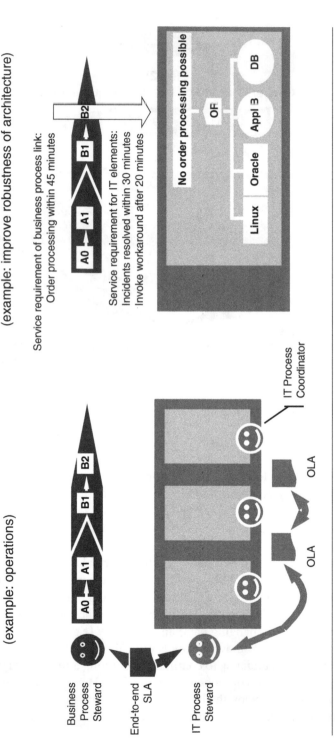

Figure 6.7c   Continuation of Figure 6.7—Integral end-to-end management, continued

Here the solution is less obvious, as investing in redundancy and other continuity improving initiatives tend to be very expensive. IT had to go back to the business to discuss the tradeoff between benefits and cost. When the IT-related cost for order processing in 60 minutes is half as much as processing in 45 minutes, the business may well opt for the second best solution.

Less isolation, more cohesion includes the need to get down to the nitty-gritty details to make it work.

REFERENCES

i. Osterwalder, A. and Pigneur, Y. (2010). *Business Model Generation: A Handbook for Visionaries, Game Changers, and Challengers.*

ii. Porter, M. E. (March 2001). *Strategy and the Internet.* Harvard Business Review.

iii. Choudary, P. S. (2013). Why Business Models Fail: Pipes vs. Platforms. Link: http://www.wired.com/2013/10/why-business-models-fail-pipes-vs-platforms/.

iv. Osterwalder, A. and Pigneur, Y. (2010). *Business Model Generation: A Handbook for Visionaries, Game Changers, and Challengers.*

v. Smith, H. A., McKeen, J. D. and Singh, S. (2007). Developing Information Technology for Business Value. Journal of Information Technology Management.

vi. Source: http://www.businessmodelgeneration.com/canvas/bmc. Accessed April 13, 2016.

vii. Maurya, A. (2012). Running Lean: Iterate from Plan A to a Plan That Works. O'Reilly Media, Inc.

viii. Henderson, J. C. and Venkatraman, N. (1993). Strategic Alignment: Leveraging Information Technology for Transforming Organizations. IBM Systems Journal.

ix. Luftman, J. (December 2000). Assessing Business-IT Alignment Maturity. Communications of AIS.

x. Stewart, W., Coulson, S. and Wilson, R. (2007). Information Technology: When Is It Worth the Investment. Communications of the IIMA.

xi. Duncan, R. (September 1972). Characteristics of Organizational Environments and Perceived Environments Uncertainty. American Science Quarterly.

xii. Peterson, R. (2004). Crafting Information Technology Governance. Information Systems Management.

7

LESS COST, MORE VALUE

Less cost, more value represents the ability to realize value from a business perspective.

Value creation is the core objective of every company. Consequently, any decision that creates new value or protects existing value is a *good* decision and vice versa. A company can create and protect value for consumers, shareholders, employees, suppliers, debt providers, government, and even society as a whole.

In the United States and several other countries, companies tend to focus on shareholder value, relying on the premise that as a result the gross domestic product per capita and employment will also grow.[i] Most European and Japanese companies adopted a more holistic approach, balancing the stakes of shareholders, customers, employees, and society as a whole (e.g., environmental pollution). With the financial meltdown of 2009 and global warming in mind, the discussion regarding the shareholder perspective of profitability over responsibility versus the stakeholder perspective of responsibility over profitability resurfaced in the United States. Supporters of the stakeholder perspective even includes former shareholder value champion Jack Welch, ex-CEO of General Electric:[ii] "*On the face of it, shareholder value is the dumbest idea in the world. Shareholder value is a result, not a strategy . . . your main constituencies are your employees, your customers, and your products.*"

From a shareholder perspective it may be best to terminate all IT systems that support consumer products that are more than three years old, but for a grandmother who does not desire the latest gadgets, it would mean a forced renewal of an otherwise perfectly functional product. In the book *The Ultimate Question 2.0*, Fred Reichland concludes that a company that favors short-term profit over customer satisfaction generates a *brand liability* that has to be repaid one day.

While this seemingly lacks any relation to this book, one has to consider that many business topics have or will soon be listed on the IT agenda. Not in a sense that businesses want to automate a new business model, but to discuss the application of current and emerging technologies in order to create new value and protect the existing company value.

Tabling such a broad strategic topic is a clear sign that the business considers IT an equal partner. It also means that the business has become less interested in direct IT cost and more interested in the added business value of technology. The utility duckling has turned into a swan. See Table 7.1 for three statements that cover the chapter as a whole.

Table 7.1   Statements to think about when reading this chapter

Statements
Benefit and risk are two sides of the same coin. The name of the coin is value.
Technology can both increase and decrease the risk profile of the business.
A business partner initiates results-driven improvements and a faithful servant initiates activity-centered improvements.

7.1 WHY THIS PRINCIPLE MATTERS

Start with the most basic question: is spending on IT even a good idea? Research by the Organization for Economic Co-operation and Development from 2004 on the impact of IT at the company level states that[iii] *"evidence suggests that IT use is beneficial, though under certain conditions, to firm performance and productivity in all countries for which micro-level studies have been conducted."* This finding is supported by various other sources including Hempel et al., who found that increased IT investments in Germany and The Netherlands raised labor productivity in service companies.[iv] A study conducted in Finland found productivity figures improved by 8–18% after employees were equipped with office automation and other IT services,[v] while research by Bosworth and Triplett indicated that IT enhanced labor and multi-factor productivity at the industry level in the United States.[vi] Last but not least, Arvanitis concluded that productivity was closely correlated with the deployment of IT in Switzerland[vii] and Clayton et al. found a positive effect on the deployment of e-commerce and productivity within the United Kingdom.[viii]

Technology in the right hands adds company value.

There is no universally accepted definition of the term *value*. It can, for example, be tangible, such as financial, speed-to-market, or customer retention, or intangible, like brand value or intellectual property. What most people agree on, however, is that at the end of the day, value is most meaningful when expressed by a financial number.

At the company level, the consolidated value of the company as a whole can be determined by selling it off to another company, an initial public offering (IPO) on a stock exchange, buyout by management or a third party, or liquidation. The last approach typically results in the lowest price, while initiating a bidding war by putting the company up for sale likely results in the highest valuation. Just think of the bidding war between Dell and HP for storage specialist 3Par in 2010. Dell initially bid $1.5 billion, but it was HP who, after a bidding war, acquired the company for $2.4 billion. The $2.4 billion represented 325 times the earnings before interest, taxes, depreciation, and amortization (EBITDA)—very different from the industry average at that time of 16 times the EBITDA. The same case also demonstrates the company-specific nature of company valuations. Compared to Dell, HP expected to realize an additional $900 million in revenue, margin, efficiency gains, improved brand value, and more.

At the business unit level, the decisions of executives and managers are driven by the first three of the four points listed here.[ix] The last is a company-level metric, solely used by business units as the discount rate in business cases:

- Enhances its profitability (e.g., margins)
- Increases its growth (e.g., revenue)
- Reduces its capital requirements
- Reduces its weighted average cost of capital (WACC)[1]

Profitability can be improved in two ways: reduce the cost of the value proposition or increase its price. The first is tied to cost leadership strategy—markets with many competitors and few possibilities to differentiate on quality or features. Here, technology is primarily used to reduce the business cost via process automation, supply chain optimizations like reduced stock levels, and improved decision making. A company can demand a high price if the value proposition offers features that are absent from the offerings of the competition, or even in markets with little or no competition. These companies see technology primarily as a potential source of new added value features.

The ability to lower the cost or increase the price is related to productivity improvements, as seen in Figure 7.1. Technology can, for example, be used to add additional channels, allowing the business to sell more products or services, thereby increasing the utilization of its (key) resources. Several emerging

---

[1] WACC is a calculation of a firm's cost of capital in which each category of capital is proportionately weighted. All sources of capital, including common stock, preferred stock, bonds, and any other long-term debt, are included in a WACC calculation (source: Investopedia).

■ Company and business unit level
■ Joint business IT domain and initiatives

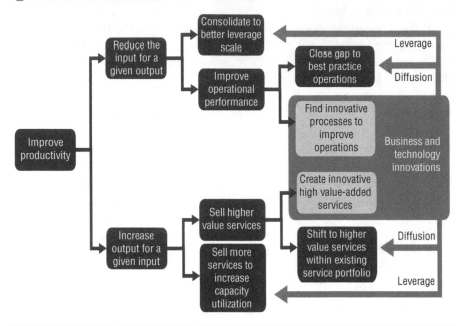

Figure 7.1   Technology-driven productivity improvement (source: Whatever Happened to the New Economy, McKinsey Global Institute, November 2002)

technologies allow for far more dramatic improvements in operational performance. Think of automating tasks requiring creative problem solving, subtle judgments, and learning. They are areas that, until recently, were thought to be exclusive to humans.

The transformative nature of technology is only partially captured by Figure 7.1. It originated in 2002, a time where companies with analog business models sought guidance on ways to *improve* their business processes and services with technology. Few existing companies at that time used technology to fundamentally *reframe* their business model as a whole. It was a time where Facebook, Uber, Airbnb, Twitter, and others that were born in a compiler were not conceived yet. For them, technology is not limited to improving two productivity performance drivers; they use it to improve productivity on all fronts simultaneously.

The second driver at the business unit level that will improve value at the company level is increasing growth. Options to increase growth are numerous, including selling more to existing customers, selling existing products in new markets, attracting new customers by investing in marketing, adding new channels, investing in new products, and creating partnerships. Realizing additional revenue by adding users or page views is actually far easier than increasing profitability, since anybody can sell a product for free or below cost. Hence, both should not be considered in isolation but in unison.

Nevertheless, there are situations when growth supersedes profitability in importance, such as introducing a new business model or value proposition. It took Amazon more than twenty years to realize any profit. Instead of focusing on earnings for shareholders, Amazon preferred to reinvest the profit of existing lines of business into new lines of business. Its sole focus was growth.

Reducing capital requirements is the driver of the third business unit level, with Uber and Airbnb as two prominent examples. Traditionally, companies such as these had to invest in taxis or build a motel or hotel to have rooms to rent out. Both businesses side-stepped this precondition by using assets that were owned by other network entities—individuals in most cases. It was, again, technology that enabled these many other disruptive *asset light* business models.

Technology can improve the profitability and growth and also reduce the capital requirements of the business.

Improving the profitability and growth while also reducing capital requirements allows the company to create additional value. As mentioned in the introduction, the executives of a company are also responsible for protecting existing value. There is a continuous stream of both expected and unexpected undesired events that require action, such as mitigation, and avoidance. To manage these risks, many companies rely on the enterprise risk management framework by the Committee of Sponsoring Organizations (COSO) of the Treadway Commission. It identifies four risk categories:

- **Strategic risk**—Includes the effect of competition on their own business model, changes in social and technological trends, and access to capital
- **Financial risk**—Includes undesirable effect on company assets, pricing, currency, solvency, and liquidity
- **Hazard risk**—Includes effects of natural disasters, property damage, and liability torts
- **Operational risk**—Includes failing business processes or products and damage to customer satisfaction or reputation

For CIOs and their team, the first and fourth category are most relevant because technology can be used to reduce the likelihood and impact of these risk categories. The strategic risk posed by competitors can, for example, be mitigated by adding digital features that are difficult or expensive to copy by the competition. Besides keeping the competition at bay, technology can also be used to mitigate the other sources of strategic business risk identified in the following points by Slywotzky and Drzik:[x]

1. **Industry margin squeeze**—At the start of a product cycle, growth and margin will be healthy, but with the product and industry evolving, commoditization, overcapacity, and substitutes will push it slowly into the no-profit zone. Technology can extend the profitable part of the life cycle by turning dumb products into smart ones, adding new channels or reducing production and supply chain cost.

2. **Brand erosion**—When existing customers are leaving, become less loyal, complain about stale products or unmet needs, those are sure signs that the company's brand is eroding. The company is losing its unique identity in the marketplace—a vulnerable position to be in. McDonalds struggled several years to formulate an effective answer to the fast-casual restaurant chain Chipotle. The latter served superior quality food at a higher price point than McDonalds, fulfilling the desire of customers to eat healthier and more environmentally friendly meals. Trucking in the United States has the image of long, boring hours and declining professional standards. Autonomously driven trucks, which only require their drivers to supervise them or perform specific tasks, may attract a new generation of drivers. Drivers raised by the iPad and thrilled by the prospect of loading, unloading, and driving a 25-meter, double-trailer combination using a couple of swipes. In this latter case, technology may well make a whole industry cool again.

3. **One-of-a-kind competitor**—Few things are as dangerous as assuming that the dominating business model and core beliefs of the industry will still be the same five years from now. Once upon a time, Walmart disrupted the retail market in the United States, only to be disrupted by Amazon, after it had comfortably settled into the dominant player role. If your company does not evolve its business model on a regular basis, it is very likely an existing competitor or start-up will come forward. In most cases, the new business model will leverage on emerging technologies or use existing ones to disrupt the status quo. Google was not the first search engine, but it used better algorithms and infrastructure to effectively take over the search market from other players.

4. **Customer priority shift**—If the company relies on a small but very loyal group of customers, it is vulnerable. Substitute products can emerge from unexpected places, suddenly and dramatically impacting the customers' preferences. Slywotzky and Drzik list *continuous creation and analysis of proprietary information* and *fast and cheap experimentation* as two powerful mitigating actions. The first can benefit from advances

in business intelligence and big data, while virtualization, simulation, and 3-D printing are some of the technologies available to operationalize the second mitigating action. Technology is also an enabler of shifting customer preferences. Why take the car to a travel agent in the city if you can book your vacation via the internet? Why lug 20 pounds of physical books in your suitcase when your e-reader can store hundreds of books? Of all the strategic business risks in this list, technology likely had, has, and will continue to have the largest impact on this one. Just like the previous point, it pays off to be an early mover.

5. **New project failure**—New products may contain flaws that failed to emerge during testing or the early stages of their life cycle. The consequent product recall would be costly, both financially and in terms of the brand equity—such as Toyota when it had to issue a global product recall in 2010 and the more recent Samsung Note 7 recall. The lower the barrier of entry, such as products that are easy for competitors to create a substitute, the larger the impact. The likelihood and impact of this risk can be mitigated by *smart sequencing, developing excess options*, and *employing the stepping-stone method*. With smart sequencing, better-understood and more-controllable products are introduced first, while an excess of functionalities increases the chance of ending up with at least one successful product. With the stepping-stone method, a series of projects is created that divide the whole endeavor into a series of sequential steps that are aimed at reducing the risk profile and thus increasing the chance of success. Here, too, the business case for business intelligence and big data is easy to make.

6. **Market stagnation**—Oil companies that are investing in solar power or other sources of renewable energy are anticipating the eventual decline of the fossil fuel market. Long-term success requires a healthy balance between *cows, dogs, stars*, and *question marks*.[2] *Demand Innovation* is mentioned by the authors as the most powerful way to counter this strategic risk. It means looking through the lens of the company's business-to-consumer (B2C) or business-to-business (B2B) customers when considering new product innovations. When your value proposition optimizes the profitability, growth, or capital requirements of the customer, it is likely to become a winner. The higher the technology density of the market, the more likely it can be of use to mitigate this strategic risk.

---

[2] These terms refer to the quadrants of the Boston Consulting Group matrix which helps business units analyze their product portfolio. More information can be found at: https://en.wikipedia.org/wiki/Growth–share_matrix.

7. **Technology shift**—Last, but not least, review the impact of technology on business models and value propositions. This strategic risk requires no further introduction considering the topic of this book. Depending on the overall strategy and positioning of the company, mitigating actions include.
    - Being first or being a fast follower, as many disrupting technologies enjoy strong network effects,
    - Investing in multiple emerging technologies simultaneously, or
    - Waiting until a dominant technology has emerged and then differentiating in other ways, such as in service or cost.

Technology can not only lower the business' strategic risk profile, as shown in Points 1 to 6, and increase it, as in Point 7, it can do the same with the operational risk profile of the business. The operational risk profile includes all losses resulting from inadequate internal business processes, IT processes, IT systems, external vendors, employees, and external events, such as flooding and hacking. As a case in point, £80 million was wasted on a failed introduction of a new transaction system at the London Stock Exchange between 1990 and 1993, while a software error in an Ariane 5 rocket resulted in a crash and loss of 500 million euro in 1996. According to Renkema, the yearly cost of poorly functioning and/or implemented IT systems runs somewhere between $60 billion to $70 billion in the United States alone.[xi] The negative impact this can have on the market value of the company is reflected by research based on 213 newspaper articles on IT failures within publicly traded companies over a period of ten years. It suggested that large IT failures result in a 2% average cumulative abnormal drop in stock prices over a two-day event window.[xii]

On the bright side, the pros of IT for the business far outweigh the cons. Neither the failed IT project at the London Stock Exchange nor the software fault in the Ariane 5 had any long-term effects on the adoption of technology. On the contrary, both stock exchanges (e.g., high frequency trading, blockchain) and space programs (e.g., SpaceX and Blue Orion) are at the forefront of inventing and adopting new technologies.

There are several ways that technology can reduce operational business risk. Given the same input, a software program will always generate the same output. Automating tasks can, therefore, improve the predictability, consistency, scalability, and quality of products and services. Other areas where digitalization can reduce the operational risk profile include regulatory compliance (such as GRC, SOD)[3], reporting tools, and fraud.

---

[3] GRC stands for governance risk and compliance; SOD stands for segregation of duties.

Technology can reduce the strategic and operational risk profiles of the business.

There is one important precondition in order to turn potential into realization: act based on the premise that risk is a two-edged sword, as risks[xiii] "*are random variables, mapping unforeseen future states of the world into values representing profits and losses.*" In other words, risk can be both rewarding and punishing, an often-overlooked fact. In the words of Funston and Frederick:[xiv] "*Conventional risk management, with its focus mainly on avoiding risk and protecting existing assets, is necessary but not sufficient. Worse, risk management as practiced rarely focuses on ways to identify, develop, seize, and exploit the most promising opportunities for the enterprise to create value. Indeed, most leaders and risk managers do not see risk management as part of value creation.*" Especially for entrepreneurial IT, it is crucial to also consider uncertainty as a positive. Risk management practices for foundation IT can stay closer to traditional practices.

The principle *less cost, more value* is therefore an invitation to regularly answer the following questions. Considering the existing speeds that markets move in, their technology density, and their maturity:

- How can IT protect the existing company value and create new value?
- How can IT increase the rewarded risk of business initiatives and decrease the accompanying unrewarded risk?
- Where are we on the road from a focus on short-term cost improvements to long-term value creation?
- Are our risk management practices holistic (e.g., able to differentiate between foundation IT and entrepreneurial IT) or narrow and traditional?

The next part of this chapter examines at least some of the answers.

7.2 FROM COST-FOCUSED TO VALUE-FOCUSED

In the old days, improving business efficiency through automation was the sole reason why business managers invested in IT. A business case to replace 100 bookkeepers with three bookkeepers and an IT system is straightforward. Being one of the first companies to offer such systems is one of the reasons IBM became *Big Blue*. Its 650, 705, and 1401 systems introduced in the 1950s—that were later on replaced by 360 and 370 mainframes—allowed for tremendous efficiency gains. This historic sweet spot of deploying technology has been mentioned by almost every scholar who was writing about the benefits of IT. Since then, much has changed. In 2010, Basahel and Irani identified 42 benefits of IT when researching recent literature and case studies.[xv]

One of those benefits—to develop new markets and products—is also mentioned by Laudon & Laudon[xvi] and Pearlson and Saunders.[xvii] Drafting a business case for this kind of initiative is far less straightforward than automating an invoice process. The same applied to the business case for *creating new strategic opportunities*, suggested by Benson et al.[xviii] and Ward et al.[xiv] Here, the contribution of business and IT blend together, requiring a different way to measure and report on the contribution of IT. For starters, the benefits tend to be for the business, while IT has to pick up the bill.

7.2.1 Four Times Upside, Two Times Downside

Every new IT value proposition and user, from the internal business user to the external customer, takes a bite out of the IT budget. Hence, if the IT budget is fixed and none of the existing IT value propositions can be retired, there will be a day when the IT team has to say *no* to the business, as can be seen in Figure 7.2. The business asking for more without helping IT by either securing additional budget or decommissioning existing value propositions results in a win-lose situation. A unilateral initiative to centralize all IT activities can have

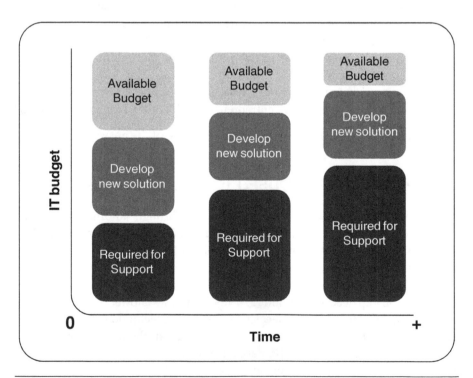

Figure 7.2   Operations and support eating the IT budget

the same effect, but with the business drawing the short straw this time. Both result in suboptimization and passive or even active resistance from the other party. Value maximization at a company level requires a more holistic approach.

The need to balance the interests of the company as a whole, individual business units, and IT are reflected in the Business Value Index (BVI) from Intel.[xx] It facilitates the decision-making process by visualizing the attractiveness of a proposed investment along three axes: business value, IT efficiency, and financial attractiveness. The latter captures the business case, such as the net present value (NPV), and the first two the positive, neutral, or negative impact of the initiative on the business and IT domains. Combined, the framework should prevent *failures*, such as a lose-lose situation, and provide decision makers with an indication as to how each investment adds value at the company level after taking into account the net effect of all three axes.

Due to its focus on IT *efficiency*, the BVI framework implicitly treats IT as a cost center—a risky assumption when dealing with hybrid and digital business models. Here, too, there should be room to differentiate between, for example, entrepreneurial IT and foundation IT. For the latter, efficiency and continuity are good proxies of IT benefits, while agility and speed-to-market are more suitable when considering an investment in entrepreneurial IT. Nevertheless, visualizing the interests of the key stakeholders[4] allows the stakeholders to quickly identify the most valuable investment opportunities and potential issues that require a solution.

Besides balancing the interests of the key stakeholders, it is equally important to act on the notion that value is a function of benefits and risks. Everybody who is familiar with NPV calculations is also familiar with discount rates, the rate reflecting the time value of money, and the uncertainty or risk of future cash flows. At the company level, investors have long since recognized that a company like Google is riskier to invest in than a water utility company. People will always need water and there are no foreseeable revolutionary game-changing technologies that will turn this business model upside down. No such luck for Google and, subsequently, investors expect a higher return on their investment. The discount rate at the company level is known as the WACC[5] and in most cases, it is the same rate used to discount cash flows of IT investments.

---

[4] May in certain situations even include the stakes of external customers and key partners since they might conflict with the interests of internal entities.

[5] If your company can borrow half of the required amount from the bank at 5% and the other half comes from shareholders who require a return of 10%, the WACC is 7.5% (5% × 0.5 + 10% × 0.5) when ignoring the impact of taxation. An investment is worth considering if the return is equal or higher than the WACC.

The interdependence between benefits and risks can also be observed in other areas. The desire of the business to launch a new digital content platform ahead of the competition has a negative impact on the project's risk profile when it requires the team to cut some corners. Speed-to-market and a thorough test program, such as unit, regression, and integration don't mix well. As long as the business makes an *informed* decision regarding this and other tradeoffs, IT is doing its job. That is, until the business wants to cross a certain line.

Some risks of the joint universe may have a spillover effect on the IT risk universe. The risk appetite of a particular business unit regarding integrity and confidentiality risk may be higher than the minimum baseline set by IT. For example, the product owner appointed by the business unit may consider allocating several development sprints to the Open Web Application Security Project (OWASP) top 10 compliancy a waste of time. A faithful servant IT team would protest a bit, but fulfill the wish of the business. A business partner straightens its back and points out that a weakness in one application may provide access to other applications or sensitive data—a risk that IT is unwilling to take, unless a board member signs off on it.

The opposite is also true; a decision beneficial to IT can negatively impact the joint domain. Think of a long-term IT outsourcing contract that trades lower IT cost for flexibility—or a unilateral decision to centralize all IT. Therefore, the trick and challenge is identifying both the positive and negative effects of a decision on the value of the company as a whole. Only investments with a positive net effect that increases company value or protects existing company value should be allowed to move to the realization phase.

The interdependent chain of benefit and risk categories or universes at the company level is depicted in Figure 7.3. On the left, the business benefits and risks span the boundary between external environment and the business

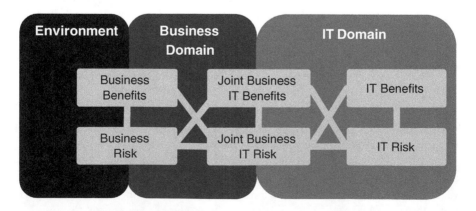

Figure 7.3   Six interdependent universes

domain. They are the sole responsibility of the business, like the value streams from an analog business model, losses related to changing customer demands, and unreliable delivery of subassemblies by suppliers. Everything outside IT's circle of influence should be treated as such, and vice versa.

From a value creation perspective that is within the scope of this book, the joint business IT benefits and risks are most relevant. The magic happens on the boundary between business and IT domains. Both parties share the responsibility for the end result. Depending on the context, such as foundation or entrepreneurial IT, the collaboration is informal-formal, iterative-sequential, etc. From a business perspective, the joint universes' risks may have a relationship with the business benefits and business, hence the connecting lines.[6] The connection between the joint universes and the IT universes on the right are irrelevant for the business. For them it is a *black box*.

Similarly, the IT team is primarily interested in its own universe and joint value propositions. Risks that are related to currency fluctuations and access to capital are considered part of the business domain. They are for IT what the OWASP top 10 is for the business: *I don't care, just fix it*. That is, until both domains fuse. At that point, the business and IT teams become one, reducing the organizational complexity (i.e., no need for the boundary-spanning joint business IT universes), but also the ability to achieve economies-of-scale.

The figure can also be translated into an formula, providing a proxy[7] of the net effects of an investment in technology for companies whereby the business and IT are separate domains. The company-level value of IT equals the sum of additional value created for the business from investments in technology and monetizable data, plus the contribution within the IT domain itself, minus the required capital expenditures (CAPEX) and operational expenditures (OPEX):

Company-level value of IT
$$= \Sigma(\text{added joint business IT benefits}) - \text{residual joint business IT risk}$$
$$+ \Sigma(\text{added IT benefits}) - \text{residual IT risk} - \Sigma(\text{CAPEX} + \text{OPEX})$$

The added joint IT business benefits include the use of technology to create either additional company value (e.g., growth in the existing market) and/or protection for the existing company value (e.g., address industry margin squeeze or brand erosion). The same applies to added IT benefits. An investment in

---

[6] From an IT perspective, there are no connecting lines between the business and joint universe. However, when calculating value at the company level, the business and IT have to look beyond their own world and accrue all sources of benefits and risks.

[7] The formula is for illustrative purpose only as it does not include the effects of time. For an actual representation, an NPV calculation should be used. However, that would make it too complex for the purpose of this book. Second, operational risk is often included as a cost in OPEX, while CAPEX is reserved for large unexpected losses.

technology can increase IT benefits (e.g., increase efficiency of support team through automation) or lower the IT risk profile (e.g., infrastructure hardening). Besides the good news, here too does the following apply: *"There ain't no such thing as a free lunch."* Every decision comes with one or more risks that need to be addressed by either avoiding it altogether (such as investing in another initiative), reducing the risk (like implementing controls), transferring the risk (through things like insurance), or accepting it.

The risk that remains after mitigation or transferring part of the impact is called residual risk. It is the expected loss that is associated with the investment and should be deducted from the expected benefits streams or added to OPEX, to create a realistic picture of the added net value. If the joint or IT residual risk remains above the risk appetite of the decision makers, the investment should be avoided. Hence, an investment in IT is a source of four types of pros and two types of cons.

The formula can be applied to individual investments and to the return of a whole portfolio (quadrant). For native digital business models, business benefits and risks become the vehicles to measure the contribution of investments in technology. When fused, most of the company-level value of an investment in IT is captured by:

Company-level value of IT
$$= \Sigma(\text{added business benefits}) - \text{residual business risk} - \Sigma(\text{CAPEX} + \text{OPEX})$$

Moving from theory to practice, let's assume that health insurance company ABC faces considerable margin squeeze due to nimbler and leaner competitors. Customers increasingly prefer lower prices over the personalized contact offered by ABC. The board, therefore, decides to transform its business model from relatively low customer volume, customer intimacy, and premium pricing to high customer volume, operational excellence, and lower pricing. In order to retain some of the customer intimacy experience, the customers will be offered a sophisticated multi-channel platform with human customer service representatives only handling the most complex cases. To existing customers, the platform presents itself as an easy-to-use self-service portal, while potential customers are enticed by seamlessly integrated channel phases, such as awareness, evaluation, purchase, and after-sales service to become a new paying customer.

Despite the considerable investment in a new platform, the business expects that a significant number of existing customers will jump ship. To offset the decline in revenue and margin, the business wants to quickly grow the number of new customers by offering aggressive discounts on three-year contracts. The net effect of the whole initiative on company value over that period is depicted in Tables 7.2a, 7.2b, and 7.2c. The table splits the benefits and risks into the three value universes that were previously introduced—one outside the scope of IT and two within. Two universes report a negative net effect, requiring the strong performance of the joint universe to push the business case into positive territory.

Table 7.2a Impact of investment in new platform on value of company

Value Universe: Business Value	Effect	Responsible
Business benefit, increase company value: • Additional customers signing up due to sponsoring several regional sports events for two years (e.g., 75% likelihood of additional 35,000 customers, total additional margin of $45) • Sponsoring and accompanying marketing costs • Impact new pricing model compared to margin of current business model	$45 – $15 – $55	COO
Business benefit, protect existing company value: • Reduced impact of industry margin squeeze. Difference between projected impact of doing nothing and the new business model	$20	COO
Residual business risk: • Existing customers leaving due to dissatisfaction with new value proposition (e.g., 10% likelihood of 5,000 customers leaving, adding $5 to the cost of remaining customers due to fixed cost)	– $5	COO
Net Effect on Business Value	**– $10**	

Table 7.2b Impact of investment in new platform on value of company ABC, continued

Value Universe: Joint Business IT Value	Effect	Responsible
Joint business IT benefit, increase company value: • Net effect of reduced headcount on companies' customer service center	$145	COO and CIO
Joint business IT benefits, protect existing company value: • Reduction in expected operational losses (e.g., fraud) due to the automation of business processes and controls	$10	COO and CIO
Joint business IT risk: • Design of self-service portal inadequate, requiring more customer service staff to stay employed (e.g., 5% likelihood, adding $10 to cost) • Introduction of copycat self-service portal by competitors, pulling customers away (e.g., 20% likelihood of 50,000 customers, adding $5 to cost of remaining customers due to fixed cost)	– $10 – $5	COO and CIO
Net Effect on Joint Business IT Value	**$140**	

Table 7.2c   Impact of investment in new platform on value of company ABC, continued

Value Universe: IT Value	Effect	Responsible
IT benefits:		CIO
• $25 added by removing existing customer service IT systems	$25	
• $70 subtracted by investment and operating cost self-service portal, including risk mitigation	– $70	
IT risk:		CIO
• Loss due to downtime of self-service portal (1% likelihood of 4-hour outage)	– $5	
• Cost of security breach (0.01% likelihood of unauthorized access to sensitive data due to high impact cost of $1,000)	– $10	
Net Effect on IT Value	**– $60**	

In real life, insurance companies have already moved beyond self-service portals. Technology is transforming their business model as a whole. In healthcare, insurance companies heavily invest in mobile health technologies, remote monitoring, drone delivered vaccines, big data, and robotics. Again, fewer employees will be able to do more activities (i.e., reduce input for a given output) of higher value (i.e., increase output for a given input).

Big data, mobile health technologies, remote monitoring, drone delivered vaccines, and robotics are an emerging joint concern, qualifying as entrepreneurial IT at this point in time. Other parts of the IT portfolio are and remain to be foundation IT. Hence, the benefit and risk universes are merely *containers* with a dynamic content. Over time, benefits can even evolve into risks and vice versa. The better the team is able to articulate and track the different benefit and risk streams, the better the quality of the investment decision.

To support the decision-making process, the next two sections cover the upside and downside of investments in technology more in-depth.

7.2.2 Add New Business Value

According to research by Forrester, an estimated $248.7 billion in revenue was generated in 2014 for the United States alone by selling food, insurance, cars, and other B2C products via the internet.[xxi] Even better news is the high growth rate of technology-enabled business models. For traditional retailers in the United Kingdom, the U.K. Office for National Statistics reported a growth of 4.4% (£29.9bn) in March 2010. During the same time period, online retail sales grew 15% (£4.5bn), according to IMRG Capgemini e-Retail Sales Index. The joint business IT universe is, therefore, the one where the CIO and their team can shine.

The higher the technology density of the business model, the higher the potential. Due to the ambiguity of the joint universe, however, it is also more difficult to pinpoint and quantify the contribution of IT. Was it the idea of the marketing department or the excellent execution of the IT department that made the difference?

In an article on CIO.com, William Blausey, Senior VP and CIO of Eaton Corporation, described how he tackled the issue by introducing the concept of *operational contribution.*[xxii] Before starting a new initiative, the IT staff of Eaton and representatives of other domains agree on both the role and contribution of IT with, in some cases, unexpected results: "*In a recent legal project, we thought that our contribution would be $750,000 in savings through expense management, but it turned out that we were able to quantify our contribution at more than $2 million per year through process improvements that we helped develop.*"

These numbers are peanuts compared the to potential of digital disruptions. Amazon's revenue per employee in 2014 accounted for $577,547 ($89 billion in revenue, 154,100 employees), more than twice as high as the $220,750 of Walmart in 2015 ($485.65 billion in revenue, 2,200,000 employees). Starbucks was one of the first food-and-beverage chains that identified technology as a source of growth and profitability. Free Wi-Fi, wireless charging, an app-based loyalty card system, indoor location beacons, coffee machines that upload their performance to the cloud, and an early adopter of mobile payments; there are few companies in that industry with a joint universe as large as Starbucks.[8] Consequently, when looking beyond business process improvements, a more holistic performance management approach is required.

The convergence of business and IT domains in, among others, the food-and-beverage industry is reflected in Table 7.3. On the left side, the business benefit universe is occupied by manifestations of the two key business benefit drivers—growth and profitability. The middle column depicts those benefits that require a joint effort, while the right column depicts benefits that are solely under the control of the IT team. In some cases, the right and even the middle columns are empty because the business benefit has no technology-augmented equivalent.

The examples in Table 7.3 are too abstract to be useful in real life. No decision maker will ever sign off on an investment in *a new hybrid or digital value*

---

[8] As analyzers and reactors are always keen to adopt the success formulas of prospectors, the industry as a whole is prone to get more technology-heavy over time—that is, until enough customers desire to go back to the basics, creating a business opportunity for one or more new (disruptive) chains with a traditional analog business model.

Table 7.3   Three benefit universes and their initiatives

Business Benefit Universe (including native digital business models)	Joint Business IT Benefit Universe	IT Benefit Universe
• Create a new, analog value proposition	• Use habit-forming technologies to create a new value proposition • Reframe the belief set of the existing business model based on a new emerging technology	• Mobilize new development team in five working days • Translate a new promising technology into a proof of concept within six months
• Company merging with a competitor to buy market share and improve economies of scale	• Create a new technology-rich value proposition through a strategic partnership (e.g., Apple + Nike)	• Access to at least ten relevant best-of-breed technology partners
• Reduce marketing cost per product	• Reduce number of overlapping CMSs, SEO, and SEA solutions and vendors[1] • Increase upselling by using advanced algorithms to better track online customer patterns	• Automate operations and support tasks related to CMS, SEO, and SEA solutions
• Extend life cycle of product by reducing the price point	• Reduce business cost through process automation • Add digital value-add features	• Reduce IT cost per product (e.g., through offshoring, IT process automation)
• Increase sales volume through analog channels	• Increase sales volume through digital channels • Create e-commerce platform for products on mobile devices • Add IoT sensors as new B2C/B2B channels	
• Enter a new geographic market using physical outlets		
Business domain ➤	◄ IT domain	

[1] CMS: Content Management System; SEO: search engine optimization; SEA: search engine advertising.

proposition, nor is it possible for IT to articulate their tangible contribution. Only items that are *SMART* can be expected to yield the desired effects and results. *SMART* items are:

- **Specific**—Is the objective unambiguous for all team members and other stakeholders?
- **Measurable**—What are the metrics used to determine that the team has achieved the objective?
- **Acceptable** or **Assignable**—Are the objectives and accompanying metrics acceptable for all stakeholders involved?—or specify who will do it. [9]
- **Realistic**—Can the team reasonably be expected to reach the objective (e.g., considering budget)?
- **Time bound**—When should the objective be realized?

The team that is responsible for realizing a new initiative should always start with replacing abstractions with concreteness and ambiguity with clarity. However, working backward from a well-defined end-point is not always possible. In some situations, the business has no more than a vision to work with. Nevertheless, even for a simulation, proof of concept, or pilot, it is possible to define tangible objectives and metrics to measure success.

Another attention point is related to team culture and the attitude of individual team members. Walmart is rooted in a time where every shop had walls and a roof. Confronted with the threat posed by Amazon, its first entrance into the digital era seemed a bit halfhearted, resulting in mediocre results.[xxiii] Only after strengthening its digital capabilities by taking over several start-up companies (such as Kosmix), and recruiting top talents, did the online performance of Walmart improved. Digitalization requires an all-in mentality and strategy.

The joint business IT universes of Chevron, BP, and Royal Dutch Shell look nothing like the examples that have been covered so far. They use predictive analysis and advanced visualization tools to optimize the production of existing oil wells and to discover new ones. The reliance on advanced technologies by these companies is reflected by the drill ship *Noble Bully 1* from Shell. It resembles more of a data center than a ship due to the technology required to survey ultra-deep waters or other previously unreachable locations. BP used similar technologies to increase the expected oil recovery from its Prudhoe Bay production facility in North America from 40 to 60%. As the 20% difference represents five billion barrels of oil, this must have been the easiest business case for any CIO ever. In the oil and gas industry, nobody has to explain the potential of big data and business intelligence. They operate at the forefront of it.

---

[9] See Appendix C—Glossary for the rationale behind the inclusion of Acceptable.

The tangible benefits of investments in social media are unfortunately more difficult to identify. Quoting David Alston:[xxiv] "*The discussion of ROI* (return on investment) *has focused mostly on the search for the Holy Grail of a metric, but adapting traditional metrics to fit social media would be akin to sticking a square peg in a round hole.*" Besides the challenge of defining suitable measurements, business and IT also have to anticipate rapidly changing customer patterns, such as teenagers moving from BlackBerry Messenger to WhatsApp. On the other hand, companies using Facebook, Twitter, Instagram, Tencent QQ, or other platforms cannot all have gotten the wrong end of the stick.

During the re-introduction phase of the Mountain Dew brand in 2008, PepsiCo relied on customer insights collected from social platforms to prioritize the introduction of new varieties. The ability to better predict the market adoption of its products turned out to be one of the key reasons that PepsiCo sold 36 million cases between 2008 and 2012. The Pretzel Bacon Cheeseburger was introduced by Wendy's in the summer of 2013. Customers loved the burgers, resulting in 7.5 million Facebook views for a series of related music videos. Shareholders took notice, pushing the stock price in a steep upward trajectory. A search for *social media success stories* will reveal many more such reports. However, examples of social media successes in combination with additional business growth or profitability remain hard to find. Success is still predominantly measured in the number of *likes*, *views*, or *followers*.

Besides adding more value at the company level, technology can also be deployed to protect existing company value—and it doesn't necessarily mean by implementing GRC and SOD tools to reduce operational risk. There is more.

7.2.3 Protect Existing Business Value

For tech companies and others with native digital business models, strategic business risk and technology are never far apart. Margins are squeezed by the ubiquity of most technologies, such as original equipment manufacturers of Windows PCs, while the brand quickly erodes when a technology shift is missed, like when Microsoft initially underestimated the mobile device, or an underwhelming product is introduced. However, fickle customers, uncertainty, and ubiquity are inherent to the industry, and companies have no choice but to play ball. These risks cannot be avoided—only reduced or accepted. On other parts of their business model, executives have more influence.

Due to the positive network effects enjoyed by many digital business models, a company can become the de facto monopolist when left unchecked. In the browser war between Netscape's Navigator and Microsoft's Internet Explorer, Microsoft used its market dominance to push its own solution until forced by regulators to level the playing field. And it is not only Microsoft that is repeatedly accused of abusing its market position; Google, Facebook, and many telecom operators are regularly scrutinized by both the public and policy makers. Another strategic risk is underestimating the bargaining power of customers and substitutes by competitors, like Netflix did in 2011. When the company increased its prices up to 60%, it lost 800,000 subscribers and 77% off its stock price in the process.

The operational business risk universe faced by this category of companies shows a similar picture. In June 2012, Amazon's cloud computing platform in North Virginia went down, taking services like Netflix, Instagram, and Pinterest with it. While cloud providers continue to reduce the likelihood of downtime by investing in business continuity, the net effect on the risk profile is limited due to the widespread adoption of cloud computing.[10] According to research by CloudHarmony on the uptime of infrastructure-as-a-service providers, Amazon AWS enjoyed the highest uptime in 2015 with *only* 56 outages, resulting in a total downtime of two hours and 30 minutes. Microsoft Azure and Google Cloud Platform fared far worse with the former experiencing 71 outages that totaled 10 hours and 49 minutes in downtime, and Google 11 hours and 34 minutes across 167 outages.[xxv] While downtime can be a major annoyance for the business, nothing is worse than insecure applications and databases.

In the 2011 report, *"Caution: Malware Ahead,"* security companies reported on software weaknesses in various parts of cars—including airbag systems, radios, power seats, anti-lock braking system, electronic stability controls, autonomous cruise controls, communication systems, and in-vehicle communication. Software glitches in Hondas have already caused millions of cars to be recalled. With IT representing some 40% of the value of a car, expect these types of recalls to become more common.[xxvi]

For now, the IT component of cars is higher than in many other products. But soon, there will be hardly any product remaining without at least some kind of internet-connected sensor in it. And that leads us to the ultimate operational risk: killed by software.

In November 2000, 21 of the patients treated at the National Cancer Institute in Panama died due to radiation overexposure. A very unfortunate combination of software failure and technicians entering incorrect patient information resulted in the radiotherapy machine delivering overdoses of Cobalt-60 radiation to the patients. Potentially much worse was a software glitch in the Soviet early warning system. In 1983, it falsely indicated the launch of several ballistic missiles by the United States. The Soviet duty officer on station kept his cool. Instead of starting WWIII, he reasoned that it was more likely to be a false

---

[10] risk = likelihood (of an undesired event) × impact (of that event).

alarm. Hence, technology itself is a source of both strategic and operational inherent[11] risk.

Proactive and reactive action, which reduces the likelihood and impact of risk respectively, from those who are responsible for managing the inherent risk of technology is only half of the story. The other half involves protecting existing business value by deploying more technology. This may sound a bit schizophrenic at first, but it is not, as the reduction in business risk will, in most cases, outstrip the increase due to the inherent risk related to technology. Just consider the net effect on the company-level risk profile of installing network-connected fire detectors, real-time forecasting, predictive equipment maintenance, and automating business controls. Their *business cases* are all solid, as is the use of IT to reduce the business risk profile of hospitals. Here, technology is used to:[xxvii]

- **Prevent errors and adverse events**—Tablets and smart phones provide the medical staff easy access to the latest patient information, anywhere and anytime (e.g., treatment plan, calculation of next drug dose using historical information).
- **Facilitate a more rapid response after an adverse event has occurred**— Response teams on-site of an accident or on the way back to the hospital with the patient use technology to send critical information back to the emergency room. This allows the staff to prepare and act more effectively when the patient arrives.
- **Track and provide feedback about adverse events**—By consolidating detailed information about a large number of patients, the effectiveness of treatments, procedures, drug doses, and more can be improved.

Even better, initiatives like self-learning manufacturing equipment and automating knowledge work can be a source of both a lower overall risk profile *and* additional benefits. Another touch point with the benefit universes covered before is the growing size of the joint domain (see Table 7.4). With the digitalization of business models, a considerable amount of business risk is substituted for joint risk. That is, until both domains fuse together.

The risk profile of the IT domain is also likely to shrink in the coming years, but in this case, it is due to several technological advances. At the bottom of the stack, concepts like software-defined networks, software-defined infrastructure, and software-defined data centers promise less *attack vectors* than the heterogeneous and hands-on infrastructures they replace. App platforms like App Engine, OutSystems, SalesForce1, and Mendix reduce the risk profile of the application layer by shielding off most of the complexity associated with

---

[11] Inherent risk reflects the likelihood of a loss in the absence of any action to reduce its likelihood and/or impact.

Table 7.4   Three risk universes and their initiatives

Business Risk Universe (including native digital business models)	Joint Business IT Risk Universe	IT Risk Universe
• Lose share in analog markets	• Lose market share in technology- and data-rich markets • Slow reaction on disrupting technology-rich business model from competitor	• Invest in the wrong technology and/or architecture • Flawed IT sourcing strategy
• Uncertain demand for analog products	• Definitional and volume uncertainty of joint value proposition	• Inflexible architecture • Technology uncertainty (e.g., embed emerging technology in existing infrastructure)
• Failure to meet yearly production target of product	• Incorrect data sent by manufacturing equipment (e.g., SCADA, PLC) to ERP system	• Downtime LAN/WAN network, application servers
• Legal fines from regulators for insider trading	• Customer class action due to data breach	• Data theft by outsiders hacking into the systems[1]
• Access to capital		
Business domain ➡	⬅ IT domain	

[1]Data theft by an internal colleague (e.g., Swiss bank employee selling financial data of American citizens to IRS) would be classified as a joint risk as the person was hired, trained, and supervised by the business.

lower-level programming. Applications are created with a *modeling language* instead of code, thereby limiting the number of attack vectors.[12] Last, but not least, many software-as-a-service providers adopt and conform to very high security standards, leveraging on a team of experts that smaller companies are unable to attract, let alone retain. Hence, risk management is more than calculating the likelihood and impact of events (e.g., the odds of a car accident and the cost of one respectively) and implementing controls.

First of all, overreliance on mathematics to calculate risk was one of the causes of the recent financial crisis and failure to detect fail-safe weaknesses at

---

[12] The disadvantages of *enterprise-application-platform-as-a-service* offerings may include less flexibility, boundaries in size, complexity and scalability of the application, fewer options for optimizations, a strong vendor lock-in and high license costs.

the Fukushima nuclear power plant in Japan, even though in hindsight, they should have seemed obvious. Second, risk taking is part of doing business. The opportunities with the greatest potential return have the highest risk profile and the most valuable lessons. Third, with business and IT converging, it is important to adopt a holistic, end-to-end perspective in order to maximize the ROI for the company as a whole.

7.2.4 From Intent to Action

The practices necessary to optimize the ROI for a company or individual initiative are part of performance management. There are many definitions of performance management, including the one from Gates:[xxviii] *"A strategic performance measurement system translates business strategies into deliverable results. Combine financial, strategic, and operating measures to gauge how well a company meets its targets."* To do so, performance management typically includes the following activities:

- Define objectives and desired results
- Provide the leadership and incentive structure necessary to ensure the stakeholders (e.g., employees, key partners) realize the objectives and results
- Monitor progress and act on deviations
- Provide the necessary resources and other required inputs
- Capture and apply lessons learned

The popularity of the topic resulted not only in many definitions, but also a broad set of models and frameworks to choose from. Most relevant is the category they belong to—result-oriented or activity-oriented—as can be seen in Table 7.5. The latter category focuses on optimizing the maturity of business and IT processes, structures, and systems. Popular occupants of this category include ISO 9001, Business Process Reengineering, COBIT, ISO 27000, and Information Technology Infrastructure Library (ITIL). Schaffer and Thomson[xxix] and Mastenbroek[xxx] are convinced that improvement programs that focus solely on structures and systems (i.e., process frameworks and tools) don't necessarily lead to an increase in performance. They suggest improvement initiatives should focus on results as *"the more the organizational change is linked to improvements in the output, the better."* John Seddon supports the argument by stating that ISO 9000-norms do not show tangible improvements in *real quality.*[xxxi]

More result-driven concepts include value-based management (VBM), the balanced scorecard (BSC), lean IT, and the Theory of Constraints (TOC). The TOC, or management by constraints, gained widespread attention after the

Table 7.5 Activity-centered transformation versus result-driven transformation

Activity-Centered Transformation	Result-Driven Transformation
Often ambitious, large-scaled, and diffused. Not oriented toward archiving specific outputs—resulting in misleading performance measurements.	Forces management to prioritize its targets and the necessary means to archive them.
Preference for orthodox approaches instead of empirical.	Empirical tests show what works and what doesn't.
Focus on long-term organizational development, not on results.	Frequent reinforcement by management provides the transformation with new energy.
Controlled by staff departments and consultants.	Management creates an ongoing learning process by leveraging on lessons learned in previous phases and uses new insight when designing and implementing the next phase.

publication of *The Goal* by Goldratt and Cox.[xxxii] The core idea of the TOC is identifying and addressing bottlenecks in the workflow. It is based on the assumption that the slowest link of the chain sets the speed for the whole end-to-end process. The capacity of the weakest link, such as functional testers, determines the amount of output the upstream part of the process can produce without creating a backlog, like the frequency and amount of new code that can be deployed at any given time. After identifying the weakest link, the team tries to maximize the throughput by analyzing and optimizing that particular constraint.

While the TOC never gained widespread traction within the IT domain, two other concepts emphasizing the importance of results and flow did: agile and lean. Lean has its roots in the manufacturing industry and its core attributes can be summarized by a relentless focus on customer value, eliminating waste, and delivery of uncompromised quality, just-in-time, and just enough. According to McKinsey, an IT team can increase IT capacity by 20 to 30% by adopting lean principles.[xxxiii] Standardization of the workflow and incremental improvement are important tools to improve the consistency, predictability, repeatability, and efficiency of the workflow. While these are all sources of customer value, they are also closely related to foundation IT. Consequently, lean IT is well equipped to handle product enhancements and process optimizations, but less suitable for companies with a value shop business model (e.g., lawyers solving specific individualized problems) or other markets with very heterogeneous and dynamic customer needs.

Starting a lean IT initiative can be as easy as focusing for a period of six to twelve months on improving the measurable performance of the following drivers:[13]

- Number of incidents,
- Resolution time of incidents,
- Time-to-market of changes,
- Effectiveness of changes, and
- Number of proactive changes.

They all represent value from a customer's perspective, as each either has a time-related bonus, such as more productive business hours, earlier access to new functionalities and less rework, or proactiveness, like the removal of recurring errors, and suggesting low-hanging fruit improvements. Solving 500 incidents 5% faster for a year may well translate into 100 or more additional productive business hours. Depending on the value of a business hour (e.g., foregone revenue), IT can draft a business case to fund one or more improvement initiatives that the business is very likely to promote. Similar cases can be made for the other benefit drivers, as they too are tangible (i.e., result-driven) and directly related to customer value.

The development teams also adopted lean, but implemented it slightly differently. Developers have no choice but to deal with uncertainty and complexity on a day-to-day basis. They translate customer focus, predictability, repeatability, and other lean values into a set of principles known as agile (see Chapter 4). It uses iterative development sprints of two to three weeks to systematically reduce the uncertainty and complexity of a business need or want. Hence, agile can be used to innovate, but still has its limitations. Agile development, for example, does not cover topics like the make-buy decision, architecture, or technology, such as C# or Java. The sweet spot of lean and agile is optimizing the operational part of the IT and/or business model.

Models to analyze the industry, markets, company, and product portfolio have been covered in previous chapters, leaving the topic of optimizing financial performance. This means entering a world occupied by EBITDA, return on invested capital, economic profit, risk-adjusted return on capital, and economic value added. They are terms used by companies to report the return at the company level of investment decisions. While they are part of the business domain, the convergence of domains may see one or more end up in more strategic discussions with IT.

To optimize these and other financial ratios, many companies compliment financial accounting, management accounting, and corporate finance practices

---

[13] A former colleague, Niels Loader, defined these and two other drivers, quality of planning and customer communication, as part of his 'IT as a Business' concept.

with management frameworks like the BSC or VBM. The BSC is a widely adopted holistic performance management framework that compliments financial performance indicators with non-financial performance indicators, such as customer perspective, learning and growth perspective, and internal business process perspective. Since its inception in 1992, the BSC has evolved into a strategic planning and management framework, supporting executives and managers to translate strategic goals and plans into day-to-day operations.

Contrary to the *balanced* approach of the BSC, VBM focuses on one metric—value. As long as the return[14] on the capital invested in an initiative exceeds the cost of that capital, it is a good decision. Decentralization, introducing a new product, implementing lean or even the BSC; all of these initiatives are judged by their ability to add value. Adopting VBM means:[xxxiv]

- Defining and implementing strategies that provide the highest potential for shareholder value creation;
- Implementing information systems that are focused on value creation and the underlying *drivers* of value across a company's business units, products, and customer segments;
- Aligning management processes, such as business planning and resource allocation, with value creation; and
- Designing performance measurement systems and incentive compensation plans that reflect value creation.

These steps and their IT specific adaptation are visualized in Figure 7.4. It starts with the business defining shareholder, stakeholder, or customer value as the overarching objective for the company.[15] All other objectives, targets, performance indicators, and incentives are chosen according to their ability to measure, evaluate, and reinforce the overall objective. As there are almost an endless number of objectives, drivers, and initiatives, focus is a crucial precondition to implement VBM successfully. The business and IT should define a limited set of truly *key* joint benefit and/or risk objectives and drivers. To quote Steve Jobs:[xxxv] *"This is how I do it. I take a sheet of paper, and I say, 'If my company can only do one thing next year, what is it?' Literally, we shut everything else down."*

As there can be more than one IT business model, it might also be necessary to create more than one BSC or VBM canvas. The performance indicators tied to optimizing the early business life-cycle phases are very different from the cost

---

[14] Measured by discounting the expected future cash flows.

[15] According to Tom Copeland et al., authors of *Valuation: Measuring and Managing the Value of Companies*, it is enough for a company to focus on shareholders as it would automatically optimize the share of the customers and other stakeholders.

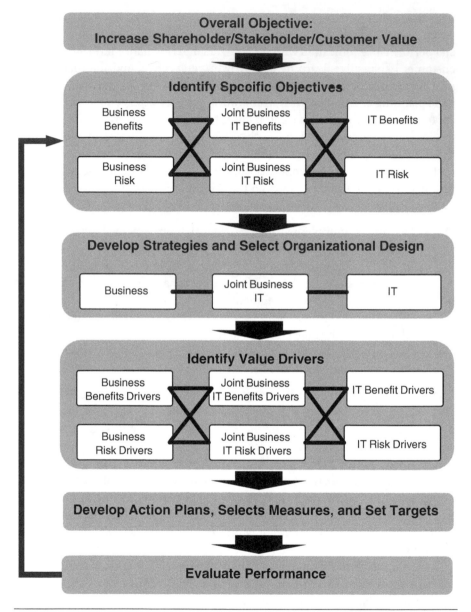

Figure 7.4   Value-based IT management (adapted from Copeland et al., *Valuation: Measuring and Managing the Value of Companies*, 1996)

leadership strategy associated with the endgame phases of a life cycle. Mixing them would inevitably lead to sub-optimization and value-leakage.

Another attention point is the top-down nature of both models. For example, contrary to agile, continuous improvement, or ITIL, the initiators of BSC or VBM implementations are, in most cases, board members or other senior executives. As a result, BSC and VBM are part of a so-called *intended* strategy: an organizational change driven by the leadership team whereby the company's mission is translated into objectives that, in turn, lead to strategies and tactics. Agile, continuous improvement, and ITIL are typically in the other corner, called *emergent* strategy. It is driven bottom-up, whereby actions taken over time condense into a strategy. They are the result of responses to unexpected opportunities and risks at an operational level. Emergent strategies and VBM/BSC are not mutually exclusive, but it is important to take into account the specific context a team faces.

Last but not least, the BSC and VBM are a means to an end. It is the tangible result that counts and that means, in this case, discounted cash flows (DCFs).

7.3 SECOND ROUND IT OUTSOURCING FOR A PHARMACOMPANY

In the old days, one company covered the whole value chain. Henry Ford's dream was creating everything from the glass windows to the smallest bolt. By keeping everything together, staff could literally walk to another department to order additional parts. In the absence of IT, it was the most efficient way of feeding the assembly line. Fast-forward a century and the complexity and variety of the individual car parts have become such that it is impossible for a single company to mobilize the capital and management to do everything in-house.

Sourcing from external key partners allows a company to specialize on those activities where it adds the most value. Identifying the accompanying capabilities is the first step in any sourcing strategy process, as these should never be outsourced. They are the core of the company, determining current and future success. Another important point is interdependency. Sourcing decisions made by the business may have a considerable impact on IT and vice versa. Some have to learn that lesson the hard way.

PharmaCompany is a leading biopharmaceutical company with a global footprint. Around the turn of the century, it decided to focus on intellectual property, research, branding, and the quality and safety measures for its products. Focus on these activities and accompanying capabilities had to provide a distinctive edge over other biopharmaceutical companies. Consequently, most other capabilities were considered indistinctive or noncritical, leading to the outsourcing of operational research and development activities, manufacturing, and IT. In one bold stroke, the IT function was completely outsourced to one vendor in 2004. In 2012, the relationship ended prematurely. Reasons cited by the CIO of PharmaCompany for this decision included:

- *It was almost impossible to change the contract even though the business was changing very rapidly.*
- *We underestimated the complexity and specific knowledge required by the procurement department to control the external partner.*

During the preparation of the deal in 2004, PharmaCompany never looked beyond the left part of Figure 7.5. It calculated the current OPEX of IT, added the cost of a procurement officer and contract manager and deducted the benefits promised by the external partner. The expected benefits were considerable, resulting in a very short decision-making process. After the transition, they slowly but surely were introduced to the right side of the figure.

In 2012, the cost-focused, one-stop-shop sourcing strategy was replaced by a best-of-breed multi-vendor strategy, emphasizing cooperation and collaboration between the parties involved. An external partner specialized in foundation IT is rarely the best choice when launching an entrepreneurial IT initiative. Not only did the sourcing strategy receive the attention it deserved, the same applied to the business case. Several of the lessons-learned are covered in the following sections.

For starters, the value of a DCF analysis is an *expectation*. The higher the level of dynamics and complexity, the larger the margin of error or *softness* of the DCF. Hence, a quantitative business case to outsource foundation IT is more likely to hit the mark than a business case for entrepreneurial IT. Due to the growing need from the business for the latter, the team responsible for sourcing IT solutions decided to introduce real options.

7.3.1 Real Options

A standard DCF calculation assumes the CAPEX, OPEX, benefits, and risks of the whole life cycle can be perfectly predicted in Year 0. Anyone who has ever been involved in an IT project, let alone a multi-year outsourcing contract, knows that the moment the project starts, the first deviations occur. Some are minor and can be mitigated by the project team; others, like unexpected new product introductions by competitors or shifting customer demand, require more drastic adjustments of the business case. Here, executives have to intervene by (partially) postponing, speeding up, or canceling the project. The ability to replace one decision in Year 0 with multiple decisions spread out over multiple years, represents a financial value. In formula form:

$$NPV^{(total)} = NPV^{(static)} + \text{value of managerial flexibility}$$

Real options provide a way to calculate the value of managerial flexibility and add that value to the business case. As a result, business cases may change from a no-go to a go.

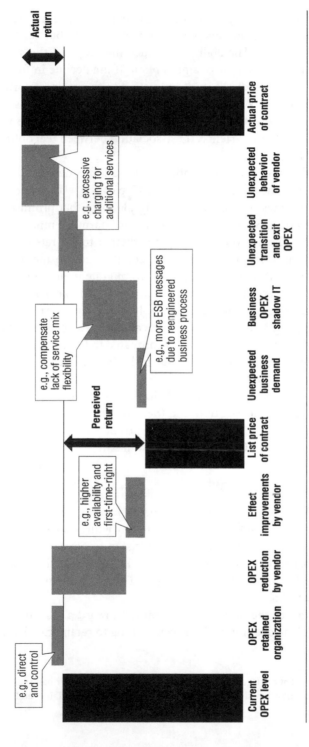

Figure 7.5 Perceived versus actual return of outsourcing

In real options terminology, the decision to expand the scope of an outsourcing contract two years from now is a *call option*; the right but *not the obligation* to change the contract. The ability to reduce the scope of the same contract during the term is an example of a *put option*. If the decline in future business volume is difficult to predict, a midterm payoff to the external partner may be more attractive than to keep on paying for services nobody needs. The higher the level of uncertainty and complexity is, the higher also is the value of the option and discount rate.[16] Hence, the association between real options and entrepreneurial IT.

A simplified example of a real options calculation is depicted in Figure 7.6. As of this writing, one of the new external IT partners was developing a revolutionary new business process outsourcing platform that promised a considerable revenue boost. Several business units of PharmaCompany have shown their interest, but the board is unsure as to whether to migrate the branches in all 34 countries at once, or start with one country and postpone the decision for the other 33 countries (the *call option*). To migrate in one country, PharmaCompany has to invest $1.5 million while the external partner will charge $46 million to migrate in all countries at once. If the new platform turns out to be a success, migrating in all countries at once generates an additional $26 million ($60 – $34 million) (see Figure 7.6) compared to the conservative scenario. However, if customer demand turns out to be lackluster, the better choice is migrating only one country.

Real options entice decision makers to look into the future and consider multiple scenarios. They translate time and the ability to postpone a decision into a monetary value that can be included in the business case. It is one of the value streams covered in the DCF analyses covered next.

7.3.2 DCFs with a Twist

Let's assume PharmaCompany is the majority shareholder of Pill & Syrup. The latter observed the struggle of PharmaCompany with its external partner from the sideline and decided to postpone its decision to outsource. Leveraging on the lessons learned from PharmaCompany, Pill & Syrup decided in 2013 to investigate the feasibility of outsourcing its IT infrastructure and part of the application portfolio.

The first draft of the business case pointed toward a disappointing return (see Table 7.6). The decision makers were willing to retain the IT function, but

---

[16] This is assuming that management has the ability to intervene. If their hands are tied (e.g., due to internal politics) the actual flexibility value is low, even though uncertainty and complexity can be high.

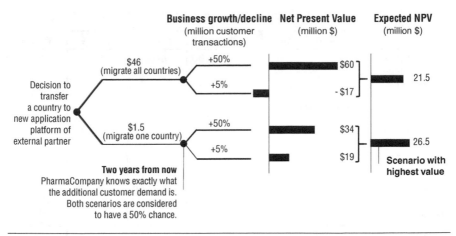

Figure 7.6   Migrate one or all countries?

they asked one of the company's financial wizards to have another go at the business case.

There are several ways to increase the attractiveness of a business case including an increase of the scope or demanding more aggressive pricing from the vendor. An alternative is identifying and contracting additional sources of benefit. At first sight, a make-or-buy decision has little in common with a merger or acquisition. This observation is true when one company buys another company with the aim to integrate both businesses (e.g., Facebook buying WhatsApp in 2014). However, private equity companies like KKR, Alpinvest Partners, and Goldman Sachs Private Equity Group buy other companies to optimize and eventually sell them again or offer the company to the public again via an IPO. They earn money by increasing the difference between the buying and selling price.[17] It means, among others, that private equity companies have a strong focus on the exit.

This is not the only similarity between M&A and outsourcing. In Table 7.7, the following M&A concepts from Craig and Willmott are applied to outsourcing, influencing the payback period (one year earlier) and cumulative NPV (which was double that):[xxxvi]

- **Option value for external partners**—the assets and people of Pill & Syrup taken over by the external partner vendor may provide the means to create new value propositions or become more successful in a certain

---

[17] The other value stream is dividends during the period the company is part of the private equity portfolio.

Table 7.6 Fictional traditional business case, amounts in 1,000, WACC of 16%

	Year 0	Year 1	Year 2	Year 3	Year 4	Year 5
Risk adjusted benefits (cost decrease) for Pill & Syrup		16,000	16,000	16,000	16,000	16,000
Necessary investment in data center if Pill & Syrup does not outsource			500		500	
Cost retained organization of Pill & Syrup		– 200	– 200	– 200	– 200	– 200
Investment in transition to external partner	– 5,750	– 3,500				
Value asset transfer	2,000					
Yearly base cost of outsourcing contract		– 14,000	– 13,500	– 13,000	– 12,500	– 12,000
Exit costs for Pill & Syrup						– 350
Net cash flow	– 3,750	– 1,700	2,800	2,800	3,800	3,450
Net present value	– 3,750	– 1,466	– 2,081	1,794	2,100	1,644
Cumulative net present value	– 3,750	– 5,216	– 3,134	– 1,340	760	2,403

customer segment (e.g., easier to close outsourcing deals with other pharma companies with Pill & Syrup as a reference). Other sources of option value include improved economies-of-scale due to the additional volume generated by Pill & Syrup and contract harvesting (e.g., upselling).

- **Option value for Pill & Syrup**—the monetary value of the asset transfer can be used to invest in capabilities with a higher expected return (e.g., invest in new promising medicine). The external partner can be a source of new capabilities, allowing for the creation of new value propositions or even a new business model. Operationally, the vendor can act as a source of volume and service mix flexibility.

Table 7.7 Fictional M&A business case, amounts in 1,000, WACC of 16%

	Year 0	Year 1	Year 2	Year 3	Year 4	Year 5
Option Value for Pill & Syrup						
• Investment in own data center in case of no-go for outsourcing			500	650	500	
• Value of innovations co-created with the external partner			450	550	750	1,000
• Quantitative effect of improved quality (e.g., improved availability)		350	450	550	550	600
• Value of transferring investment risk to external partner (e.g., volume flexibility)		500	200	100	200	100
Intrinsic Value						
• Value asset transfer	2,000					
• Return on re-investing capital asset transfer (@ net ROI 20%)		400	400	400	400	400
• Transition cost	– 5,750	– 3,500				
• Interest cost transition (10% per year)		– 575	– 925	– 925	– 925	– 925
• Benefits (cost decrease) for client company		16,000	16,000	16,000	16,000	16,000
• Yearly base cost of outsourcing contract		– 14,000	– 13,500	– 13,000	– 12,500	– 12,000
• Cost retained organization of client company		– 200	– 200	– 200	– 200	– 200
Exit Costs for Client Company						– 350
Value Related to Sourcing Risk						
• Strategic risk (*lock-in*)			– 10	– 20	– 30	– 45
• Operational risk		– 50	– 25	– 10	– 5	– 5
• Reputation/legal risk		– 30	– 15	– 8	– 4	– 4
Net cash flow	– 3,750	– 1,105	3,325	3,537	4,736	4,571
Net present value	– 3,750	– 953	2,472	2,267	2,617	2,178
Cumulative net present value	– 3,750	– 4,703	– 2,231	36	2,653	4,830

- **Embedded value for external partners**—the regular revenue stream from Pill & Syrup for the term of the contract (the value of an extension can be included as an option). By rationalizing the delivery model, the external partner can generate additional revenue by assigning part of the transferred staff and assets to other contracts.
- **Embedded value for Pill & Syrup**—the difference in CAPEX and OPEX between making and buying, supplemented by the monetary value represented by improvements, either enforced or non-enforced, in speed-to-market and availability levels. More intangible in nature is less management attention due to, in the best case scenario, dealing with a mature and professional external partner and access to a larger and more diverse skill set.
- **Exit costs for external partners**—the revenue foregone if Pill & Syrup decides to switch to another supply source at the end of the contract term.[18] A direct source of negative value is spending more resources on the exit transition than the external partner is able to recover from Pill & Syrup.
- **Exit costs for Pill & Syrup**—Pill & Syrup has to cover the exit costs of the existing partner, and the cost to either re-transition the activities back in-house (*insource*) or transfer them to another external partner.

The exit-related costs are not the only negative value streams Pill & Syrup has to take into account. Other sources of negative value include opportunistic behavior by the external partner, underestimating the required future flexibility when drafting the contract, and lower than promised quality levels. Depending on the life-cycle phase and other properties of the buy initiative, the optimal control strategy and accompanying cost can be determined, such as in trust-based soft controls versus a strict GRC regime.

As with any business case, it is important to understand its limitations. If the board demands a return of at least 20% on every business case, they all miraculously will. Especially in companies where monitoring of the actual benefit realization is weak, business cases tend to promise the moon and the stars, regardless of the initiative. When people are held accountable for the actual outcomes—within reasonable limits as the future cannot be predicted—the projected cumulative NPV is likely to be more realistic.

---

[18] The possibility to exit a contract is an option from the perspective of Pill & Syrup.

REFERENCES

i. Copeland, T., Koller, T. and Murrin, J. (1996). *Valuation: Measuring and Managing the Value of Companies.* 2nd edition.
ii. Financial Times article, March 12, 2009.
iii. Pilat, D. (2004/1). The ICT Productivity Paradox: Insights from Micro Data, OECD Economic Studies No. 38.
iv. Hempell, T., Van Leeuwen, G. and Van der Wiel, H. (2004). ICT, Innovation and Business Performance in Services: Evidence for Germany and the Netherlands.
v. Maliranta, M. and Rouvinen, P. (2004). ICT and Business Productivity: Finnish Microlevel Evidence.
vi. Bosworth, B. and Triplett, J. (2003). Services Productivity in the United States: Griliches' Services Volume Revisited.
vii. Arvantis, S. (2004). Information Technology, Workplace Organisation, Human Capital and Firm Productivity: Evidence for the Swiss Economy.
viii. Clayton, T. and Waldron, K. (2003). E-Commerce Adoption and Business Impact.
ix. Brigham, E. and Ehrhardt, M. (2010). *Financial Management: Theory and Practice.*
x. Slywotzky, A. and Drzik, J. (April 2005). *Countering the Biggest Risk of All.* Harvard Business Review. Link: https://hbr.org/2005/04/countering-the-biggest-risk-of-all.
xi. Charette, R. (2005). Why Software Fails. We Waste Billions of Dollars Each Year on Entirely Preventable Mistakes.
xii. Bharadwaj, A., Keil, M. and Mähring, M. (2009). Effects of Information Technology Failures on the Market Value of Firms.
xiii. McNeil, A. (1999). Extreme Value Theory for Risk Managers.
xiv. Funston, F. and Wagner, S. (2010). Surviving and Thriving in Uncertainty: Creating the Risk Intelligent Enterprise.
xv. Basahel, A. and Irani, Z. (2010). Examining the Strategic Benefits of Information Systems: A Global Case Study.
xvi. Laudon, K. and Laudon, J. (2004). *Managing the Digital Firm.*
xvii. Pearlson, K. and Saunders, C. (2000). Managing and Using Information Systems: A Strategic Approach.
xviii. Benson, R., Bugnitz, T. and Walton, W. (2004). From Business Strategy to IT Action: Right Decisions for a Better Bottom Line.
xix. Ward, J. and Peppard, J. (2002). *Strategic Planning for Information Systems.*
xx. Nisman, M. (2005). IT Business Value Index, *Managing IT Investments for Business Value.*

xxi. Forrester. (March 2010). Data Essentials: U.S. Retail—A Technographics Dashboard.

xxii. CIO Executive Council, Communicating IT Value, December 18, 2009. Link: http://www.cio.com/article/2421917/leadership-management/com municating-it-value.html.

xxiii. Manjoo, F. (November 26, 2012). Walmart's Evolution from Big Box Giant To E-Commerce Innovator. Link: http://www.fastcompany.com/3002948/walmarts-evolution-big-box-giant-e-commerce-innovator.

xxiv. Alston, D. (2009). Social Media ROI—What's the 'Return on Ignoring'? Marketing Profs.

xxv. Butler, B. (January 7, 2016). And the cloud provider with the best uptime in 2015 is . . . , January 7, 2016. Link: http://www.networkworld.com/article/3020235/cloud-computing/and-the-cloud-provider-with-the-best-uptime-in-2015-is.html.

xxvi. Blanco, S. (June 8, 2010). How much does software add to the cost of today's vehicles? How about tomorrow's electric cars? Link: http://green.autoblog.com/2010/06/08/how-much-does-software-add-to-the-cost-of-todays-vehicles-how/.

xxvii. Bates, D. and Gawande, A. (2003). Improving Safety with Information Technology. New England Journal of Medicine.

xxviii. Gates, S. (1999). *Aligning Strategic Performance Measures and Results*.

xxix. Schaffer, R. and Thomson, H. (January–February 1992). *Successful Change Programs Begin with Results*, Harvard Business Review.

xxx. Mastenbroek, W. (1997). Verandermanagement. Holland Business Publications.

xxxi. Seddon, J. (2000). The Case against ISO 9000, How to Create Real Quality in Your Organization.

xxxii. Goldratt, E. and Cox, J. (1984). *The Goal*.

xxxiii. Roberts, R., Sarrazin, H. and Sikes, J. (December 2010). Reshaping IT Management for Turbulent Times. Link: https://www.mckinseyquarterly.com/Business_Technology/Reshaping_IT_management_for_turbulent_times_2707.

xxxiv. Ittner, C. and Larcker, D. (2001). Assessing Empirical Research in Managerial Accounting: A Value-Based Management Perspective.

xxxv. Feloni, R. (2015). Steve Jobs Used This Simple Productivity Hack to Hone Apple's Focus. Business Insider. Link: http://finance.yahoo.com/news/steve-jobs-used-simple-productivity-175545445.html.

xxxvi. Craig, D. and Willmott, P. (February 2005). Outsourcing Grows Up. McKinsey Quarterly.

8

THE DIGITAL MANIFESTO

This chapter covers the Digital Manifesto itself. The Digital Manifesto is a growth path, consisting of six *interdependent* principles. Turning the potential value of the Digital Manifesto into realized value starts with capable and *intrinsically* motivated team members, embodied by the first principle—you can lead a horse to water, but you can't make it drink. Personal development, growing as a team, and eventually, change at the company level all start with an individual whose motivation comes from inside rather than external *sticks and carrots*. The sixth principle—*less cost, more value*—is an outcome or result.

The Digital Manifesto is not a normative framework, a new standard to certify against. There are plenty of those—more often than not, promising more value than they deliver.

The six principles, and the frameworks, models, and best practices used to operationalize them should be considered a source of guidance and structure—preventing teams from reinventing the wheel. Depending on the specific context and maturity of the company, carefully pick one or more models, never forgetting that the actual world is too complex to fit exactly into four quadrants or a standardized set of processes. Furthermore, the more sophisticated the model, the more mature both business and IT have to be to extract its inherent value. Maturity is, therefore, also one of the topics covered in this final chapter.

Last, but certainly not least, the Digital Manifesto is about diversity. Quoting Stephen Covey: "*Strength lies in differences, not in similarities.*" Diversity increases the adaptability of the company, as the team covers a broader set of viewpoints, skill sets, experiences, and attitudes. It enables a company to react faster and more effectively on unexpected opportunities and threats—a precondition for a sustainable and growing business. Nobody wants their company to be a one-hit wonder. Table 8.1 provides three statements that cover the chapter as a whole.

Table 8.1   Statements to think about when reading this chapter

Statements
Value is created when crossing the finishing line.
The more dynamic the market, the more a company can bonofit from diversity.
IT can act as a child, adult, or parent.

8.1 THE DIGITAL MANIFESTO IS A SET OF INTERDEPENDENT PRINCIPLES

Spending more on IT does not automatically create additional company value or protect existing value. Emerging technologies and concepts like Scrum, software as a service, DevOps, and big data all have tremendous *potential* value but only when applied by the right hands does *potential* turn into *realized*. IT is not a neatly packaged box with a guaranteed return on investment stamped on it. IT is like a kitchen: spending $25,000 on a new kitchen does not automatically result in a great dining experience—you also need a cook.

In this case, the cook is the IT professional, embodied by the principle *less defensive, more offensive*. The IT team no longer delivers a piece of hardware or software to the business, but a solution—or even better: a value proposition. A value proposition fulfills a specific want or need of a customer, allowing that customer to create value (e.g., additional benefits, less risk). While advanced automation and robots are substituting for humans in several service-related areas of the value chain, employees remain necessary for truly added value activities like strategy setting, innovation, performance improvement, and exception handling.

These activities all draw on the human capability for out-of-the-box thinking, creativity, and entrepreneurship. Computers can be programmed to generate new ideas, products, and strategies, but will always operate within predefined patterns and boundaries. In other words, they can only fulfill the existing needs of customers. Predicting and fulfilling future customer needs—a precondition for a sustainable business model—remains the exclusive domain of humans, as seen in Figure 8.1.[1]

---

[1] For the foreseeable future that is. In 2016, Google launched a research project to see if computers can be truly creative. It is only one of the projects that are part of a global effort to create machines with artificial intelligence and *deep learning* capabilities.

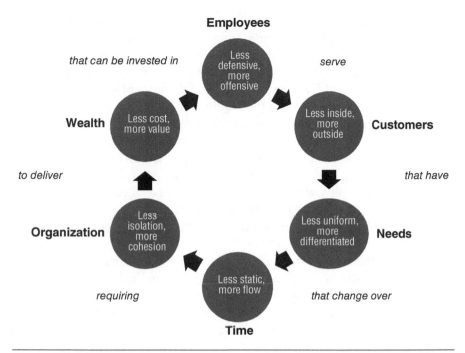

Figure 8.1   The Digital Manifesto is a set of interdependent principles

The constantly evolving technology landscape also has a profound impact on the value propositions offered to the company's customers. Music lovers used to record their favorite music on tape, replacing them over time with DVRs, hard drives, MP3 players, and more recently, streaming from the cloud. Technology is also busy transforming the way we travel (e.g., autonomous cars), communicate (e.g., chatting via WhatsApp, even when in a bar), and inform ourselves. Today, people eat considerably less salt and sugar than ten years ago, forcing companies to adjust or suffer the consequences. McDonalds moved slowly on the desire of customers for healthier and more natural food, allowing new entrants to grab a considerable slice of the market. Only after changing dozens of menu items, did the company start to report improving sales numbers again.

The rate of change is not constant, but increases both in volatility and complexity. The tape recorder was invented around 1930 and enjoyed a stable and predictable life cycle for almost half a century—no such luck for more recent substitutes. More generally, every new product is more capable than its predecessor, but also more difficult and expensive to design and produce. This translates into a network of hundreds, if not thousands, of specialized companies to deliver one coherent value proposition from a customer perspective.[2] Together, these companies form a virtual entity, bundling a broad set of capabilities, skill sets, and other assets to realize one or more shared objectives. The larger and more complex the value proposition and network, the more organization (as in *"the act or process of planning and arranging the different parts of an event or activity"*[i]) is necessary to achieve the required effectiveness and efficiency. Do this well and the result is wealth for all of the stakeholders involved.

By investing part of that wealth into the quality of the working environment, employee satisfaction is improved—the first step in the so-called service-profit chain.[ii] The service-profit chain establishes relationships between value creation, customer loyalty, and employee satisfaction. Loyal customers buy more and generate referrals—both key drivers of growth and profitability. To become loyal, they need to be consistently satisfied by the value proposition offered by the company.

The larger the service component of the value proposition, the higher the impact of those who are responsible for designing and delivering the service. Hence, the emphasis on employee satisfaction because content employees are more productive, go that extra mile, and are less likely to look around for other job opportunities. The end result is a positive feedback loop, from which all stakeholders benefit.

8.2 THE DIGITAL MANIFESTO ENCOURAGES DIVERSITY

Every individual has their own strengths and development points. A business analyst may be blessed with the skill to quickly gain trust in a one-on-one conversation with the customer, but struggle when asked to put his or her thoughts on paper. Some score high on IQ tests, while others excel in activities that benefit from emotional intelligence. Every individual is blessed with her or his strong points and specific areas for learning and development. Hence, creating teams that cover all of the capabilities that are required to realize a certain result is one of the key responsibilities of those holding leadership positions.

---

[2] Sustainable success requires companies to invest the available resources (e.g., available budget, management attention) in their distinctive or core competencies. Other competencies should be sources from external partners. Prahalad and Hamel consider a competency as *core* when it is not easy to copy by competitors, it can be used for other products and markets, and it contributes to the end consumer's experienced benefits and value. See also: https://en.wikipedia.org/wiki/Core_competency.

While some managers may consider solving this kind of puzzle a burden, diversity is an important source of variety. It enhances the capability of a company to innovate and create new value propositions, allowing a company to act more effectively on external stressors, random shocks, and unexpected events. The end result: companies with more diverse workforces perform better financially.[iii] So while solely hiring the top students from the same Ivy League university year in and year out may seem a smart move, it results in a very smart but *homogeneous* organization, along with a restrictive homogeneous decision-making *spread*.

The optimal level of diversity fluctuates per company, driven by its external environment, strategy, and business model. The more dynamic and complex the market, the more a company can benefit from investing in a diversified team and partner network.

The various layers of diversity and variety requiring attention are depicted in Figure 8.2. The most outer layer of the onion is the market, which properties shape all other layers. Any misalignment inevitably leads to value leakage like using a *mechanistic* IT organization that is optimized for stable analog markets

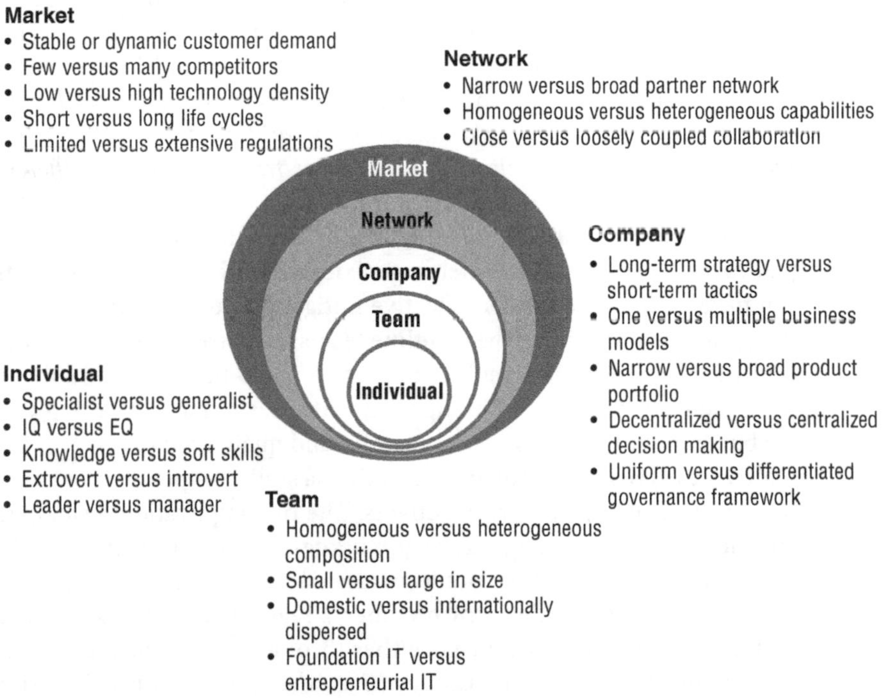

Market
- Stable or dynamic customer demand
- Few versus many competitors
- Low versus high technology density
- Short versus long life cycles
- Limited versus extensive regulations

Network
- Narrow versus broad partner network
- Homogeneous versus heterogeneous capabilities
- Close versus loosely coupled collaboration

Individual
- Specialist versus generalist
- IQ versus EQ
- Knowledge versus soft skills
- Extrovert versus introvert
- Leader versus manager

Company
- Long-term strategy versus short-term tactics
- One versus multiple business models
- Narrow versus broad product portfolio
- Decentralized versus centralized decision making
- Uniform versus differentiated governance framework

Team
- Homogeneous versus heterogeneous composition
- Small versus large in size
- Domestic versus internationally dispersed
- Foundation IT versus entrepreneurial IT

Figure 8.2 The Digital Manifesto encourages diversity

to enter a dynamic digital market. A mechanistic worldview comes with a highly structured and controlled IT operating model, authority that is based on the formal line-management position, and standardized procedures.[iv] In contrast, an *organic* IT organization is characterized by an open and informal operating model, whereby authority is based on individual expertise who are focusing on getting things done instead of following formal procedures.

The relationship between (in)stability and diversity can also be observed in biology and evolution. The evolution of an ecosystem in a remote cave system evolves at a snail's pace compared to a rain forest. The latter's ecosystems will also contain far more species and subspecies than that little acidic lake that is hidden in a cave at the base of an old volcano. In his book *Out of Control*, Kelly describes the similarities between biological ecosystems and markets and economies—embodied by nine *incubation* principles:[v]

- **Distribute being**—The book uses beehives, the economy, intelligence, and evolution as examples of systems where the sum of the parts create more than all of the individual parts can (e.g., brain cells versus the brain as a whole). A company that is part of a broad and heterogeneous network can switch faster from one value proposition to another compared to a company that is part of a narrow and homogeneous network. Similarly, by working together, business and IT experts can create more value compared to working in isolation. Or as Marissa Mayer, CEO of Yahoo, said at an HR conference in Los Angeles: *"People are more productive when they're alone, but they're more collaborative and innovative when they're together. Some of the best ideas come from pulling two different ideas together."*

- **Control from the bottom up**—In large diversified companies or companies that are part of a large heterogeneous network, unexpected events can have large ripple effects. Effective mitigation does not only require delegation of authority to the frontline teams and a free flow of information, but also a team that is able to think out-of-the-box. Problem solving is most effective when combining trust with a team that is covering varied but complimentary experience, skills, and qualifications.

- **Cultivate increasing returns**—Each time a skill, competency, or capability is used, it enjoys learning effects. The first application developed after learning a new language is the hardest—any consecutive application will benefit from its predecessors. Here, diversity increases the chance that at least one team member already has some experience with the new program language, either through a previous job or personal interest. In their book *Competitive Advantage Through Diversity*, Herrior and Pemberton argue that *"organizational diversity is not a* *disadvantage to be overcome, but a key resource facilitating creativity and learning."* [vi] According to the authors, an effective organization requires collaborative learning, leveraging on the capacity of every team member to *know beyond* existing facts and experience. A company's governance and management framework can either frustrate or strengthen the ability to learn as an individual, team, and organization.

- **Grow by chunking**—With markets, technology, data, and processes becoming increasingly complex, it is now more important than ever to keep it as simple as possible. Quoting Nassim Taleb from his book *Antifragile*: *"A complex system, contrary to what people believe, does not require complicated systems and regulations and intricate policies. The simpler the better. Complications lead to multiplicative chains of unanticipated effects."* [vii] Hence, a successful value proposition should be based on a simple and elegant solution that fulfills a clear-cut need of a customer. Based on the initial success, new elements can be added that strengthen the market differentiators (e.g., Google diversifying from free, ad sponsored search functionalities to free, ad sponsored e-mail). Radical big-bang change programs should be avoided, unless the company has its back to the wall (see Chapter 2).

- **Maximize the fringes**—Traditional governance and management practices try to reduce the number of loose ends because they are considered a source of unrewarded risk. It is often forgotten that these organizational outskirts, isolated teams, nonconformist employees, and forgotten customer segments are also a source of adaptation, resilience, and innovation. Google allows its employees to experiment and chase novel ideas during working hours, thereby stretching the boundaries of Google's portfolio. Especially in markets with a high level of uncertainty, variety is an important mitigating control to prevent obsolesce.

- **Honor your errors**—Entrepreneurs accept a calculated amount of both rewarded and unrewarded risk. A culture that punishes errors can only survive in a stable environment, as everybody will try to maintain the equilibrium. Evolution is the prime example of advancing through trial and error. Variation enables species to enter new habitats or become more successful in exploiting existing ones. Similarly, prototyping, proof of concepts, and pilot projects allow a company to test new ideas and learn from them. Failing to do so inevitably results in the company heading for the *red ocean*: competition solely on price. [viii]

- **Pursue to optima; have multiple goals**—Until the arrival of solar and wind power, the business model and technology portfolio of utility companies enjoyed decades of stability. As covered in Chapter 3, technology and deregulations transformed the market, forcing utility companies to adapt to new customer demands, technologies, and innovative business models launched by start-ups. It is a challenge requiring a broad and evolving set of skills, competencies, and knowledge.

- **Seek persistent disequilibrium**—A defender strategy is not sustainable. The needs and wants of customers change over time and competitors will one day inevitably introduce a viable substitute or even disrupt the whole business model. Eternal stability is a mirage. A company with a prospector strategy that is expecting to introduce one disruptive business model after another is in for a similar disappointment. Companies should seek a continuous flow between both extremes, whereby companies in highly competitive and uncertain markets should surf closer to the disruptive edge of the wave, and other companies are better off pursuing a more efficiency-focused strategy. Depending on the level of disequilibrium, the team should be more or less diverse.

- **Change changes itself**—When distributing tasks, solutions, value propositions, or business models, the parts will influence each other. Apple requires its business partners to manufacture and assemble its products according to very strict functional and non-functional requirements. Nevertheless, if Sony's new camera module holds the promise of a new awesome feature, Apple may well be willing to adjust the design of next year's iPhone. More generally, as the complicated components that are required to create complex products evolve, they influence and eventually change the product, organization, and network. Depending on the business model and strategy of the company, the change is more dedicated (top down) or emergent (bottom up) in nature.

Using diversity and variety to increase the company's ability to react quicker and more effectively on unexpected opportunities and threats can be achieved by: (a) adjusting existing hiring and talent management practices, (b) building a new organizational entity from scratch, or (c) buying another company. At first sight, the latter option looks like the easiest and quickest solution, as it saves time. However, many buyers overestimate the synergies that an acquisition will yield (e.g., sharing customer portfolios, complementary product portfolios, sharing capabilities, economies of scale).[ix]

Between September 1997 and August 2013, Yahoo bought 87 companies—including GeoCities for $3.57 billion and Tumblr for $1.1 billion. Nevertheless, it was not enough to change the fortunes of the company, and Verizon bought Yahoo's core business in 2016 for $4.8 billion. Microsoft bought aQuantive for $6.3 billion in 2007, valuing the company in its books at $100 million five years later. Search engine Excite acquired @Home in 1999 for $6.7 billion and then filed for bankruptcy in 2001 after losing $7.4 billion in the previous year.

With an active M&A strategy not being a universal ticket to diversity (and its benefits of variety, innovation, and agility), companies either have to adjust their existing organization or invest in a completely new entity. The latter allows the company to experiment with new brands, leadership styles, business models, value propositions, organizational designs, skill sets, cultures, and technologies. If the existing company has a reputation of preferring men over women or people with a certain background, a new entity provides a fresh start. By installing a diverse leadership team from the start, talent management (e.g., attracting, developing, and retaining) will be shaped according to their belief set and background.

The behavior of the *mother company* is often key to the success of these new entities. Especially when they were very successful or after missing a financial target, executives from the mother company struggle to keep their distance. They want to help, but often, *slowly but surely*, the boundaries between the two companies will fade. As a result, *fast, hip, diverse, and variated* turns into robust, predictable, and homogeneous. High potentials and customers start to leave, and three years later, the remaining team is formally integrated into the mother company.

Most difficult to achieve is increasing the level of diversity in companies with a long and stable history. Here, patterns, values, and practices had the most time to engrain themselves. As mentioned in Chapter 2, effective change starts with a leader who is consistent (e.g., walk the talk) and focuses on results (e.g., from 20 percent women in leadership positions to 30 percent in three years). Diversity has to be part of a dedicated strategy, a bottom-up approach takes too much time. Markets and customer behavior change too fast for an evolutionary approach.

8.3 THE DIGITAL MANIFESTO IS A GROWTH PATH

Several years ago, I received the book, *The 7 Habits of Highly Effective People* by Stephen Covey, as a gift from a colleague. I read parts of the book with interest, and it eventually ended up in the bookcase with all of my other books. It came to my attention again when I was doing my research for this book. While leafing through the book, I was struck by the overlap between the seven habits and the growth of an IT function.

The book by Covey focuses on increasing one's personal effectiveness, emphasizing the importance of attaining tangible goals. We all start as a child, depending on our parents for food, safety, and guidance. Without it, a person cannot build the self-worth required to become independent, let alone interdependent. The latter is the highest state, feeling comfortable enough to share wealth, recognize the value of others, and take responsibility for the well-being of others.

A child is reactive, acts on stimuli from its environment, and tends to point at others when things don't go according to plan. The parent tells the child what to do and what the priorities are (*wash your hands before eating*). IT teams that are stuck at this maturity level are rare, but can still be found in some smaller companies. Like a fire brigade, these teams run from one incident to another. New business demands are met on an ad hoc basis and the quality of the result depends solely on the skills of the individuals involved. Actions are dictated by external stimuli and job burnouts are considered a badge of honor. The business defines the objectives and is the sole source of structure (e.g., budget policy, basic investment process).

For any business model that is more complex than baking bread, this level of maturity is unsustainable. An IT team should be able to act at least independently, as depicted in Figure 8.3. It is the level whereby the business is the client and IT is the supplier, a type of relationship that is embodied by the business IT alignment paradigm. The IT team is in control; able to deliver new and existing services according to pre-agreed quality, time, and budget levels. To achieve the next step on the ladder, IT as a business partner, IT has to be able to anticipate future situations, making things happen rather than waiting to be asked by the business. The essence of beginning with the end in mind starts with defining the desired result or effect in business terminology and considering technology as a means to an end.

Last but not least, we'll discuss what is called, in agile terminology, the *product backlog*. The business demand for new functionalities or solutions is always larger than the available budget, thus, requiring prioritization. Similar to agile Scrum projects, the business and IT have to draw a line after the lowest of the high-priority investments that both feel they can complete. It also means rescheduling an internal meeting or training when the business faces an unexpected and urgent issue. Putting first things first is applicable to both strategic and operational topics.

For many companies with an analog business model, IT as a reliable and predictable servant will do. When technology evolves from an operational business utility to a strategic business asset, both business and IT have to evolve further. Interdependence is tied to the convergence or even fusion of business and IT domains (see Chapter 6). At this level, business-savvy technologists and perceptive business professionals are able to successfully realize new business initiatives and evolve them into *stars* and eventually *cash cows*. Interdependence means thinking win/win instead of focusing solely on your own team.

Another crucial capability that is tied to interdependence is understanding the actual need or want of the internal or external customer. Too often, the

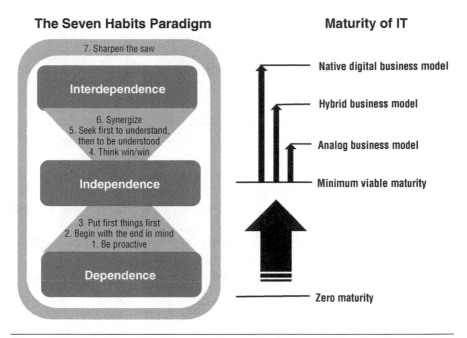

Figure 8.3 The Digital Manifesto is a growth path

analyst or engineer starts proposing solutions before truly understanding the underlying business problem. The customer often falls for the same trap, dictating the IT solution instead of explaining the challenge at hand. It is in the nature of people to be understood, before we fully understand the other person. However, like a doctor, both business and IT first have to agree on the diagnosis before exploring potential solutions.

Synergize, or in other words, *to combine or work together in order to be more effective*[x] is the gateway to value that business and IT are unable to create in isolation. Synergy requires mutual trust, close collaboration, and valuing each other's differences. It is a precondition in order to be successful in native digital and hybrid markets, as neither domain can prosper independently in an Internet of Things world.

The seventh habit is called *sharpen the saw*, and it surrounds the other habits because it recommends that an individual should continuously improve and renew. Applied to a company, it can be translated in a combination of regular strategic reflection (e.g., do we need to reframe the existing business model?) and continuous improvement at an operational level. Complacency inevitably leads to obsolescence. Sharpen the saw represents a balanced program for organizational, team, and individual self-renewal.

REFERENCES

i. Source: Merriam Webster dictionary.
ii. Heskett, J. L., Jones, T. O., Loveman, G. W., Earl Sasser, W. Jr. and Schlesinger, L. A. (2008). *Putting the Service Profit Chain to Work*. Harvard Business Review.
iii. Hunt, V., Layton, D. and Prince, S. (2015). Why Diversity Matters, McKinsey. Link: http://www.mckinsey.com/business-functions/organization/our-insights/why-diversity-matters.
iv. Slevin, D. and Colvin, J. (1990). Juggling Entrepreneurial Style and Organizational Structure: How to Get Your Act Together.
v. Kelly, K. (2008). Out of Control: The New Biology of Machines, Social Systems, and the Economic World.
vi. Herriot, P. and Pemberton, C. (1995). *Competitive Advantage through Diversity: Organizational Learning from Difference.*
vii. Taleb, N. (2012). *Antifragile: Things That Gain from Disorder.* Random House.
viii. Kim, W. and Mauborgne, R. (2005). *Blue Ocean Strategy.* Harvard Business Review.
ix. Christofferson, S., McNish, R. and Sias, D. (2015). Where Mergers Go Wrong. McKinsey Quarterly. Link: http://www.mckinsey.com/business-functions/strategy-and-corporate-finance/our-insights/where-mergers-go-wrong.
x. Source: Cambridge dictionary.

Appendices

Introduction

As pointed out in the preface, digitalization starts with the business and IT reframing their current belief set and operating model. Isolated initiatives inevitably result in value leakage as a successful transformation touches on the companies' leadership style, culture, skill sets, strategy, business model, sourcing strategy, and process model.

This broad scope resulted in several tough choices regarding the topics covered in the previous chapters.

The objective of the appendices is filling in some of the resulting gaps. By looking from make-or-buy and architecture perspectives, these appendices provide a slightly different angle on the six principles of the Digital Manifesto.

The last appendix provides a glossary with definitions and explanations of terms, concepts, methods, and technology.

A

MAKE-OR-BUY REVISITED

We live in a world of perpetual evolution and disruption. Only a network of interdependent companies that are committed to continuous innovation and improvement can turn the accompanying waves of short-lived opportunities into company value.

A traditional manufacturer of race bikes considers its website non-core, as it only provides generic and static information. For a webshop selling the manufacturer's race bikes to customers, the website is one of its primary sales channels. To differentiate itself from other webshops, the owner heavily invests in search engine optimization (SEO)—a smooth order-to-cash workflow and integration with various social media channels.

IT is responsible for the make-or-buy decision of the manufacturer's website. The business oversees everything that is even remotely related to the online presence of the webshop. The manufacturer outsources all development and support activities, using price as the primary selection criteria. Only a small retained IT organization remains. The webshop is constantly on the lookout for external partners with either scarce expertise (e.g., marketing automation, SEO) or complementary value propositions (e.g., a state-of-the-art mobile platform providing access to a new customer segment). Price is of secondary importance because it considers the online platform a source of differentiation, as depicted in Table A.1.

Attracting customers by investing in new technologies and other innovations is one of the three basic strategies that a company can choose in order to compete. Covered in Chapter 4, a company can either offer:[i]

- The latest and the greatest features, technologies, and insights (*product leadership*),
- A value proposition, tailored to the specific needs and wants of a customer (*customer intimacy*), or

Table A.1   Differentiated sourcing objectives and economics

	Strategy		
	Win Customers through Innovation	**Win Customers through Customer Intimacy**	**Win Customers through Lowest Cost**
Business Economics	Early market entry enables charging premium prices and acquiring large market share. Speed-to-market is key value driver.	High cost of customer acquisition results in focus on increasing share-of-wallet. Economies-of-scope are key value driver.	High fixed costs make large volumes essential to reduce cost. Economies-of-scale are key value driver.
Context of Business Demand	Most innovative and breathtaking features, speed-to-market, and brand image.	A seamless extension of customers' business process or journey through domain knowledge, customization, and flexibility.	Cost, cost, and cost; supplemented by scalability, predictability, and reliability.
Key Outsourcing Economics	• Increase margin through differentiation • Increase revenue by being early to the market	• Decrease cost of customer acquisition and management • Increase revenue/decrease *churn* through value-add services (e.g., buy top-rated mobile e-commerce app)	• Decrease cost per transaction • Increase revenue/decrease *churn* through value-add services (e.g., telco contracting start-up to launch own chat app)
Key Outsourcing Objectives	• Augment distinctive capabilities • Access complementary capabilities/innovations (e.g., content) • Access scarce skills and expertise • Improve speed-to-market	• Augment distinctive capabilities (e.g., advanced analytics capabilities and value-added services) • Reduce cost of indistinctive and non-critical capabilities • Access to first class CRM and/or channel platform • Access new customer segments (e.g., through Facebook)	• Reduce cost of indistinctive and non-critical capabilities • Access complementary capabilities/innovations (e.g., security services)

- A product at a lower price point than the competition (*operational excellence*).

Companies competing on price seek economies-of-scale—either through the acquisition of competitors and/or by outsourcing non-core activities. These companies make the headlines with large-scale offshoring to India, the Philippines, and other countries that offer *labor arbitrage*. But even this traditional outsourcing model is changing quickly due to the advances in artificial intelligence and advanced robotics, as explained in the following paragraphs.

The objectives and economics that drive the sourcing decisions of companies pursuing a product leadership or customer intimacy strategy, in combination with a hybrid or native digital business model, are very different.[1] When business and IT capabilities converge or possibly fuse, individual sourcing strategies for the business and IT are replaced by one integral sourcing strategy—a sourcing strategy that considers external partners first and foremost as a source of complementary capabilities.

Small, highly innovative external partners provide larger, slower, but cash-rich companies access to emerging technologies and capabilities. Quoting Su et al.:[ii] *". . . today, more than ever, as rapid technological changes disrupt industries, established companies need access to fresh ideas, new technologies, and cutting-edge expertise. In IT, these capabilities are often found among smaller, more agile suppliers."* To better leverage their capabilities and deny the competition access to them, many established companies use their often considerable cash reserves to acquire one or more of these highly valuable external partners.[2]

The first part of this appendix emphasizes the importance of a differentiated sourcing strategy, captured by the principle *less uniform, more differentiated*. The second part combines the principles *less static, more flow* and *less cost, more value* to describe the evolving benefits and risks over the sourcing life cycle. The third part covers several relevant trends that are shaping current and future sourcing engagements. Table A.2 provides three statements that cover this appendix as a whole.

---

[1] IT in a company with an analog business model *supports* business activities. Consequently, even the technology that is used to automate the company's core business is considered non-core and is, therefore, a candidate for traditional outsourcing arrangements.

[2] The downfall of Yahoo demonstrates that an active merger and acquisition strategy cannot replace a viable business strategy and value proposition. Acquisitions and selective sourcing can only strengthen existing distinctive capabilities and core competencies.

Table A.2   Statements to think about when reading this chapter

Statements
External partners are a source of commodities and cost reduction.
The client company always dictates the rules to the external partner.
Resource-centric offshore contracts remain the dominant sourcing model for the foreseeable future.

A.1 KEY PARTNERS VERSUS SUPPLIERS

The IT business model introduced in Chapter 6 includes the building blocks called key activities and key partners. The key activities are an integral part of the company's distinctive capabilities, providing a competitive advantage. Also known as core activities, key activities should never be outsourced. They can, however, benefit from key partners.

Renamed key partnerships in the book *Business Model Generation* (what's in a name), this building block describes the network of external partners that make the digital business model work. A company has dozens or even thousands of external partners, but only a few have a considerable impact on the *future* cash flows of the company. In most cases this is not the business process outsourcing (BPO) deal with a large supplier in India or the $20+ million low-end information technology outsourcing (ITO) contract, but the niche player with the new, disruptive, augmented reality platform. It is the latter that will make or break the company's market position three years from now.

The net present value (NPV) or other metric that reflects the added value of an external partner is one of the aspects that can be used to differentiate between a key partner and supplier. Other aspects include the mutual dependence and ability to find substitutes, as seen in Figure A.1.

The sourcing approach for suppliers is closely related to traditional procurement practices, which in turn, are based on the systems theory. In its most basic form, the system theory describes the behavior of an entity consisting of an input, process, output, and objective. By combining them into a self-correcting feedback loop, the system automatically adapts to accomplish the predefined objective.

Here is an example of the theory applied to the previously introduced manufacturer of race bikes: The IT director of the company asks the procurement officer to reduce the cost of the existing IT outsourcing contract by 10 percent in six months (objective). The procurement officer needs to spend his own time, retain involvement from a legal counsel, and review the existing contract

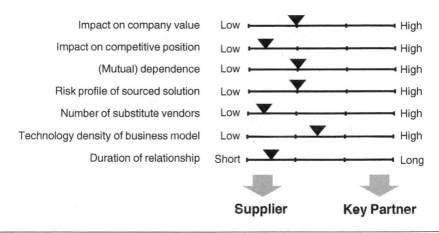

Figure A.1   The difference between a key partner and a supplier

(inputs). After the negotiation (process), a new contract is signed by both parties (output). The loop is closed by addressing any difference between the agreed and actual cost reduction.

The attractiveness of standard procurement practices and the underpinning system theory lies in their relative simplicity. However, as practitioners know, sourcing a custom IT solution or enterprise resource planning implementation is very different from buying chairs and staplers. With the digitalization of business models, the complexity, dynamics, and chance of mutually exclusive[3] objectives only increase further. The key partners involved in introducing a new business model, adopting a new emerging technology, or an investment in a new customer-facing platform must, therefore, be managed differently than the suppliers.

To effectively manage key partners, traditional procurement practices need to be mixed with elements from conflict management (e.g., address the inherent conflict of interest between both parties), game theory (e.g., *'the best result comes from everyone in a group doing what's best, both for themselves and the group'*[4]) and decision-making theories (e.g., why outsource, what to outsource, which sourcing options are available, and how to outsource).

---

[3] Think of the business demanding a best-in-class solution from an IT team that is faced with budget cuts.

[4] A historically wrong, but nevertheless explanatory quote from John Nash (played by Russell Crowe) in the movie *A Beautiful Mind*.

Regardless of the label *supplier* or *key partner*, every external partner represents an investment, each with a specific risk and return. Consequently, they must be managed accordingly.

A.2 MANAGING A BASKET WITH THE KEY PARTNER AND SUPPLIERS

A popular model among sourcing practitioners to manage external partners is the Kraljic matrix[iii] that is depicted in Figure A.2. It categorizes external partners based on their added value and risk profile. A power imbalance, supply-side resource constraints, low solvency and/or liquidity ratios, and high agency cost[5] are indicators that the external partner inhabits one of the quadrants on the right. Depending on the impact on the bottom line of the client company, a high-risk profile is either a serious nuisance (*bottleneck*) or, in the worst case, a potential ticket to a Chapter 11 bankruptcy filing (*strategic*).

Somewhere in the future, the board of the manufacturer of race bikes decides to focus on product development, marketing, sales, and after sales, while outsourcing its entire product line to one external business partner. The external business partner who won the contract would be a true key partner. While it may deliver on the promised 20 percent cost reduction per bike, if the key partner delivers a sub-par product, or fails to deliver completely, both business-to-business and business-to-consumer customers will call the manufacturer (technically speaking: ex-manufacturer at that point). The decision of the board puts the company at the mercy of an external business partner.

Since Apple, Google, and many other companies have outsourced their production to external business partners, it is a viable business model—that is, if the associated risks are managed effectively. Foxconn, TSMC, and Samsung depend on Apple for a substantial part of their revenue and profit. Combined with a multi-vendor strategy, the mutual dependency ensures that Apple, and not an external partner, holds the reins.

Nevertheless, distinctive capabilities should always be retained. Apple will never outsource its design function, nor will Google outsource anything even remotely related to its search and ad targeting algorithms. The strategic quadrant is, therefore, either empty or occupied by a few true key partners. As mentioned

---

[5] Within the context of this topic, agency costs arise from the conflicts of interest between the buyer and supplier (e.g., each party wants to maximize their profit and revenue). Think of the capital expenditure (CAPEX) and operating expenditure (OPEX) needed to establish and operate the retained organization, auditing fees, benchmark fees, and the invoice from the legal counsel.

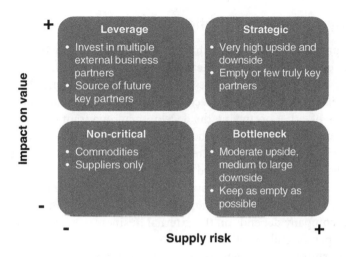

Figure A.2   The Kraljic matrix (adapted from: Kraljic, P. [1983]. Purchasing Must Become Supply Management. *Harvard Business Review*. 61 (5), pp. 109–117)

before, large ITO or BPO contracts don't qualify as value in the Kraljic matrix, and should be interpreted in terms of additional future market share, profit, and revenue.

The non-critical quadrant is solely populated by suppliers, leaving two quadrants filled with a mix of suppliers and potential key partners.

Looking at the matrix from an IT perspective, most external IT partners of companies with an analog business model are in the non-critical quadrant because the accompanying positioning of IT as an Average Joe or faithful servant is reflected in the sourcing strategy. The business demand can be fulfilled with commodity solutions that are sourced from a broad supplier market. However, analog business models are going the way of the dinosaurs, turning long-term, cost-driven outsourcing contracts into a risk proposition, as was described in Chapter 7. When the winner is primarily selected on price, then flexibility, innovation, and proactiveness lose out.

IT teams that enjoy a business partner position collaborate with several potential key partners that are located in the leverage quadrant, while a prima donna finds it difficult to resist contracting external business partners with a high supply risk. A prima donna wants the latest and the greatest—regardless of cost and risk. Hence, expect several bottleneck contracts when faced with a prima donna.

To reduce the impact of these and other *sourcing accidents*, those who are responsible for the sourcing strategy should always take notice of, at least, the two following key drivers of sourcing risk: power imbalance and unequal maturity.

A.2.1 Symmetrical Relationships Add the Most Value

The key partner who is dominating the client company is in the exploitable quadrant of Figure A.3 since the asymmetrical relationship allows the key partner to optimize its own interests (e.g., profit).[iv] Depicting the relationship from the external partner's perspective, this matrix from Buchanan signals the importance of either occupying the development quadrant or core quadrant as a client company. In the development quadrant, the external partner is willing to invest in the relationship to increase the revenue and profit streams, thereby shifting the client company toward the core quadrant. Again, referring to Covey's *Seven Habits of Highly Effective People*, in the development and nuisance quadrants, the external partner and client company are independent, while the client company depends on the external business partner in the exploitable quadrant (parent-child relation). The most value is created when both consider the relationship a win-win: when both the client company and the external partner are interdependent and rely on each other for future success.

To achieve company objectives, the client company not only has to ensure strategic and financial symmetry, but also symmetry regarding organizational maturity, as seen in Figure A.4. While some client companies use outsourcing to leverage on the best practices of the external partner (e.g., governance framework, process models, and tooling) to increase the quality and efficiency, this approach is not without risk. I have experienced several cases whereby fast-paced and dynamic business teams got extremely frustrated after the CIO

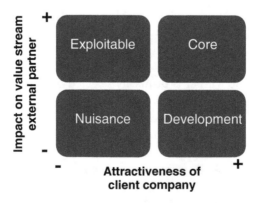

Figure A.3 The importance of mutual dependence between client company and external partner (source: Buchanan, L. [1992]. Vertical Trade Relationships: The Role of Dependence and Symmetry in Attaining Organizational Goals. *Journal of Marketing Research*, 29. pp. 65–75)

decided to outsource the IT function to a *mature* external partner. Captured by the principle *less uniform, more differentiated* that was discussed in Chapter 4, the 26 ITIL v3 processes and 34 COBIT v4.1 processes add value in some, but certainly not in all scenarios.

Here too, there is a risk of exploitation if the maturity of the external partner far exceeds the organizational maturity of the client company. The client company will not know what hit it, both operationally and financially, when they get steamrolled by the bureaucratic machine of the external partner.

Almost every country has associations governing the pedigree of cats, dogs, or horses. These associations are responsible for the welfare, breeding guidelines, and promotion of one or more species. Shows and events allow the breeders to show and sell their animals, heavily relying on passionate volunteers for the judging and accompanying administration.

When an association invited me to a horse show in 2014, I felt as though I had traveled back to 1980, due to the amount of handwork and overlap. Scores were manually written down on forms, manually consolidated on other forms, and eventually keyed into an Excel spreadsheet. Not only were the shows a blast from the past, the association itself was run in a similar fashion, spending more than $250,000 per year on stamps to communicate with the breeders and other stakeholders. Of the 85 employees, more than half were dedicated to opening and responding to the thousands of letters.

One of the key objectives of the new director included the digitalization of the operating model. Due to the relatively small size of the organization and the nature of its core activities, it was quickly decided to heavily rely on external IT partners to design and execute the program. To do so without ending

Impact of maturity

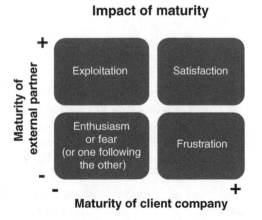

Figure A.4   The importance of the client company and external partner sharing an equal maturity level

up in the exploitation quadrant in Figure A.4, the association invested in both the creation of a small but highly skilled retained IT organization and carefully planned and executed sourcing strategy.

A symmetrical relationship between the client company and the external partner is an important precondition in order to optimize the return on the decision to buy instead of make.

A.2.2 Maximizing the Return of the Basket

Complacency is enemy number one for every commercial company. The same applies to the sourcing strategy and the external partner portfolio. Some optimizations focus on shifting an external partner from one quadrant to the other, while others aim to strengthen its current position, as seen in Figure A.5. Caniëls and Gelderman took the Kraljic matrix and defined nine growth paths or optimization strategies[v] that sourcing professionals can use to optimize the return of the portfolio:

1. **Maintain strategic partnership**: Strategic partnerships are costly to build and maintain. For this reason, both parties should pursue a strategy focused on increasing the scope of the collaboration. Foxconn has been a strategic partner for Apple for more than a decade, reflected in the ever-expanding partnership. In 2016, reports hinted at Apple looking to work with Foxconn to open new research centers in several locations in Southeast Asia and India. There is even talk about Foxconn investing in a display plant in the United States, a deal believed to be worth $7 billion and 50,000 jobs.[vi]

2. **Accept lock-in partnership**: If the key partner owns a difficult-to-substitute patent that is crucial to the client company's value proposition, the latter has little choice but to accept the lock-in. Small app developers consider Apple and Google to be key partners as they provide low-friction gateways to a large customer base. Here, too, the relationship is asymmetric. The app developer has no choice but to accept the rules and guidelines of Apple's App Store or Google's Play Store.

3. **Terminate partnership, find new key partner**: In a case where the key partner structurally underperforms and fails to show improvement, the client company has no choice but to end the relationship. At that point, the client company has three options: (1) source for an external partner with a suitable substitute, (2) invest in internal delivery capabilities, or (3) adjust the feature set of the value proposition. In 2014, Apple terminated its relationship with GT Advanced Technologies after extending

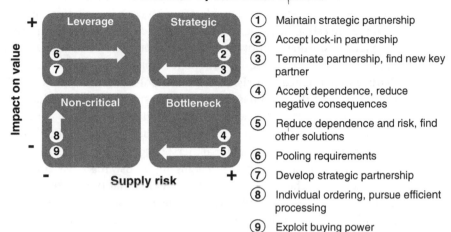

Available optimization actions

Figure A.5 Optimization Strategies in the Kraljic Matrix (source: Caniëls, M. and Gelderman, C. [2005]. Purchasing Strategies in the Kraljic Matrix—A Power and Dependence Perspective. *Journal of Purchasing & Supply Management 11*, pp. 141–155)

a loan of $578 million to manufacture sapphire display covers for the iPhone and Apple Watch. A sapphire display would provide Apple with considerable competitive advantage, like the introduction of the aluminum unibody in 2008. (It took HP, Dell, Acer, and other competitors several years to introduce laptops with a similar design because Apple had secured all of the available *computer numerical control (CNC) lathes* capacity in the market required to make magnesium-aluminum unibodies with a thickness of less than 0.8 of an inch. For several years, Apple offered a unique product, allowing the company to demand a premium price.) However, GT Advanced Technologies failed to meet Apple's expectations and Apple had no choice but to continue using Gorilla Glass from Corning.

4. **Accept dependence, reduce negative consequences**: In 2011, China was the largest maker of hard disk drives, followed closely by Thailand. When large parts of Thailand flooded during the monsoon season, the output fell by 30 percent, causing worldwide hard drive shortages as most PC and server makers had only four to six weeks, on average, of inventory. Hence, the key phase of this optimization strategy is

contingency planning. Those undesired events, which in all likelihood can be predicted with a reasonable certainty, can be mitigated by, for example, investing in stock or consigned stock agreements with other suppliers. Risks that cannot be mitigated should either be accepted or transferred (e.g., insurance) by the client company.

5. **Reduce dependence and risk, find other solutions**: For this optimization strategy, the key phase is: source for substitutes. To reduce the dependence on the external bottleneck partner, the client company adjusts its value proposition or business model in such a way that a broader portfolio of external partners becomes available to select from. The simplest strategy is replacing high-cost, high-risk products or services with cheaper alternatives, provided that the cost reduction justifies the decrease in added value. Referring back to the aluminum unibody laptops, customers expect a lower price point for a plastic laptop because customers perceive a metal body as a value add. When introducing a new innovative application platform, the start-up needs customers, as they are a source of references who are fueling a positive feedback loop. The license fee is of secondary importance. This policy changes when the customer base reaches a certain size. I have experienced several occasions whereby the external partner suddenly increased their license fee threefold or even fivefold, undermining the business case of the client company. More than once, the client company decided to disinvest and transfer the applications to the platform of a less opportunistic supplier.

6. **Pooling requirements**: Managing five external partners is cheaper than managing 500 external partners. This optimization strategy increases the purchasing power[6] of the client company by increasing the scope of the contract and reducing the number of external partners. To execute this strategy effectively, the client company needs a mature procurement and contract management function to prevent an undesired shift in the power balance.

7. **Develop strategic partnership**: In case the external partner has the potential to strengthen the client company's strategic position or distinctive capabilities, both parties should explore the transition from the leverage quadrant to the strategic quadrant. Interdependency is an important precondition to prevent the client company from ending up in the exploitation quadrant of Figure A.3. Another option that is

---

[6] Purchasing power is the quantity, quality, or added value that the client company can buy for a certain amount of money.

available to the client company is acquiring the external partner, removing the risks related to an asymmetrical relationship altogether.

8. **Individual ordering, pursue efficient processing**: For commodity services or products that cannot be pooled, the client company has to focus on minimizing the transaction cost. Think of investing in centralized e-sourcing and procurement management systems, allowing users to electronically source, order, and track their purchase. To reduce search time and stress, consider using social media, content aggregators, and specialized search portals.

9. **Exploit buying power**: In this quadrant, both the supply base and range of substitutes are wide. As a result, the client company is the dominant party and is in the position to exploit this advantage. Think of enforcing unfavorable contract terms (e.g., price, termination, liability, and duration). With this strategy, it is the external partner that is at risk of being pushed into the exploitation quadrant.

It is important to emphasize that these nine growth paths (or optimization strategies) target the performance of the external provider, not the performance of existing contracts. Both are required, whereby the first focuses on future *growth* (assuming the current performance is satisfactory) and contract management focuses on *control*.[vii]

To select the right external partner and optimization strategies, it is important to understand the evolving business and IT demands. Captured by the principles *less static, more flow* that was covered in Chapter 5 and *less cost, more value* that was covered in Chapter 7, a sourcing strategy not only has to add value today, but also three years down the road.

A.3 MAKE-OR-BUY DECISIONS FLOW

Regardless of the life-cycle phase that a value proposition or business model is in, the decision to buy instead of make is primarily driven by economics. There are two key economic differences in the transactions that take place between two departments that are part of the same commercial entity, and transactions between the two entities that each strive for value maximization. The first is beneficial to the client company.

Unlike most internal departments, an external partner is exposed to competition. To stay competitive, the external partner must invest in the following capabilities that are valuable to client companies:[viii]

- **Specialization**: Even a *full-service provider* like IBM must choose which areas to invest in and which to disinvest due to eroding margins and revenue. While writing this book, IBM identified the cloud, artificial intelligence, and Blockchain as key growth areas, while CEO Ginni Rometty has divested $8 billion worth of business activities since she was appointed head of IBM.[ix] Similarly, Amazon, Google, and Microsoft invested billions in data centers, allowing these companies to create platforms and infrastructure-related capabilities that individual client companies are unable to match.

- **Market discipline**: The Darwinistic forces that are governing capitalistic markets force external partners to create new innovative value propositions, improve existing ones, and act on moves and countermoves by competitors. The more lucrative and dynamic the market, the higher the price to pay for a wrong decision—very different, especially from IT departments supporting analog business models. They enjoy a protective shield that is provided by the business.

- **Flexibility**: Nobody can predict the future, despite the efforts of NPV-based business cases, real options, and other financial tools. A large investment remains a risky decision, requiring the responsible executive to *put his big-boy pants on*. For non-core business activities, client companies can offload this risk to external business partners. Infrastructure as a service (IaaS) and software as a service (SaaS) are two popular value propositions from external IT partners that fulfill the client company's desire for low investment risk and volume flexibility (e.g., pay-per-use model). Besides volume flexibility, external partners are also a source of service mix flexibility (e.g., free versus premium offerings) and speed (e.g., source specific entrepreneurial IT-related capabilities externally).

- **Cost savings**: Last but not least, the classic reason why client companies outsource is to improve efficiency by leveraging on the scale and/or best practices of the external partner. The more generic the activity and higher the volume, the faster an external partner can achieve economies-of-scale by bundling the demand of multiple client companies. This way, the external partner can spread fixed operating costs and capital investments over more client companies. Besides scale, external partners also use labor arbitrage and, more important and more sustainable innovations like automation of knowledge work and advanced robotics to lower the cost of an activity.

The bad news is that both the client company and the external partner want to maximize their share of the benefits while minimizing the associated cost and risks. The second key economic difference is, therefore, not beneficial to the client company. More specific, the client company is faced with transaction costs and agency costs when sourcing from an external partner.

Agency costs reflect the tendency of external partners (and individuals) to act in their own best interest, affecting the value of the client company. Transaction costs include searching for suitable sources of supply, deal making, and contract enforcement. Both types of cost increase when shifting work from internal departments to external partners.

The more symmetrical the relationship, the lower the information asymmetry,[7] and more stable and straightforward the demand, the lower these costs will be. For example, the agency and transaction costs of a commercial off-the-shelf SaaS solution are lower than the costs to source a custom e-commerce platform that is based on several promising but risky emerging technologies.

A.3.1 Mapping the Buy Decision to the Business Life Cycle

The more uncertain, complex, and dynamic the situation faced by the client company, the more interesting it becomes to offload part of the investment risk.[8] Introducing a new value proposition in a new market using a new emerging technology is as risky as it gets. By collaborating with external partners, the client company can not only reduce the required CAPEX by leveraging on their capabilities and innovations, but also benefits from a higher speed-to-market as *buying* tends to take less time than investing in *making*.

Hence, during the introduction phase of the business life cycle, external business partners and, in case of hybrid and digital business models, external IT partners are a potential source of innovation and differentiation.

However, every upside has its downside, as seen in Table A.3. If the client sources an emerging technology or other recent innovation, the external partner cannot be expected to fall back on a mature and scalable delivery organization (regardless of what the sales rep promised during his best sales pitch ever). There will be operational issues.

Another, more strategic risk that is inherent to the introduction phase of the business life-cycle is captured by the following two phrases: *bet on the wrong horse* and *jumped on the bandwagon too late*. When is the right moment

---

[7] Theories related to information asymmetry cover decisions in transactions where one stakeholder has more or better information than the other. The resulting imbalance of power may push either the client company or the external partner toward the exploitable quadrant, shown in Figure A.3.

[8] Investment risk can be defined as the likelihood and impact of undesired events affecting the expected return of an investment.

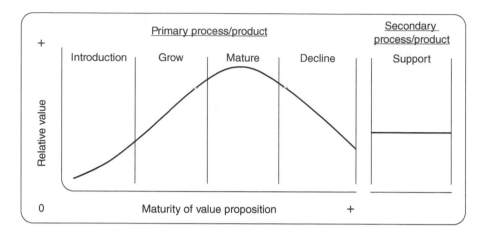

Table A.3   Mapping sourcing benefits and risks to the business life cycle

	Key Sourcing Objectives	Sourcing Benefits	Specific Sourcing Risk
Introduction	Augment distinctive capabilities (product): • Source technology and other innovations to increase differentiation • Boost speed-to-market • CAPEX spread	Primary: • Create new value propositions • Reduce investment risk Secondary: • Access to complementary expertise, skills, and solutions	• Operational issues (e.g., availability, delivery times, and quality) • No or limited substitute external partners • *Bet on the wrong horse*
Grow	Augment ability to execute and improve (volume and features): • Scalability and flexibility • Access to differentiating product features	Primary: • Grow market share fast • Add new features fast Secondary: • Fast up- and down-scaling of resources (e.g., developers)	• External partner's ability to scale quickly while maintaining quality levels • Strategic dependence on external partner (composite and concentration risk)
Mature	Augment ability to retain high margins (efficiency and quality): • Reduce business and IT cost while maintaining quality levels	Primary: • Increase/maintain margin through lower cost Secondary: • Access to process innovations and enhancements	• Overestimating maturity of external partner and its ability to reduce cost beyond initial agreement • Underestimating the required residual flexibility (in the future)

Decline	• Extend life cycle • Aggressive reduction of business and IT costs • Eliminate CAPEX	Primary: • Revenue and margin foregone compared to in-house scenario[1]	• Underestimate cost of (premature) exit
Support	Reduce business and IT cost while maintaining quality levels	Primary: • Increase/maintain margin through lower cost Secondary: • Access to process innovations and enhancements	• Underestimating the required flexibility • Integrating and/or data exchange between SaaS solutions

[1] In case the cost of making exceeds the cost of buying, outsourcing allows the client company to extend the life-cycle of the value proposition.

to adopt virtual reality? Or, is it better to invest in augmented reality? Oculus Rift (owned by Facebook), Google, Microsoft, HTC, Magic Leap, Samsung, and several other companies invest heavily in often incompatible virtual reality or augmented reality solutions. Nobody knows who will win, but everybody wants to catch the right wave at the right moment. Wait too long and the opportunity may pass. Go all-in too early and risk a considerable write-off.

There is a reason why the challenges that are faced by the IT team during the introduction phase are best reflected by the term entrepreneurial IT. The converged or fused business and IT team is launching a new business.

Those client companies that successfully introduce a new value proposition face a new set of challenges when entering the growth phase. External partners can contribute here, too.

Both during the introduction phase and the growth phase, it makes good business sense to use IaaS instead of investing in a dedicated environment. Google's load balancers can scale to one million+ users instantly and its infrastructure has a global network footprint with over 100 points-of-presence across more than 33 countries.[x] Best off all, Google, Amazon, and Microsoft allow you to pay only for actual use. Hence, if the value proposition fails to gain traction in the market, you just close the account. No CAPEX, just OPEX until the moment you stop using it.

The main downside of every life-cycle phase beyond the introduction phase is the inability to make instead of buy (*composite risk*). If the external partner has all the capabilities to perform certain activities, it will be very costly to reverse the sourcing decision, even though some capabilities turn out to be distinctive for the client company during the growth phase. At that point, the external partner has been promoted to a de facto key partner (or takeover target). Also related is concentration risk, a term that originates from the financial industry.

During the growth phase, the value proposition quickly expands in market share, revenue, profit, and consequently, in strategic importance. If a considerable part of the business model is outsourced to one or two external partners, the client company should either accept or mitigate the accompanying concentration risk. Mitigating actions include expanding the number of external partners (e.g., Amazon Web Services (AWS) *and* Microsoft Azure, instead of AWS *or* Azure for IaaS), differentiation and substitution (e.g., LCD screens for Apple 8 and OLED screens for iPhone X), and signing a Build Operate Transfer (BOT) contract. With a BOT contract, the external partner is payed to set up a captive unit for the client company, transferring the ownership after a pre-agreed period. In case the value proposition fails to reach the growth phase, the external partner should be able to salvage and reuse part of the assets, reducing the write-off faced by the client company.

The mature phase shares several properties with the sourcing objectives of secondary processes and products. Both strive for achieving cost leadership while maintaining quality and output levels. The most important risk factor of the mature phase is underestimating the required flexibility. The longer the contract term and the more aggressive the agreed cost, the lower the flexibility and level of innovation. Repeating a quote that was used when describing the PharmaCompany case from Chapter 7: "*It was almost impossible to change the contract, even though the business was changing very rapidly.*"

At the end of the business life cycle, external partners are still a potential source of added value since they allow the client company to postpone the inevitable end. Economies-of-scale and labor arbitrage are two examples of the tools available to an external partner to create a win-win.

A.3.2 Sourcing Strategy 101 for Hybrids and Native Digitals

For companies with a hybrid or native digital business model, the technology life cycle is as relevant as the business life cycle. To succeed in the marketplace, both must be carefully integrated and orchestrated, as covered in Chapter 5.

It's to nobody's surprise that the same applies to the accompanying sourcing strategy. Combining an innovative business model with an emergent technology that is sourced from an external partner is a popular way to create new sources of future company value. Depending on the technology density, dynamics, and complexity of the existing business model, the client company is either well-equipped to manage the accompanying risks effectively or prone to grossly underestimate them and end up in the valley of despair, which is often followed by the trough of disillusionment.[9]

When Oculus Rift introduced its virtual reality solution, Facebook faced the choice to either defend its current business model and channels (e.g., website, app) or embrace the new technology as an additional channel to reach existing and new customers. Facebook chose to embrace the channel and bought the company in 2014. Founded in 2004 and, thus, a relatively young native digital company itself, Facebook understands how to turn an emergent technology into NPV-positive cash flows.

Client companies with a long and stable history that either acquire a born digital start-up or collaborate with an external partner with a similar background and capabilities must find an effective way to bridge the considerable cultural and organizational gap. As mentioned before, foundation IT is fundamentally different from entrepreneurial IT and must be sourced and managed accordingly.

In time, the emerging technology either commoditizes, is replaced by a better substitute (e.g., Windows CE by iOS and Android), or becomes obsolete before reaching commodity status (e.g., Microsoft Surface table). The sourcing strategy for the technologies that survive the shakeout slowly shifts from product innovation toward product features and enhancements to eventually cost reduction, as seen in Table A.4.

Unfortunately, obsolesce before reaching commodity status is on the rise. Repeating a quote from Chapter 1 of *The End of Competitive Advantage: How to Keep Your Strategy Moving as Fast as Your Business* by Rita McGrath:[xi] *"The list of once-storied organizations that are either gone or no longer relevant is a long one. Their downfall is a predictable outcome of practices that are designed around the concept of sustainable competitive advantage. The fundamental problem is that deeply ingrained structures and systems designed to extract maximum value from a competitive advantage become a liability when the environment requires instead the capacity to surf through waves of short-lived opportunities."*

Every business model will eventually be disrupted. In time, no competitive advantage is sustainable—they are transient. The only variable is the velocity of change in that particular industry or market segment.

---

[9] The valley of despair refers to the performance dip that companies should expect to experience during and after a large change is implemented. The lower the technology density, dynamics, and complexity of the current business model, the longer and more severe the performance dip. If you fail to recover from the dip before the patience of the board runs out, the investment will slide down the trough of disillusionment of the Gartner hype cycle that was covered in Chapter 5.

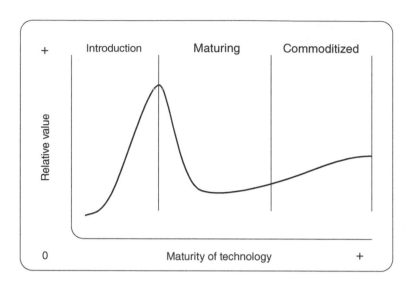

Table A.4   Mapping sourcing benefits and risks to the technology life cycle

	Key Sourcing Objectives	Sourcing Benefits	Specific Sourcing Risk
Introduction	• Quickly launch a (disruptive) digital or hybrid business model and/or value proposition • Add differentiating technology features to existing value proposition	Primary: • Speed-to-market • Create or enter new market • Reduce investment risk Secondary: • Access to disruptive/innovative expertise, skills, or solutions	• Unrealistic expectations of benefits • Operational issues (e.g., availability of expertise, quality) due to lack of practice for external partner • No or limited substitute external partners
Maturing	• Leverage on technology that *won the race* (e.g., process innovation, aggressive cost reduction, differentiating features, and enhancements) • Fast follow successful start-ups	Primary: • Additional revenue (e.g., enter adjoining market) • Improve margins Secondary: • Access to complementary expertise, skills, and solutions	• If technology *lost the race*: cost and risks related to exiting current contract and transition to *winner*. • Operational issues

Commoditized	• Augment non-distinctive business and IT capabilities • Reduce business and IT cost while maintaining quality levels	Primary: • Additional revenue (e.g., enter adjoining market) Secondary: • Access to best practices (e.g., productivity, quality, and security)	• Hold on to custom (proprietary) solution for too long • Integrating and/or data exchange between SaaS solutions

A symmetric, innovative, and win-win orientated network of external partners allows the client company to surf more effectively through those waves of short-lived opportunities, while sharing the accompanying risks and benefits with the other network partners. To do so, the client company needs to invest in professionals who are capable of deploying agile, innovation-driven sourcing processes; professionals who are able to provide the client company with scalability without traditional linear investments in human resources and assets; and professionals who use automated processes to source and settle non-critical services and manage their performance and spending.

The future belongs to sourcing professionals who continuously invest in honing their skills and knowledge; while the future looks grim for those procurement officers who are perpetuating what worked in the past.

The external partner faces a similar challenge—captured by the following quote from Phil Fersht and Jamie Snowdon from the services research company Horses for Sources:[xii] *"The difference between a new style of automation-rich intelligent operations and offshore-centric traditional operations is growing. It's a bit like comparing the growth of Walmart to that of Amazon—(although it has started to change with its belated online strategy and acquisition of Jet.com)."*

A.4 FROM THE FAR EAST TO THE ONSITE ROBOT

Coca Cola was relatively late to adopt cloud computing when it started moving non-critical applications to a private environment at the beginning of 2014. The move was part of a broader transformation that was initiated by CIO Onyeka Nchege in order to change the focus from technology to business value.

As explained in Chapter 2, these transformations require, first and foremost, team members with the right attitude and skill set—reflected by the following quote from Nchege:[xiii] *"What I will be looking for in my team are IT associates that are facing my business partners and spend all of their time understanding business processes and translating that to services. That's essentially what we're recruiting for today—resources that can span from business perspective and have a strong technical aptitude."*

When these business-savvy resources decide to buy instead of make, they will be looking for an external partner that both talks the same talk and walks the talk. Talk that is flavored not only by the emphasis on delivering tangible business value, but also by the state-of-the-art technologies that are required to do so. Augmented reality, artificial intelligence, big data, and robotics are shaping and reshaping both analog and digital business models. Quoting an article from McKinsey on workplace automation:[xiv] *". . . researchers at Oxford University, collaborating with Google's DeepMind division, created a deep-learning system that can read lips more accurately than human lip readers—by training it, using BBC closed-captioned news video. Similarly, robot 'skin' is able to 'feel' textures and find objects by touch, and robots are becoming more adept at physical tasks (such as tying a shoelace) that require fine motor skills."*

External partners with a long history and delivery model that is based on labor arbitrage have the choice to either embrace this new reality and reinvent their business model or try to stay afloat in a red ocean with its race-to-the-bottom tactics.

Automation Anywhere, IPSoft, IBM, and Blue Prism are part of a fast-growing group of external partners who are investing in potential blue oceans. IBM is clearly trying to dominate the artificial intelligence market by investing billions in its Watson platform. Many of the 6,000+ client companies that are using the cognitive platform even keep their use under wraps to remain ahead of the competition.[xv] This is what it means to add business value as an external partner.

These and other technology-enabled business models are reshaping the traditional sourcing market. With robotic process automation and cognitive computing, labor and business output are decoupled, dramatically reducing the cost per transaction. Computers don't need to sleep, don't get sick, nor do they go on vacation. Infosys partnering with IPSoft and Genpact with Automation Anywhere are only two of the dozens of partnerships that are aimed at staying competitive in the BPO space.

The Internet of Things (IoT) is another battleground. To counter the declining revenue and profit streams from AT&T's traditional business model, the company decided around 2014 to invest in the IoT to turn the tide.[xvi] With AT&T Digital Life services, customers are offered highly automated home security and climate control services, using Infosys to provide billing and web solutions on a pay-per-use basis. For several years, General Electric (GE) and its external partner Genpact processed and analyzed the data sent back by sensors that were embedded in jet engines powering Boeing and Airbus airplanes. In 2016, GE took the next logical step when it announced the GE Digital Alliance Program, a digital industrial platform dedicated to connecting its network of external partners.[xvii] *"The program is designed to connect systems integrators, telecommunications service providers, independent software vendors, technology providers, and resellers with the technology and digital industrial expertise of GE."*

Ethereum, Hyperledger (Sawtooth Lake), Multichain, IBM Bluemix Blockchain, HydraChain, and Open Chain invest millions in Blockchain platforms—each striving for a dominant position in this emerging market. Blockchain holds the promise of reshaping the organization of supply chains, frictionless multi-party financial transactions, decentralization of business processes, and more effective tracking of tangible assets. Which client company can resist its promise?

As these and other waves are still gaining momentum, many opportunities remain unidentified and unfulfilled. It is, therefore, still undecided which incumbent external partners or new entrants will dominate in the coming years. The winners in the *as-a-service* world are the ones who are able to turn technology into a blue ocean. External partners who are able to:[xviii] create and capture new demand, break the value-cost trade-off, and create uncontested market space will make the competition irrelevant.

REFERENCES

i. Treacy, M. and Wiersema, F. (January–February 1993). Customer Intimacy and Other Value Disciplines. Harvard Business Review.

ii. Su, N., Levina, N. and Ross, J. (Winter 2016). The Long-Tail Strategy for IT Outsourcing. *Sloan Management Review Magazine*. Link: http://sloanreview.mit.edu/article/the-long-tail-strategy-for-it-outsourcing/.

iii. Kraljic, P. (1983). Purchasing Must Become Supply Management. Harvard Business Review. 61 (5), pp. 109–117.

iv. Buchanan, L. (1992). Vertical Trade Relationships: The Role of Dependence and Symmetry in Attaining Organizational Goals. *Journal of Marketing Research 29*, pp. 65–75.

v. Caniels, M. and Gelderman, C. (2005). Purchasing Strategies in the Kraljic Matrix—A Power and Dependence Perspective. *Journal of Purchasing & Supply Management 11*, pp. 141–155.

vi. Reuters, (January 22, 2017). Foxconn CEO Says Investment for Display Plant in U.S. Would Exceed $7 Billion. Fortune website. Link: http://fortune.com/2017/01/22/foxconn-ceo-says-investment-for-display-plant-in-u-s-would-exceed-7-billion/.

vii. Rietveld, G. (2009). Purchasing, A New Paradigm. https://www.bol.com/nl/c/algemeen/gerco-j-rietveld/6190325/index.html?lastId=8299.

viii. Seddon, P., Cullen, S. and Willocks, L. (2007). Does Domberger's Theory of 'The Contracting Organization' Explain Why Organizations Outsource IT and the Levels of Satisfaction Achieved? *European Journal of Information Systems 16*, pp. 237–253.

ix. Shah, R. (2015). Divestures Key Part of Strategy: IBM CEO Rometty. CNBC website. Link: http://www.cnbc.com/2015/11/03/ibm-ceo-said -sometimes-size-matters.html.

x. Future proof infrastructure, the cloud for building what's next. (Accessed July 2017). Link: https://cloud.google.com/why-google/future-proof/.

xi. McGrath, R. (2013). *The End of Competitive Advantage: How to Keep Your Strategy Moving as Fast as Your Business.*

xii. Fersht, P. and Snowdon, J. (January 2017). Offshore has become Walmart . . . as Outsourcing becomes more like Amazon. Link: http:// www.horsesforsources.com/offshore-walmart_011817.

xiii. Murphy, M. (June 17, 2014). Coca-Cola CIO: Cloud Allows Me to Transform My IT Team Into Business Professionals. Computerworld UK online. Link: http://www.cio.com/article/2375411/cloud-computing/ coca-cola-cio—cloud-allows-me-to-transform-my-it-team-into-business -professionals.html.

xiv. Chui, M., George, K. and Miremadi, M. (July 2017). A CEO Action Plan for Workplace Automation. McKinsey Quarterly. Link: http:// www.mckinsey.com/global-themes/digital-disruption/a-ceo-action -plan-for-workplace-automation.

xv. Technative, IBM UK's Watson Lead Explains Why AI Offers an Edge on Competitors (Accessed: June 2017). Link: https://www.technative.io/ibm -uks-head-of-watson-explains-why-ai-offers-an-edge-on-competitors/.

xvi. Sood, V. (September 2014). Wipro, Infosys Turn to Centralised Computing as Telcos Cut Spend on Common Outsourcing Deals. Link: http:// articles.economictimes.indiatimes.com/2014-09-10/news/53770470 _1_infosys-and-wipro-tom-reuner-revenues.

xvii. Sarosiek, A. (February 2016). GE Digital Unveils Global Alliance Program, Forms New Collaborations on the Heels of Predix Platform General Availability, to Spur Industrial Internet Growth,' GE Digital Press release. Link: http://www.genewsroom.com/press-releases/ge-digital-unveils-global -alliance-program-forms-new-collaborations-heels-predix

xviii. Kim, W. and Mauborgne, R. (2005). *Blue Ocean Strategy.*

B

WANTED ALIVE: ARCHITECT WHO LOOKS BEYOND TOGAF

"Architecture is a rare collective profession: it's always exercised by groups. There is an essential modesty, which is a complete contradiction to the notion of a star."
Rem Koolhaas—architect, architectural theorist, and urbanist.

In some aspects, the building block of *Key Resources and Architecture* is the most important one of the IT business model (see Figure 6.2) because it forms the foundation from which to create new innovative strategies, business models, and value propositions. The first part of the building block, key resources, is embodied by the principle *less defensive, more offensive* and was covered in Chapter 2. However, besides leadership, culture, and skills, there is also a *hard* part to this building block—architecture.

Architecture as a discrete topic is one of the fruits of the effort to govern and manage IT more effectively. It was first mentioned by Amdahl et al. in the IBM research paper 'Architecture of the IBM System/360' in 1964 and defined as:[i] *"the conceptual structure and functional behavior, distinguishing the organization of data flows and controls, logical design, and physical implementation."* Since then, architecture has matured into an impressive body of knowledge, used and continuously refined by thousands of practitioners and academics.

Decisions that are based on the advice of architects have a tremendous impact in terms of both money and time. The decision to choose SAP over Oracle has a lifespan of at least a decade. Should we make the decision to adopt .NET, Java, or PHP to develop future business applications? The implications of this choice can be even longer lasting, as COBOL (short for common business-oriented language) was designed in 1959, but many critical back-office processes still rely on applications that were written in this venerable language.

Consequently, investing in the wrong emerging technology or a botched enterprise resource planning (ERP) implementation tend to be tremendous drains on money, time, energy, and motivation.

Spending $400 million to upgrade Nike's supply-chain systems was *rewarded* with class-action suits, $100 million in lost sales and a 20% stock dip.[ii] Corporations loved the enterprise server approach of BlackBerry because it allowed the security team to control almost every aspect of the mobile communication by employees. Selling more than 50 million devices in 2011, BlackBerry, however, failed to keep up with the times, forcing companies to write off the platform and invest in the Apple and/or Android ecosystems.

A paper by Yampolskiy and Spellchecker provides several examples of artificial intelligence (AI) gone wrong. Mistakes during the design phase (e.g., algorithms) or learning phase (e.g., lack of diverse data) resulted in a bias or even racism (e.g., Microsoft's chat bot Tay, First International Beauty Contest judged by AI, Northpointe's crime prediction system).[iii] AI is still an emerging technology. For at least another century, the catchy headline *"robots will wipe out humans"* is just that—a catchy headline.

While it would be unfair to blame the architect for any of these failures, it would be an equally bad practice for an architect to solely focus on technology and technology standards. Like everybody else in the team, the architect must add tangible business value as the company moves from opportunity to opportunity. This includes opportunities within the traditional boundaries of its own industry, and increasingly, outside of those boundaries. Amazon, for example, started as an online bookstore, but now competes with Apple and Google in the consumer electronics space, with Microsoft for cloud domination, and has become a direct challenger of Walmart after acquiring Whole Foods Market in 2017. Amazon is not the only one. Of the 300 CEO's across 37 sectors that were interviewed by McKinsey about data analytics, one-third had cross-sector dynamics at the top of their agenda.[iv]

Only for the most stable secondary business processes can the architect fall back on the traditional practices that are related to foundation IT and the accompanying strictly enforced rules. However, this is a small and declining part of the technology garden. The largest and most productive part of the garden is faced with a difficult-to-predict combination of sun, rain, and the occasional hail storm. The future looks grim for the introvert, ivory-tower architect and bright for the holistic, extrovert, business-savvy technologist and *team player*. Like urban development, digitalization is also exercised by groups.

The good news is that the architects themselves are questioning their traditional practices. In their blog post *In Praise of Heuristics—or Saving TOGAF from Its Friends* on Opengroup.org, Boardman and Harrington emphasize the need for enterprise architects to be critical thinkers instead of blindly slapping

TOGAF standards[1] onto their organizations. The world has become too unpredictable for this approach, as they argue that[v] *"understanding, accepting, and taking advantage of the presence of uncertainty is essential for any organization today. This would be true even if it were only because of the accelerating rate of change. But more than that, we need to recognize that the way we do business is changing, that agile organizations encourage emergence, and that success means letting go of hard and fast rules. Enterprise architects, to be useful, have to work with this new model, not to be risk averse, and to learn from (shared) experience."*

Hence, the job of an architect is far from boring and the first part of this appendix is dedicated to the opportunity to develop from a bureaucratic policy enforcer into a leader who adds tangible business value. The second part explores ways to push architecture beyond the traditional practices, a key requirement when the external environment is in a state of constant flux. The appendix ends with several key technology-driven trends that require an effective response from the architect. See Table B.1 for three statements that cover the chapter as a whole.

Table B.1   Statements to think about when reading this chapter

Statements
The architect is responsible for the technology portfolio of the company.
Every IT project should comply to the same set of company-wide architecture principles.
Because they are best practices, every company should implement TOGAF or a similar architecture framework.

B.1 FROM ENFORCING POLICIES TO LEADING THE WAY

The technology domain expands at light speed in two dimensions. First, is the variation of technologies. From the choice between COBOL or FORTRAN (derived from formula translation) to hundreds of development languages; or going from mainframes to the options of thousands of mobile and non-mobile computing devices.

Second, the update frequency for each technology increases exponentially. In the old days, it was common to have one or two application releases per year.

---

[1] TOGAF stands for The Open Group Architecture Framework and provides an approach to design, implement, and govern a multilayered architecture (e.g., business architecture, application architecture, data architecture, and technical architecture).

Today, the Microsoft team deploys up to 15 new Azure releases per month. In an article on release frequencies in general by Novak,[vi] 11% of the respondents released multiple times per day in 2015 (from 4% in 2014), 19% released multiple times a week (from 7%), and 27% released on a weekly basis (from 17%). There is even talk about release cycles of minutes.

Due to these two trends, the architect risks an *information overload*: "*a term used to describe the difficulty of understanding an issue and effectively making decisions when one has too much information about that issue.*"[vii] Which of the thousands of articles, social media feeds, and books should I read or which YouTube videos should I watch? How can I identify those technologies and innovations that are most relevant to my company? When is the right moment to invest in a proof of concept? What is the best approach to convince the rest of my organization of the business value of a new technology or innovation?[2]

Depending on the technology density of the company's business model, the architect's ability to answer these questions is either a *nice-to-have* or a crucial *must-have*.

The business perspective of the technology garden cultivated by the architect is also captured by Figure B.1. It uses the analogy of home construction to translate changes in the external environment to the domain of the architect. Assuming the house is built near the sea, this includes mitigating the risks related to sea level rises.

Depending on the likelihood and impact of the scenario, the current owner, his children, or his grandchildren should worry. A 50% chance of a one-meter rise in the next 20 years is a very different scenario than a 5% chance of a one-centimeter rise in the next 200 years. In the latter case, no immediate action is required, while an investment in a dike around the house would be adequate to mitigate the impact in the first scenario. However, there is also a tiny chance of a positive feedback loop in nature whereby the whole arctic ice shelf would eventually melt. If this Black Swan event were to become a reality, the sea level at that particular location would rise by more than ten meters.[3]

---

[2] Even something as technical as an application programming interface (API) can be a huge driver of business value. According to Iyer and Subramaniam, Salesforce generated 50% of its revenue through APIs in 2015, and Expedia 90%. (Source: Iyer, B. and Subramaniam, M. "The Strategic Value of APIs," Harvard Business Review, January 2015. Link: https://hbr.org/2015/01/the-strategic-value-of-apis).

[3] The actual definition of a Black Swan is: "*the impossibility of calculating the risks of consequential rare events and predicting their occurrence. Sensitivity to harm from volatility is tractable, more so than forecasting the event that would cause the harm.*" Hence, the likelihood of the occurrence itself, the number of meters, and the time frame of this type of sea level rise cannot be accurately predicted. Only the harmful impact of such an event on the house can be forecasted. (Source: Taleb, N. *Antifragile: Things That Gain From Disorder*, 2012).

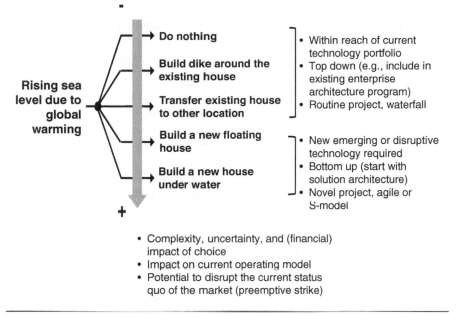

Figure B.1   How a holistic architect tackles a problem

No technology in the current portfolio of the construction company that was hired to advise the homeowner can mitigate the effect of this Black Swan event. It is completely outside of the capability of its current technology portfolio. A floating house would already stretch the available emerging technologies, but would be feasible if the company is willing to invest.

Building a house underwater requires the company to start with a clean sheet of paper, inventing many of the necessary technologies from scratch. It would be a *bet-the-company* business decision for the construction company.

A small investment in a proof of concept to demonstrate the feasibility of the technology that would be required to build a floating house would already position the company well ahead of most competitors in case of a sudden and dramatic sea-level rise. Based on the current climate models, only the most bullish investor would sign the check that would be required to establish a sustainable underwater community.

The IT architect faces a similar challenge. Here, a combination of emerging technologies, disruptive business models, and customers faced with an abundance of choice and desire for instant gratification generate a wider spread of more extreme business scenarios.

The line between a flop and a runaway success is very thin these days. Hence, the more technology rich the business model, the more important the ability of the architect to think strategically, including scenario planning.[4]

In addition to the tools provided in the previous chapters, Table B.2 depicts the key focal points and the likely role of the architect based on the technology density of the business model and the three basic strategic choices that are available for a company to compete. The investment orientation (e.g., experiments, transformation, renewal, and process improvement) is covered in Chapter 4 and Figure 4.2c, while the roles of the architect (e.g., innovator, strategist, technologist, and enabler) are based on Figure 2.2 in Chapter 2.

The application of the situational roles of a CIO to the architect is a conscious decision. In companies that depend on technology for their future success, all human key resources must demonstrate situational leadership. The architect is one of those key resources.

The two diagonally most opposite quadrants in Table B.2 are *product leadership—digital business model* and *operational excellence—analog business model*. The first has the strongest focus on technology-enabled innovation and entrepreneurship. The architect and the other team members fuse business and technology capabilities to create new products or to access new markets, spending a considerable part of the available budget on experiments (e.g., low-cost, rapid-fire proof of concepts, and pilot projects on popular platforms) in order to stay ahead or at least on par with the competition. Consequently, the most important situational role of the architect in this quadrant is the innovator, due to its focus on generating business value from technology in a dynamic and difficult-to-predict business environment.

In a company with an analog business model striving for cost leadership, IT supports the business. The convergence or fusion of the previous quadrant is replaced by the business IT alignment paradigm, including the accompanying focus on efficiency, risk-averseness, robustness, and use of mature commoditized technologies. The centralized IT function spends most of its available investment and operating budget on renewal: shared applications with a long life cycle. However, as analog business models are heading the same way the dinosaurs did some 66 million years ago, the architect must track and act on those technologies and digital business models that may disrupt the current operating model. The architect is a technologist and potential future strategist.

To complicate things further, situational leadership—or in this case, situational architecture—implies that there is no single *best* architecture.

---

[4] Also called scenario analysis or scenario thinking, scenario planning is a strategic method to make flexible long-term plans. It provides senior decision makers with a structure to think about the future. See also the real options approach covered in Chapter 7, as it has a similar objective.

Table B.2   From business context to the role of the architect

	Product Leadership	Customer Intimacy	Operational Excellence
Digital	• Inventor or early adopter/fast follower of new technologies that enable new products or access to new markets • Invest in experiments • Architect is an innovator	• Early adopter/fast follower of new technologies that transform customer experience • Invest in experiments (customer-facing) and process improvements (back end) • Architect as a strategist	• Early adopter/fast follower of new technologies that decouple labor and business output (e.g., robotic process automation) or break the value-cost trade-off • Invest in transformations • Architect as an enabler and part-time innovator
Hybrid	• Fast follower new technologies enabling differentiating new product features • Invest in mix of experiments (digital products, features, and channels) and process improvements (back end) • Architect as a strategist and part-time innovator	• Fast follower new technologies for customer-facing part of the business model • Invest in experiments (customer-facing) and process improvement (back end) • Architect as a strategist and part-time technologist	• Fast follower new technologies promising a dramatic increase in productivity • Invest in transformation and renewal • Architect as an enabler
Analog	• Sense and act on technologies that may disrupt the product portfolio and business model • Invest in process improvements and occasional experiment • Architect as a technologist and potential future innovator/strategist	• Sense and act on technologies that may disrupt the customer-facing part of the business model • Invest in process improvements and occasional experiment • Architect as an enabler and potential future strategist	• Sense and act on technologies that may disrupt the current operating model • Invest in renewal and occasional experiment • Architect as a technologist and potential future strategist

B.1.1 Situational Architecture

An effective architecture is context-aware; and the most successful architects are those who adapt their leadership style, vision, principles, and solutions to the continually evolving external environment, business strategy, and business model. An effective architect understands the (im)possibilities of the existing architecture and can anticipate both the short- and long-term business objectives that need to be accomplished.

A simple example of a context-aware architecture is the practice to separate internet-facing business-to-consumer (B2C) and business-to-business (B2B) portals and apps from the back-office applications that contain most of the data and business rules. Especially in technology-rich markets with supply outstripping demand, customers expect a digital *wow* factor. An easy to navigate, responsive website and a regularly updated mobile app are mere dissatisfiers. To satisfy, let alone delight, the company must anticipate the wants and needs of every individual customer, which requires a 360-degree customer view. Needs and wants are in a constant state of flux—requiring a continuously evolving flow of new features, content, and technology.

The rate of change faced by the average back-office application is a magnitude lower. At the latest, two or three years after the initial development started, the release frequency can be scaled down to monthly or even quarterly releases. Compared to the customer-facing functions like marketing, sales, outbound logistics,[5] and after-sales service, the business activities that are related to manufacturing, inbound logistics, and human resources are relatively stable.

To make entrepreneurial IT and foundation IT play nicely together is complicated enough in a *green-field* situation. It gets really complicated for companies with a long history as they are *blessed* with a diverse and aging application landscape. Those applications that were built before the late 1980s pre-date the dawn of the Information Age and the accompanying internet technologies. Besides lacking modern communication mechanisms (e.g., API's using REST or SOAP),[6] they also come with aging user interfaces and a traditional authorization structure.

Nevertheless, the business case to convert the legacy code or replace the application with a standard commercial off-the-shelf (COTS) solution is not straightforward.

With a one-on-one conversion, the user gets exactly the same from a functional standpoint. Only the underpinning technology and user interface are modernized (e.g., from a server-client application in COBOL to a web front end in PHP and a back end written in Java). For this reason, it is a scenario that is typically only considered when the last two remaining application engineers start to celebrate their 60+ birthdays. At that point, the operational risk becomes too high to maintain the status quo.

---

[5] Think of using drones, robots delivering packages, blockchain, Amazon Prime, and Amazon Go.

[6] API: Application programming interface; REST: Representational state transfer; SOAP: Simple object access protocol. See also Appendix C—Glossary.

Replacing a custom legacy back-office application with a state-of-the-art standard COTS, software as a service (SaaS), or on-premise solution seems, at first sight, a far more attractive scenario—and dozens of external IT partners are ready to promise you the sun, the moon, and the stars.

However, the stories about failed SaaS and on-premise ERP and customer relationship management initiatives are abundant enough to illustrate the actual risk profile of the initiative. In many cases, the external IT partner either underestimates the complexity of the business rules and functionalities that are embedded in the existing custom application or they overestimate the ability of its own platform to configure or model them. While a 20-year-old legacy application likely contains *dead code* and rarely or never-used features, there will still be a huge number of features that are used on a daily basis. And as practitioners know, with custom applications, the devil is in the details.

A context-aware or situational architecture from a strategic perspective is captured by Figure B.2. The vertical axis captures the maturity of the technology-related capabilities that are relative to the maturity that is required to remain competitive. The latter, represented by the market perspective on the horizontal axis, is an indicator of the technology-related rate of change induced by existing competitors and new entrants.

Established companies with analog business models reside in the bottom left quadrant and get disrupted by start-ups that are entering the bottom right quadrant. At that point, the incumbent is forced toward the top right quadrant, as seen in Figure B.3. The company must change, but is unsure of what to do. It suddenly went from independent to dependent and the business and the IT team are both desperate for a paternalistic or even authoritarian leader to guide them safely out of the sudden hailstorm.

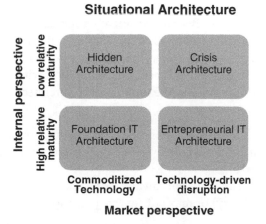

Figure B.2   Situational architecture

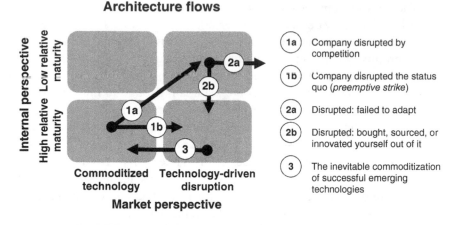

Figure B.3   Several scenarios that an architecture can evolve

In the quadrant called foundation IT architecture, the architect focuses on efficiency, predictability, control, and standardization. The architect manages. When faced with a technology-induced crisis, the company looks at the architect for leadership. Which emerging technologies should be invested in? Is it best to build, source, or buy the necessary capabilities and competencies? While the architect may not make the final decision, the executives who do will be all ears.

Hence, the future belongs to architects who can both manage and lead, as according to Peter Drucker:[viii] "*Management is doing things right; leadership is doing the right things.*" Due to advances in AI and cognitive computing, the management component will slowly shrink, emphasizing the ability of an architect to lead.

Moving back to Figure B.3, the arrows are a representation of the principle *less static, more flow* that was covered in Chapter 5. Both the architect and the company's architecture must evolve, driven by the technology life cycle and/or the business life cycle. As mentioned, the center of gravity of the incumbents' IT landscape tends to reside in the foundation IT architecture quadrant. From there, the incumbent can either:

- Reframe its belief set, expand beyond existing boundaries, and pursue new opportunities—thereby proactively disrupting the status quo (*preemptive strike*), or
- Be disrupted by a new entrant and face a crisis—which the company may (e.g., BlackBerry) or may not survive (e.g., Kodak and Yahoo).

For the survivors, the circle of life and death is never-ending. Even Yahoo, a native digital company, was unable to innovate and buy itself out of the crisis that was caused by the rise of Google and Facebook. Their technology-enabled business models turned out to be more effective in monetizing online advertising. However, there is no telling whether Google or Facebook face a similar fate somewhere in the coming two decades; hence, the *relative* maturity on the vertical axis in Figures B.2 and B.3.

A side effect of this technology-driven circle of life is the increased added value of architects. The impact of the architect's decisions and advice on the company's future revenue and profit streams shows a strong upward trend with no indication of leveling off. That is, *if* the architect is up to the task—which brings us to the next topic.

B.1.2 Hidden Architecture

A special place in Figure B.2 is reserved for the quadrant *hidden architecture*. It refers to a relative immaturity at two levels: business unit and corporate. At the business unit level, the consumerization of B2B IT solutions that are enabled by the cloud and other technologies allows the business to buy and use without even informing the corporate IT team. Technology has democratized and continues to do so.

While the cloud and other IT solutions provide a quick fix, there are several caveats of these often hidden, feudal, or even anarchistic governance archetypes.[7] The first downside of cloud solutions is captured by Michael Relich, the former CIO of clothing retailer Guess:[ix] *"It's getting more complex because it's proliferating. I call it cockroach technology."*

The SaaS market particularly is highly specialized, resulting in fragmentation, duplication, and integration issues. Of the 674 senior executives who participated in a KPMG survey conducted in 2013, 31% found the integration of the cloud to be more difficult than anticipated and 33% reported higher than expected implementation costs.[x] Even more tangible are the following two quotes from business executives who rely on multiple SaaS solutions for their day-to-day activities:[xi]

---

[7] Weill and Ross introduced six governance archetypes in their article 'A Matrixed Approach to Designing IT Governance,' published in the *MIT Sloan Management Review* magazine in 2005. Quoting from the article: "*In a feudal system, business unit or process leaders make separate decisions on the basis of the unit or process needs. [. . .] the most decentralized system is anarchy, in which each individual user or small group pursues his, her, or their own IT agenda.*" Link: http://sloanreview.mit .edu/article/a-matrixed-approach-to-designing-it-governance/.

- *"The frustration is to get everything to talk with each other and sync. Everything is manually entered. It is hours every day for sure."* The owner of Arctic Spas Utah, a company that specializes in spa installations, requires eight SaaS applications to automate the company's end-to-end value chain.
- *"It is very difficult to move data, and very easy to lose it. I spend at least an hour each month maintaining the data between just two of the cloud-based apps I use."* The marketing director of Tour Operator GoCar must use seven SaaS business applications on a daily basis to do his job.

Besides the waste resulting from the introduction of non-value-add complexity, many business executives tend to underestimate the risks associated with the cloud. On paper, you own the data and company-specific business logic, but the reality is more complex and expensive. If you use proprietary application-specific services—such as databases and application development platforms from Microsoft, Amazon, or Google—you get locked in. These features are a great source of short-term benefit, but an equally great source of long-term risk.

Here is another example. For Azure, availability levels max out at 99.9% for single virtual machines, while Amazon S3 uses a service-credit mechanism to compensate for any availability below 100%. As these numbers are impressive enough for all but the most demanding business applications, business executives may decide to move all of their business unit specific applications to the cloud.

However, while the internet itself is designed to reroute around damage, the cloud is not. Due to a scripting error by an Amazon engineer, SoundCloud and Imgur were offline for more than three hours in February of 2017, while Pinterest, Airbnb, Netflix, Slack, and Spotify experienced slowdowns. According to Dave Bartoletti, a cloud analyst with Forrester, the outage took 148,213 sites down, including three to four trillion pieces of data.[xii] When a large Amazon S3, Google, IBM, or Azure site goes down, the impact is immense.

What if one of your SaaS providers went bankrupt? Code Space is a former SaaS provider that failed within six months after it got hacked via its Amazon Web Service (AWS) control panel. According to *SC Magazine*,[xiii] *"the hackers erased data, backups, offsite backups, and machine configurations before attempting to extort the business by claiming a "large fee" would resolve their issues."* Just imagine the impact if Code Space was a key partner of one or more business units for your company.

Another example is the failure of cloud storage firm Nirvanix. When it decided to close its virtual doors, customers were given two weeks to move their data out of its data centers.[xiv] With some business units sitting on Petabytes of data, two weeks allows you to transfer maybe 5%. Can the business unit and the parent company survive without the other 95%? As both the application and data are kept off-premise, the bankruptcy of a SaaS provider can push a company toward an earnings crisis or even liquidity crisis.

Cloud computing is not alone; AI, Blockchain, Robotic Process Automation, and other promising technology-enabled concepts are a source of both considerable future benefits *and risks*. In an ideal world, they would be treated accordingly, with the business executives seeking advice from the architect, sourcing professional, and other specialists.

However, most front-line business executives are too busy with achieving their short-term business goals and profit targets to comprehend the long-term consequences of their IT decisions. Furthermore, over the years the architects slowly but surely created an ivory tower image—*extending* rather than *closing* the gap between the business and IT. As a result, the architect is in a pickle.

The business needs speed-to-market and flexibility in order to react effectively on new market opportunities and threats, and won't accept the top-down strait jacket of the traditional ivory tower architect. The *do nothing* scenario is equally unattractive, as an unmanaged feudal or anarchy governance structure results in an unsustainable mishmash of centralized and decentralized technologies, architectures, solutions, and external partners.

How does a business find the right balance between a bottom-up or emergent business strategy[8] with the accompanying emergent architecture and a top-down intended business strategy with the resulting more mature architectures?

First and foremost, a successful outcome depends on the leadership qualities of the architect. As was covered in Chapter 2, highly skilled, creative, and motivated team members don't accept an authoritarian approach. They are no longer impressed by the fact that you are from *headquarters* and do not believe that you should, therefore, be obeyed blindly and unconditionally. High-performance business professionals want to be treated as equals and expect the architect to understand and appreciate the day-to-day business challenges that they face. They expect an architect who scores high on both intelligence quotient and emotional quotient.

In addition to highly developed soft skills, the architect should be able to select the optimal mix of soft controls and hard controls in order to ensure *most* of

---

[8] With an intended strategy, the company's mission is translated into objectives, which in turn, are translated into strategies and tactics in order to realize them. An emergent strategy is more bottom-up, whereby actions and decisions taken by frontline teams over time condense into a strategy. According to Mintzberg and Waters, five kinds of strategies can be identified: emergent strategy, intended strategy, deliberate strategy, realized strategy, and unrealized strategy (Source: Mintzberg, H. and Waters, J. [1985]. Of Strategies, Deliberate and Emergent. *Strategic Management Journal, 6*, 257–72).

the architecture of the business units and, thus, the company as a whole resides in one or two of the mature quadrants of Figure B.2.

To support an architect who possesses the required soft skills, the second part of this appendix introduces several practices and tools to fulfill the desire of the customer facing business units for speed-to-market, agility, and innovation in combination with the company-wide need for control, effectiveness, and efficiency.

B.2 ARCHITECTURE BEYOND BUSINESS IT ALIGNMENT

Arisen from the same cradle as the business IT alignment framework from Henderson and Venkatraman,[xv] most architecture frameworks (e.g., Zachman Framework, TOGAF, EA3, and ISO/IEC 42010:2007) are optimized for a relatively stable external environment and, consequently, share the breadth and depth of the Control Objectives for Information and Related Technology, the Information Technology Infrastructure Library, and the ISO 27000 family.[9]

The core element of every modern architecture framework is the enterprise architecture (EA) and according to Bernard,[xvi] an EA is "*an ongoing management program that provides a strategic, integrated approach to capability and resource planning/decision making. An EA program is part of an overall governance process that determines resource alignment, develops standardized policy, enhances decision support, and guides development activities.*"

The definition of EA that is found on Wikipedia is equally comprehensive:[xvii] "*a well-defined practice for conducting enterprise analysis, design, planning, and implementation, using a holistic approach at all times, for the successful development and execution of strategy. Enterprise architecture applies architecture principles and practices to guide organizations through the business, information, process, and technology changes necessary to execute their strategies.*"

Hence, both definitions ooze the business IT alignment paradigm and thus foundation IT. As stated before, this is not necessarily a bad thing, unless you apply EA out-of-the-box on entrepreneurial IT, that is. But before covering that topic in more detail, let us first take a trip to the restaurant.

B.2.1 More Than One, Part 1

In Figure 8.2, the onion is used as a metaphor to translate the diversity and dynamics of the external environment into, eventually, the required skills and

---

[9] See the glossary in Appendix C for additional information on architecture standards.

competencies of individual team members. In a similar fashion, a drill down can be made from the company's strategy to the physical rack space in the data center, as seen in Figure B.4. To visualize the relation between the value streams of the business and underpinning IT architecture, the figures map the architecture domains (e.g., business, information, and technology) to the three benefit and risk universes introduced in Chapter 7—business, joint, and IT.

In architecture jargon, the business universe is governed by the business strategy and a set of underpinning principles and objectives (e.g., business, financial).[10] The joint universe is governed by information principles and objectives and, unsurprisingly, the IT universe by technology principles and objectives.

To operationalize this simplified version of the extensive theoretical body of knowledge on architecture, let's assume there are two restaurants in the same street, each with its own business strategy:

- Restaurant A: operational excellence strategy
- Restaurant B: customer intimacy strategy

In accordance with its strategy, the owner of Restaurant A defines the following key business principle for his restaurant: *"Meals are designed in such a way that they are cheap to produce and serve."* To operationalize this strategic business principle, it must be made *smart*:[11]

- Offer customers a maximum of ten standard meals to choose from.
- Sell the meals at or below the price point of the three nearest competitors.
- Serve the meals via only two channels: eat in the restaurant or use a drive-through for vehicles.

The key value driver of this business model's building block *revenue streams* will be the number of meals sold, and all of the marketing efforts are focused toward achieving that objective (e.g., *Wednesday: 10% discount on all meals,* and *Thursday: 15% discount on drinks).* The information principles and technology principles fit perfectly in the foundation IT domain, as will the sourcing strategy (e.g., lowest bidder passing the minimum qualitative score wins).

Due to the different business strategy, the principles of Restaurant B follow a different path. Not customer volume, but the customers' share of wallet is

---

[10] In real life, creating a business architecture is far more complex and, when applying TOGAF, includes activities like developing a baseline description, developing a target description, business modeling, gap analysis, defining road maps, resolving impact across the architecture landscape, a stakeholder review, and accessing and updating the architecture repository. The outputs of these activities include dozens of documents, diagrams, catalogs, process descriptions, and so on. However, due to the objective of this book, I took the liberty of minimizing the amount of architectural breadth and depth.

[11] Specific, measurable, acceptable, realistic, and time bound. See also Chapter 7.

Restaurant B

Business strategy

Customer Intimacy

Business principles

Meals are designed in such a way that customers can customize them (e.g., customer can select the ingredients of a meal).

Financial principles

Revenue streams are based on *lifetime value* for the customer (e.g., the more times the customer visits, the higher the discount).

Information principles

User-centered design is mandatory for all front-end applications (e.g., the design has to score at least 4 out of 5 stars or usability and simplicity)

The information presented to the customer is tuned to its preferences channel, and life-cycle phase (e.g., using the mobile phone, the customer can create custom dishes up to two days in advance and request the restaurant to start cooking when leaving the house).

Information regarding the *lifetime value* and life-cycle phase the customer is in is available to relevant employees at every touchpoint (e.g., the waiter is notified using near-field technology when the customer enters the parking area).

Technology principles

Application functionalities are structured in logical components and follow service oriented architecture principles (e.g., the payment module communicates via the shared enterprise service business with the other application components).

All technology platforms that offer digital B2C channels with more than 10% market share are supported with native apps. Others are enabled via a responsive website (e.g., native apps for Android and iOS, generic web apps for other platforms).

Business universe. Key components: business model (e.g., value propositions, key activities)

Joint universe. Key components: customer journeys, user stories, interaction design, data, and information flows/models

IT universe. Key components: applications, middleware, operating system, and infrastructure

Figure B.4   From business architecture principles to technology architecture principles

the key business value driver. Every technology investment should directly or indirectly contribute to the restaurants capability to (a) deliver a highly tailored and personalized service and (b) serve meals adapted to the specific needs and wants of the individual customer, as seen in Figure B.4.

In contrast to Restaurant A, Restaurant B has the choice to either pursue an analog or a hybrid customer intimacy strategy. There is a customer segment that seeks a classic old-school dining experience while another well-to-do customer segment wants an experience that combines a great meal with the convenience enabled by the consumerization of technology.

Restaurant A has no choice but to embrace technology to reduce cost (e.g., replace cashiers with kiosks that use touchscreen technology to order and pay). It is a prime example of the fundamental difference between a company pursuing a cost leadership strategy or a differentiation strategy. With the latter, the owner has more options available to set his business apart from the competition.

The overarching objective of the information architecture is providing an interface layer between the business team and IT. Both teams have to understand each other, regardless of the business strategy. Workshops, interviews, and desk research are used to translate the business objectives, business context, and high-level requirements into road maps, customer journeys, epics, user stories, interactive designs, data models, and other inputs that are required to develop both effectively (e.g., which user stories have the highest business value, relative importance of scalability, security, and reliability) and efficiently (e.g., optimal mix between senior and junior developers, optimal on-site/offshore mix).

It is the information architecture that transforms business demand and technology into a *form* that customers or business users are happy to use. Furthermore, the information architecture shields the business executives and business users from the technical complexity (e.g., two Java applications, one PHP application, four databases, six virtual machines, two firewalls) and organizational complexity (e.g., two internal development teams, one externally sourced development team, hybrid operations team). For the business, only the result matters: does the solution deliver on the promised business value, customer experience, and/or user experience?

The technical complexity and organizational complexity is the exclusive domain of the IT team, using practices that are related to the technical architecture to reduce the complexity to manageable proportions, as described in the following sections.

Compared to the difference between operational excellence and customer intimacy strategies, the difference between entrepreneurial IT and foundation IT is even more distinct.

B.2.2 More Than One, Part 2

To balance flexibility, speed-to-market, and innovation on the one hand and reliability, low risk, and efficiency on the other, Prahalad and Krishnan introduced the applications-infrastructure scorecard.[xviii] The scorecard provides the business team and IT team with a common framework to understand the capabilities, impediments, and risk profile of the company's information infrastructure.

Applications evolve from a high variance in user expectations and required innovation (*evolving domain*) to a focus on efficiency and accompanying low variance in user expectations (*stable domain*). According to the authors, three criteria are important when creating an application infrastructure that can accommodate evolving applications:

- The ability to connect seamlessly with existing applications,
- The ability to accommodate changes without incurring significant cost or time, and
- The ability to connect with multiple technology platforms to mitigate the risk of a vendor lock-in.

Often easier said than done when faced with a pre-Information Age application landscape, these criteria are nevertheless useful entrepreneurial IT architecture principles, as pointed out in the ensuing text.

The ability to deal with a high variance in user expectations and other sources of uncertainty and complexity is also at the core of lean architecture. In their book *Lean Architecture for Agile Software*, Coplien and Bjørnvig apply lean principles to architecture to make it less rigid and more porous. They champion a lightweight, up-front architecture that evolves over time, based on new insights—an architecture guided by the following principles:[xix]

- **Architecture is more about form than structure**: Focus on the shape and arrangement of the solution and less on methods, data members, and other expressions of structure. The latter evolve over time, reducing the risk of early architecture decisions becoming inhibitors of progress further down the life cycle.
- **Architecture is more about compression than abstraction**: It is much easier to write thick documents than express something in a few words. By ensuring that all team members share a vocabulary that captures relevant standards and domain knowledge, architectural expressions can be kept condensed.
- **Much architecture is not about solving user problems**: Quoting the authors: "*A good system form gives the vendor enough flexibility to respond to new end-user expectations within a given problem space. Much software architecture has evolved to the point where we focus on properties*

that we believe to reduce cost in the long term, such as coupling and cohesion, without much regard for function." Especially for entrepreneurial IT, the value streams are tied to functions, features, and user interaction design. They determine whether the solution even gets the chance to evolve from the introductory life-cycle phase to the growth and mature phases. Consequently, when moving through the high potential quadrant toward the strategic quadrant, coupling, cohesion, scalability, and all of those other aspects that are related to foundation IT slowly increase in importance.

- **Architecture has both a static and dynamic component**: A prime example of this principle is the difference between internet-facing front end apps and back end systems. The principle is also closely related to the key principle *less static, more flow*, as it captures the ability of an architecture to *grow*. If there is a good chance of a new high potential initiative evolving toward the strategic quadrant, I always opt for dedicating the first three to four development sprints to building a reasonably scalable architecture (both functionally and technically) and a solid automated deployment process. Additionally, solutions expected to remain within the entrepreneurial IT architecture quadrant (e.g., fire-and-forget proof of concepts) or the foundation IT architecture quadrant in Figure B.2 must be able to land on architectures and platforms that are optimized for their respective context from day one.

- **Architecture is everybody's job**: Too often, architecture is considered the sole responsibility of the architect, while it should be exercised by groups. The adoption of agile development by the IT service provider described in Chapter 2 demonstrates the waste resulting from isolated initiatives. Especially for companies with a hybrid and digital business model, architecture is an organizational capability, not the task of a single individual.

- **Architecture need not be hard**: Architecture is a *hard control*; and reading a book about traditional architecture practices is not something for the fainthearted. However, the tide is turning. The relative importance of producing an extensive set of documentation is diminishing due to the inability of the business to predict an increasingly volatile market. With the business surfing waves of short-lived opportunities, the IT team has to formulate an EA that enables the business to do so at an acceptable risk level. The front-line teams can benefit from platform as a service (PaaS) platforms and other tooling that allow business stakeholders, solution architects, user interaction (UX) designers, and developers to visualize and collaborate more effectively from the conceptualization phase to the deployment of the end result.

Again, the common thread of these principles is the skills and knowledge of the individual team members: extrovert and business-savvy enterprise architects, lead developers who understand the value of an adequate solution architecture, junior developers who are passionate about the latest and greatest AWS and Azure PaaS features, UX consultants with an inspiring vision for the company's future multi-channel customer experience, and open-minded and forward-looking decision makers—in other words, professionals who understand the importance of thinking before acting because decisions always have consequences.

B.2.3 Wrapping a Differentiated Architecture

The focus on *thinking before doing* may result in some tension with development teams that blindly apply the agile practice of *do, inspect, adapt* in order to please the focus of the business on features and visuals. Even though the more senior developers and Scrum Masters know that the approach will only please the business in the short term, due to the extensive rework that will be required to resolve the shortcuts and weaknesses. With a vanilla form of agile, the business initially only sees the *tip of the iceberg.* The true total cost of ownership remains hidden until the development team asks for another year of development to solve the technology debt (see upcoming text).

To prevent the team from developing a *skyscraper* the same way they would a *one-story house,* every company with a substantial demand for entrepreneurial IT should adopt a lean set of guidelines and principles to balance the sometimes conflicting desire for speed-to-market, flexibility, acceptable risk profile, and tolerable waste (e.g., only partial reengineering of architecture, or tooling allowing easy migration from Azure to AWS or vice versa). For this reason, Figure 5.3 is extended with an architecture layer, as seen in Figure B.5.

The company's mission, vision, and strategic themes; core business principles; and context (e.g., level of uncertainty, technology density of the market) shape the strategic IT themes and core principles that are driving the IT business model. These, in turn, shape the minimum[12] set of core architecture principles that are applicable to both entrepreneurial IT and foundation IT, preventing a business unit or the company as a whole from ending up in the hidden architecture quadrant or, even worse, the crisis architecture quadrant.

In addition to a set of overarching core architecture principles, the architect should also define specific principles for entrepreneurial IT and foundation IT. As

---

[12] In my vocabulary, 'minimum' means five to ten core principles, not fifty to one hundred. With websites and books offering 100+ examples, it is all too easy to get carried away in your private Ivory Tower. However, *less is more* applies here too.

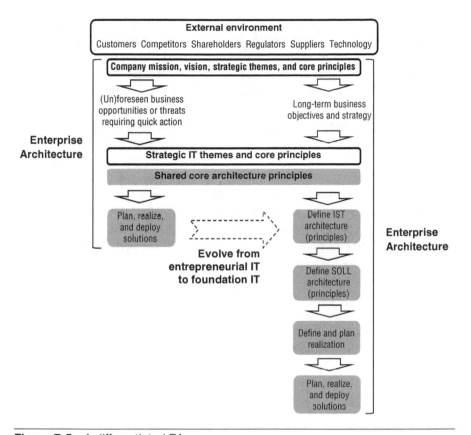

Figure B.5   A differentiated EA

the following example of architecture principles for agile software development from Scaled Agile demonstrates, these specific sets can also be limited in size:[xx]

- *"Design emerges; architecture is a collaboration*
- *The bigger the system, the longer the runway*
- *Build the simplest architecture that can possibly work*
- *When in doubt, code or model it out*
- *They build it, they test it*
- *There is no monopoly on innovation*
- *Implement architectural flow"*

Compared to these principles that target entrepreneurial IT, the list for foundation IT can be slightly longer—due to its predictability, business value (e.g., multiple *cash cow* value propositions), and longer duration of the accompanying business life-cycle phases.

Another difference is the enforcement policy. When developing a new core banking system, the relevant architecture principles should be rigorously enforced. There is little room for interpretation; and the architecture will be a multi-year road map that is based on a big up-front design.

These and other aspects are depicted in Table B.3, providing a consolidated overview of EA, foundation IT architecture, and entrepreneurial IT architecture. In an ideal world, every new app development or sourcing initiative adheres to the core set of company-wide EA principles, resulting in an empty hidden architecture quadrant. They should be abstract enough to be applicable to both entrepreneurial IT and foundation IT, robust enough to be applicable over a longer period, and either a source of additional benefits or risk reduction.

Due to their strategic nature, these EA principles are the most difficult to implement. The classic approach of sending a memo to the whole company proclaiming their existence and importance (*the board signed off on them!*) is unlikely to lead to a high adoption rate. Unless the whole organization is governed by the fear that noncompliance leads to being terminated as an employee.

With low added-value business activities being automated and highly skilled, creative, and motivated people in short demand, compliance through fear is not a sustainable option. Therefore, the architect must convince the team to adopt the core EA principles. The architect must be able to lead and manage organizational change.

At first sight, the hardest-to-convince teams are those that are responsible for entrepreneurial IT. When called *cowboys* by the rest of the organization, they consider it a badge of honor. However, looks can be deceiving, as the more experienced developers of these teams understand the value of architecture. They script, reuse code, use generic platform services, build APIs instead of *hard-wiring* applications, apply OWASP10 best practices, and think before coding. Grouped together, these more technical best practices form a valuable body of knowledge and reusable components known as a reference architecture, or in TOGAF terminology, technology architecture.

Due to the high level of variation, architecture principles for entrepreneurial IT should cover principles that are related to the (a) low-level technical reference architecture, and (b) high-level and more abstract principles like the example from Scaled Agile. Spending time on anything in between will most likely result in waste due to the inability to predict the future.

For entrepreneurial IT, the architect should focus on a lean and flexible set of technical and high-level *must-haves*.

In contrast to the proof of concepts, mashups, and composite applications that dominate the entrepreneurial IT universe, the multi-year IT programs that are necessary to automate the stable primary and secondary business processes can benefit from an additional level of control.

Table B.3   A differentiated architecture

	Enterprise Architecture Principles	Entrepreneurial IT Architecture Principles	Foundation IT Architecture Principles
Application	Company-wide	Company-wide, refinements at business unit level	Company-wide, refinements at business unit level
Horizon	Long-term	Short-term	Medium- to long-term
Enforcement	Comply or explain	Lenient comply or explain	Strict comply or explain
Business Context	External environment and companies' business model drive IT positioning and relative stability and complexity	Both current and future state are dynamic and diffuse	Current and future state are stable and well defined
Key Objective	• Prevent waste • Stay below companies' risk appetite • Learn from the past	• Innovation, speed, and flexibility in a controlled manner • Learn from the past	• Maximize efficiency and predictability • Minimize IT risk profile • Learn from the past
Key Inputs	• Trends external environment • Business strategy and business model • Strategic IT themes and IT business model	• Business opportunities and threats • Emergent technologies	• Business strategy, change programs, and road maps • Strategic IT themes and existing IT portfolio • Mature technologies
Key Constraints	• Leadership skills of architect	• Available capacity of scarce skills and knowledge • Integration with legacy applications (e.g., pre-SOAP and REST)	• Business domain knowledge • Existing application landscape • Ability to change
Image of Architect	Depends on business context	A flexible and proactive business savvy technology leader	A professional and reliable, but often too theoretical, technology manager

For nuclear power plants, fighter jets, and core banking systems, this additional layer of control looks different from the additional control required to optimize most other applications. The risk appetite of utility companies operating nuclear power plants and fighter pilots who are operating at 30,000 feet in a hostile environment may even warrant a full-fledged implementation of TOGAF or other frameworks.

For other applications, the discounted cash flow of an investment in foundation IT architecture most likely peaks well before reaching the full scope of such frameworks due to the (a) growing uncertainty faced by the company as a whole, and (b) the increasing dependency of companies that are on external IT partners to automate the stable parts of their manufacturing, supply chain, and customer relationship processes.

One effect of the growing business uncertainty is a shorter lifespan of foundation IT applications, reducing the relative importance of some software quality aspects (e.g., resource utilization, maintainability), while increasing the importance of others (e.g., modularity, modifiability, usability). Also, changing is the importance of security, effectiveness, and user experience.

Even though the back end systems target internal business users and external network partners, these customer segments expect a smooth, visually pleasing, secure, and effective workflow, as described in Chapter 3. They, too, are used to an abundance of choice and have therefore little patience with subpar IT solutions—foundation IT or not.

Hence, the principles driving the foundation IT architecture should balance the desire for efficiency and a low risk profile with the ability to agree on an experience level agreement instead of the traditional, IT-oriented service level agreement—among others, as the architect also has a debt to pay.

B.3 ECOSYSTEM ENTROPY AND TECHNICAL DEBT

Some incumbents acted quickly on the digitalization of their analog business models, but most moved too slow. Failing to sense disruptive *waves* and organizational inertia, and focusing on short-term financial results will turn leaders into followers or even defenders. The list of challenges that are faced by companies with a hybrid or digital business model is even longer because they are more directly impacted by hardcore IT topics such as software entropy and technical debt—two topics that rarely reach the business domain in companies with an analog business model.

In time, every piece of software or hardware declines in quality as the disorder of a closed system can only remain unchanged or increase. This principle is known as the Second Law of Thermodynamics and a measure of this disorder is called entropy. Entropy cannot only be observed at system level (e.g., declining quality of the operating system on a particular device due to the never-ending stream of updates with modifications), but also in ecosystems and platforms.

Microsoft relies on a global network of external IT partners to turn its products and platforms into business value for the end customer (e.g., develop custom solutions with .NET, implement SharePoint or Dynamics 365). While I admire the strategic turnaround that was initiated by Satya Nadella, I wonder whether the high-frequency release policy of so many products (e.g., Windows 10, SharePoint, Windows Server, Visual Studio, System Center, SQL, BizTalk, Dynamics 365, Microsoft Teams, Azure, and Azure Stack) is sustainable. Microsoft's strategy is quickly increasing the entropy of its own ecosystem and, consequently, also the entropy of its external IT partners and end customers.

Entropy, or disorder, is like a debt; it is a sum of company resources that is owed to other stakeholders. More importantly, the sum accumulates interest until the company takes action. Take Google for example.

Gartner estimated that Android reached 1.1 billion users in 2014, a 26% increase from 2013.[xxi] According to the same analyst firm, Android was installed on more than 80% of the devices sold in 2015 and 2016, further extending its leading market position.[xxii]

The cornerstone of this growth is Google's strategy to allow any manufacturer of mobile phones, media streamers, TVs, car systems, smart watches, or other supported devices to use its software. Download, install, and start selling. The strategy allowed Google to quickly catch up and surpass Apple after the latter's iPhone and iOS ecosystem turned out to be a runaway success. However, its strategy also resulted in innumerable combinations of CPUs, screen sizes, cameras, and memory sizes that must be supported in new software versions, as the users of the devices expect Google to provide them with the latest and greatest features and eye candy.

Google's strategy made Android the dominant player in terms of number of devices, at the cost of moving the ecosystem from an ordered state to a disordered state. The company has recognized the risk and has started to tighten its grip on the ecosystem, as unmanaged entropy inevitably results in errors and a degraded user experience, which in turn, results in customers and revenue leaving the ecosystem.

The diversity of the Microsoft and Android ecosystems is only the start of what is coming. Moore's law ensures that devices will continue to reduce in size, while becoming cheaper and more powerful, eventually resulting in literally every physical object becoming *smart*. The Internet of Things, the convergence of administrative IT and industrial IT, and the adoption of Blockchain technology within the supply chain networks and the financial services industry create new ecosystems that move from a relatively ordered state to one of disorder, *if not managed effectively*.

To minimize the impact of the Second Law of Thermodynamics, the architect has to fight back on two fronts:

- Entropy created by external partners in the companies' network (e.g. Microsoft, Google), and
- Entropy introduced by the company itself, effecting both internal and external stakeholders (e.g., customers and external partners).

Every company with a dynamic hybrid or digital business model generates a never-ending stream of new apps, modifications, add-ons, and withdrawals that must be governed and managed in an orderly and controlled way, in order to minimize entropy. As it is easier to accelerate the creation of disorder (e.g., focus on short-term benefits, do-check-adapt instead of thinking before doing) than minimize it, the leadership skills of the architect are again called upon to ensure that the responsible executives make an informed decision. Choosing short-term gain is fine if they understand the long-term pain of their decision. A similar message applies to technical debt.

Software entropy and technical debt are related, but are not the same. A clean install of an operating system on a device can often fix issues that are related to software entropy, but if the quality of the code itself is the problem, a fresh copy won't help. In that case, the issue is technical debt. Quoting Cunningham:[xxiii] "*Shipping first-time code is like going into debt. A little debt speeds development so long as it is paid back promptly with a rewrite . . . The danger occurs when the debt is not repaid. Every minute spent on not-quite-right code counts as interest on that debt. Entire engineering organizations can be brought to a stand-still under the debt load of an unconsolidated implementation, object-oriented or otherwise.*"

The main causes of technical debt are easy to define. With speed-to-market being a crucial precondition in order to remain competitive in many markets, the development team often has no choice but to promote code to production status before it is ready (e.g., complete, consistent, no major defects). The longer the company continues to borrow on the technical debt for short-term gain, the larger and more expensive the eventual refactoring effort.

However, the payback period of a secure, modular, and scalable architecture is always longer than some cool visual gimmick that catches the eye of potential customers. So, guess which item is most likely to make it to the top of the backlog.

Depending on the technology literacy of the product owner and/or business executive and on the power imbalance between the business and IT, the technology debt either stays within manageable proportions or spirals out of control. Worse case—the business forces the development team into the role of faithful servant, a position described by Han Van der Zee[xxiv] as "*Always helping, wherever possible, no questions asked.*" Yet asking questions and having discussions are a precondition in order to maximize the *total* cost of ownership.

Worst case—the business is the most important source of technology debt, not IT.[13] The development team is not off the hook, however. If the team consists of junior developers and one very outspoken senior developer with autocratic tendencies, then duplications, errors, and questionable design decisions (e.g., lack of attention for decoupling and cohesion) likely remain undiscussed.

Laziness (*there is always another sprint, so let's apply the easiest instead of the most cost-effective fix*) and too much focus on stand-ups, backlogs, and burndown charts instead of adding tangible business results are other causes of IT-induced technology debt.

Hence, Cunningham's statement that "*entire engineering organizations can be brought to a standstill under the debt load*" is not an imaginary scenario. Too much technical debt kills agility, sprint velocity, motivation, and consequently value.

Fowler identified four types of technical debt,[xxv] each with its own dynamics, as seen in Figure B.6. If the team is *unable, but confident* in situational leadership terms, they are unable to take on the responsibility for the task—but proceed anyway, regardless of the risk. Their lack of skills is masked by bravura (*we don't have time for design*). Also reckless, but easier to forgive, is a lack of knowledge (*what is layering?*).

A prudent example of technical debt is the business and the development team deciding to release despite several defects in rarely used parts of the code. In that case, both the principle and the interest are sufficiently small to deploy.

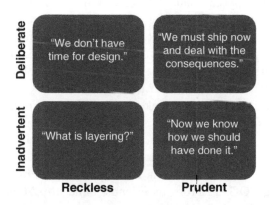

Figure B.6   Technical debt quadrants by Martin Fowler (source: Fowler, M. [October 2009]. TechnicalDebtQuadrant. Link: https://martinfowler.com/bliki/TechnicalDebtQuadrant.html)

---

[13] See also my three blogs with the title Agile: Creator and Destroyer of Value on my website. Link: https://www.digital-manifesto.org/blog/.

Due to their relative simplicity, the quadrants from Fowler can be used to communicate the challenges faced by the development team to the business. Depending on the seniority of the developers, either they or the architect can take on this task. The common thread running through software entropy, ecosystem entropy, and technical debt is the need to actively manage decisions that are related to architecture and software development, since they affect value, cost, productivity, and motivation. Every decision has both short- and long-term consequences, and the business and IT must be ready to face them.

There is no silver bullet architecture, development approach, or technology platform that can magically produce the best, most flexible, and scalable solutions *yesterday* and at *no cost*. There are—and always will be—trade-offs.

Architecture development is an ongoing process, and it is up to the architect to lead the rest of the team through that journey as effectively as possible.

As said before, architecture is a group effort.

REFERENCES

i. Amdahl, G., Blaauw, G. and Brooks, F. (1964). Architecture of the IBM System/360, *IBM Journal for Research and Development*.

ii. Fruhlinger, J. and Wailgum, T. (July 2017). 15 famous ERP Disasters, Dust-ups and Disappointments. CIO.com. Link: http://www.cio.com/article/2429865/enterprise-resource-planning/enterprise-resource-planning-10-famous-erp-disasters-dustups-and-disappointments.html.

iii. Yampolskiy, R. and Spellchecker, M. (2016). Artificial Intelligence Safety and Cybersecurity: A Timeline of AI Failures. Link: https://arxiv.org/ftp/arxiv/papers/1610/1610.07997.pdf.

iv. Atluri, V., Dietz, M. and Henke, N. (July 2017). Competing in a World of Sectors Without Borders. *McKinsey Quarterly*. Link: http://www.mckinsey.com/business-functions/mckinsey-analytics/our-insights/competing-in-a-world-of-sectors-without-borders.

v. Boardman, S. and Harrington, E. (May 2015). In Praise Of Heuristics—or Saving TOGAF® From Its Friends. Link: http://blog.opengroup.org/2015/05/06/in-praise-of-heuristics-or-saving-togaf-from-its-friends/.

vi. Novak, A. (February 2016). Going to Market Faster: Most Companies Are Deploying Code Weekly, Daily, or Hourly. New Relic blog. Link: https://blog.newrelic.com/2016/02/04/data-culture-survey-results-faster-deployment/.

vii. Wikipedia article on Information Overload. (Accessed July 2017). Link: https://en.wikipedia.org/wiki/Information_overload.

viii. Source: https://en.wikiquote.org/wiki/Leadership.

ix. Wladawsky-Berger, I. (June 2013). Cloud Computing and the Changing Role of the CIO. *USC Annenberg Innovation Lab*. Link: http://blog .irvingwb.com/blog/2013/06/cloud-computing-and-the-changing-role -of-the-cio.html.

x. Merrett, R. (February 2013). Third of IT Execs Face Cloud Integration, Implementation Issues: survey. CIO.com. Link: http://www.cio.com.au/ article/453252/third_it_execs_face_cloud_integration_implementation _issues_survey/.

xi. Boyd, M. (May 2013). Why SaaS Fragmentation Is Giving Rise to New Markets. Link: http://venturebeat.com/2013/05/31/why-saas-fragmentation -is-giving-rise-to-new markets/.

xii. Weise, E. (February 2017). Massive Amazon Cloud Service Outage Disrupts Sites. *USA Today*. Link: https://www.usatoday.com/story/tech/ news/2017/02/28/amazons-cloud-service-goes-down-sites-scramble/ 98530914/.

xiii. 3 Companies that Went Out of Business Due to a Security Breach. (November 2014). Pro OnCall Technologies blog post. Link: https://prooncall .com/3-companies-went-business-due-security-breach/.

xiv. Robinson, S. (September 2013). Nirvanix Failure—a Blow to the Cloud Storage Model. ComputerWeekly.com. Link: http://www.computerweekly .com/opinion/Nirvanix-failure-a-blow-to-the-cloud-storage-model.

xv. Henderson, J. C. and Venkatraman, N. (1993). Strategic Alignment: Leveraging Information Technology for Transforming Organizations.

xvi. Bernard, S. (2012). *An Introduction to Enterprise Architecture*.

xvii. Enterprise architecture, Wikipedia. (Accessed July 2017). Link: https:// en.wikipedia.org/wiki/Enterprise_architecture.

xviii. Prahalad, C. and Krishnan, M. (July 2002). The Dynamic Synchronization of Strategy and Information Technology. *MIT SLOAN Management Review, Volume 43, Number 4*, pp. 24–33.

xix. Coplien, J. and Bjørnvig, G. (2010). *Lean Architecture for Agile Software Development*.

xx. Agile Architecture, Scaled Agile (June 2017). Link: http://www.scaled agileframework.com/agile-architecture/.

xxi. Gartner (2014). Gartner press release, Gartner Says Worldwide Traditional PC, Tablet, Ultramobile and Mobile Phone Shipments On Pace to Grow 7.6 Percent in 2014. Link: http://www.gartner.com/newsroom/ id/2645115.

xxii. Gartner (February 2017). Gartner press release, Gartner Says Worldwide Sales of Smartphones Grew 7 Percent in the Fourth Quarter of 2016. Link: http://www.gartner.com/newsroom/id/3609817.

xxiii. Cunningham, W. (1993). The WyCash portfolio management system. *ACM SIGPLAN OOPS Messenger, vol. 4(2)*, pp. 29–30.

xxiv. Van der Zee, H. (2003). *Measuring the Value of Information Technology*.

xxv. Fowler, M. (October 2009). TechnicalDebtQuadrant. Link: https://martin fowler.com/bliki/TechnicalDebtQuadrant.html.

C

GLOSSARY OF TERMS, CONCEPTS, METHODS, AND TECHNOLOGY

This appendix contains an alphabetical list of terms used in this book that deserve an explanation. Most explanations are short, while other definitions are more elaborate, as several topics deserved more attention than the chapters and other appendixes allowed for.

Term	Description and Further Reading
3-D printing	With 3-D printing or additive manufacturing, a solid object is created by laying down successive layers of material based on a digital file.
3rd-party logistics	If the company uses an external partner to fulfill activities related to supply chain management (e.g., distribution, fulfillment), the external party is often referred to as a third-party logistics provider (abbreviated 3PL).
Administrative IT	Administrative IT consists of the value propositions (e.g., CRM, ERP), processes, people, and technology used to digitize the administrative processes of a company. Due to the digitalization of industries including manufacturing, chemicals, and oil and gas, the administrative IT domain and industrial IT domain are converging toward each other. See also Industrial IT.
Advanced robotics	Until recently, robots were restricted to automating repetitive work in static environments, as they were unable to adapt. Advanced robotics refers to robots that are able to work effectively in dynamic and complex environments. To do so, they have the capability to learn, have access to a broader set of more capable sensors, and can share knowledge with other robots. Another development is adding *personalities* to robots by teaching them social and emotional interactions. See also Artificial intelligence.

Agency costs	Agency costs are the costs that are related to information asymmetry or the inherent conflicts of interest between *principles* and *agents* of a company. Think of executives (agent) who are optimizing their share at the cost of the shareholder (principle). All costs that are required to manage the relationship between the principle and agent and that solve any issues are called agency costs.
Agile	The higher the uncertainty and complexity of a market, the more relevant the capability of a company to rapidly change or adapt its business model and/or value propositions. To translate organizational agility to software development, seventeen experienced software practitioners defined the Agile Manifesto (agilemanifesto.org/) as four main values and twelve principles to guide the development of software. The most popular way to operationalize the Agile Manifesto is Scrum (Kanban is another). With Scrum, the end-product is specified, prioritized, coded, tested, and deployed in a series of fixed-length iterations (*sprints*). You can find an elaborate narrative of the (mis)use of the Agile Manifesto in software development at: https://www.digital-manifesto.org/blog/
Analog	In the context of this book, analog refers to business models with a low technology density. Think of companies that use IT exclusively to automate administrative processes and rely solely on distinctive *business* capabilities to differentiate themselves in the market. In most cases, they have a *brick and mortar* business model like physical retailers, hairdressers, and bakeries.
Application containers	The containerization started with the operating system (OS) to reduce the performance overhead that is related to hypervisor-based virtualization. OS containers allow multiple isolated *user space instances* to share the same kernel. Where OS containers can run multiple services and processes, application containers are designed to run a single application, application service, or application component, using APIs to talk to each other.
Applications-infrastructure scorecard	This tool from Prahalad and Krishnan is designed to facilitate the dialogue between the business and IT by dynamically synchronizing the capabilities of the IT team with the evolving demands from the business. To do so, the authors suggest business and IT executives should regularly discuss (a) an application's role in the business strategy; (b) the stability of the business processes; (c) the degree of change in the application; (d) the application sourcing; (e) the data privacy level; and (f) the quality level. Source: Prahalad, C. and Krishnan, M. (July 2002). The Dynamic Synchronization of Strategy and Information Technology, *MIT Sloan Management Review, Volume 43, Number 4*, pp. 24–33.

Application programmable interface (API)	When software components need to communicate with each other, the components must be able to *understand* each other, requiring a predefined method. An API is such a method—consisting of protocols and subroutine definitions. APIs are not restricted to a single development language or technology.
Architecture	Architecture is the art of transforming functional and technical complexity into an elegant and pleasant-to-use form. Unfortunately, there is no such thing as *the* architecture. The list includes, but is surprisingly not limited to: • **Business architecture**: *"a blueprint of the enterprise that provides a common understanding of the organization and is used to align strategic objectives and tactical demands."* Source: Wikipedia. • **Common systems architecture**: *"guides the selection and integration of specific services from the foundation architecture to create an architecture useful for building common (i.e., highly re-usable) solutions across a wide number of relevant domains."* Source: TOGAF, OpenGroup.org. • **Enterprise architecture**: *"an ongoing management program that provides a strategic, integrated approach to capability and resource planning/decision making. An EA program is part of an overall governance process that determines resource alignment, develops standardized policy, enhances decision support, and guides development activities."* Source: Bernard, S. *An Introduction to Enterprise Architecture*, 2012. • **Foundation architecture**: *"is an architecture of generic services and functions that provides a foundation on which more specific architectures and architectural components can be built."* Source: TOGAF, OpenGroup.org. • **Industry architecture**: *"guides the integration of common systems components with industry-specific components, and guides the creation of industry solutions for targeted customer problems within a particular industry."* Source: TOGAF, OpenGroup.org. • **Information Architecture**: *"is the structural design of shared information environments; the art and science of organizing and labeling websites, intranets, online communities, and software to support usability and findability; and an emerging community of practice focused on bringing principles of design and architecture to the digital landscape."* Source: Wikipedia. • **Lean Architecture**: *"provides a firm foundation for the ongoing business of a software enterprise: providing timely features to end users."* Source: Coplien, J. and Bjørnvig, G. (2010). *Lean Architecture: For Agile Software Development*.

	• **Organizational architecture**: *"has two very different meanings. In one sense it literally refers to the organization's built environment and in another sense it refers to architecture metaphorically, as a structure which fleshes out the organizations."* Source: Wikipedia. • **Reference architecture**: *"A reference architecture is the part of an EA that provides standards and documentation for a particular type of capability throughout the enterprise—such as mobile services or cloud computing."* Source: Bernard, S. (2012). *An Introduction to Enterprise Architecture.* Enterprise architecture is by far the most important definition on the list and most other architectures can be considered its *children.*
Architecture standards	There are many architecture standards and best practices, including: • **Zachman Framework**: Published by John Zachman in 1987, and considered the *mother* of all other frameworks created since. It focuses on creating a shared vocabulary and set of perspectives to rationalize the design of a complex solution. It helps the architect to make the right decisions by answering the following six basic questions: what, how, where, who, when, and why. • **The Open Group Architectural Framework (TOGAF)**: This framework has emerged as the industry-wide standard, like COBIT for IT governance and ITIL for service management. It includes both an implementation process [Architecture Development Method (ADM)] and necessary content (e.g., principles, vocabulary, tools). • **EA3**: The architecture framework described in the book *An Introduction to Enterprise Architecture* by Scott A. Bernard. It too provides both a process and necessary content to implement an enterprise architecture. • **ArchiMate**: Like TOGAF, ArchiMate is published by the Open Group and provides an open modeling language for enterprise architecture, allowing the architect to analyze, describe, and visualize relevant aspects. • **ISO/IEC 42010:2007**: This is an ISO standard for architecture, using the following definition: *"Architecture is the fundamental organization of a system embodied in its components, their relationships to each other and the environment, and the principles guiding its design and evolution."* Source: IEEE 1471:2000. • **Standards from government bodies within the United States**: Federal Enterprise Architecture Framework (FEAF), Treasury Enterprise Architecture Framework (TEAF), and Department of Defense Architecture Framework (DoDAF).

	Of the 334 individuals that responded to a survey conducted in 2013 by Cameron and McMillan on EA, 20% of the participants used the open standard TOGAF. Next in popularity was DoDAF with 2% and FEAF with less than 1%. Source: Cameron, B. and McMillan, E. (February 2013). Analyzing the Current Trends in Enterprise Architecture Frameworks. *Journal of Enterprise Architecture.*
Artificial intelligence	When devices and systems can perceive their environment and act based on those stimuli to maximize their chance of achieving a predefined goal, they possess artificial intelligence. The closer the devices and systems mimic the cognitive functions that people associate with the human mind, the more *intelligent* they are.
As-a-service economy	The as-a-service economy refers to (a) the shift from ownership to access and (b) a cloud-enabled business processing outsourcing concept. The cloud, artificial intelligence, data analytics, and other technologies enable external IT partners to create new value propositions that promise pay-per-use, agility, robustness, efficiency, and innovation—all at the same time. The first interpretation of the as-a-service economy is better known as the sharing economy, as the latter also emphasizes access instead of ownership, a focus on service, and is enabled by cloud-based platforms. See also Shareconomy.
Attack surface Attack vector	Both attack surface and attack vector are related to information security. Attack vector refers to the means or paths that a hacker can use to gain unauthorized access to an application, data, and/or infrastructure. Attack vectors include viruses that are embedded in e-mails or websites and deception (e.g., click on a link that refers to a rogue website). The sum of all of the attack vectors forms the attack surface.
Augmented reality	See Virtual reality.
Balanced scorecard (BSC)	The balanced scorecard is a performance management framework that was made popular by Kaplan and Norton's book *The Balanced Scorecard: Translating Strategy into Action.* Managers use it to define objectives and track their progress; it also can be applied both to the implementation of a strategy and for operational management.
Big data	Advances in technology allow companies to collect and analyze extremely large data sets. Advanced algorithms are used to expose trends, associations, and other patterns that allow the company to optimize its business model (e.g., market research, customer targeting, product quality, logistics). Related is business intelligence—the process of turning data into actionable information, which allows executives to make better informed decisions.

Big-up-front-design (BUFD), Big-design-up-front (BDUF)	A BUFD makes sense if (a) the requirements are stable and known up-front and (b) the acceptable risk level is very low. With a BUFD or BDUF, the architecture and design of the whole application is perfected and accepted by the business before the realization starts. For this reason, it is associated with waterfall software development.
Black Swan	The definition of a Black Swan is: *"the impossibility of calculating the risks of consequential rare events and predicting their occurrence. Sensitivity to harm from volatility is tractable, more so than forecasting the event that would cause the harm."* It is a metaphor for events with a very low likelihood and a very high impact that, in most cases, can only be rationalized with the benefit of hindsight. Source quote: Nassim Nicholas Taleb (2014). *Antifragile: Things That Gain from Disorder.*
Blockchain	Quoting Iansiti and Lakhani, *"The technology at the heart of bitcoin and other virtual currencies, blockchain is an open, distributed ledger that can record transactions between two parties efficiently and in a verifiable and permanent way."* The transactions are not limited to financial transactions, but can be used for everything of value (e.g., healthcare patient records, supply chain transactions, *smart grid* electricity transactions, property transactions). Source quote: Iansiti, M. and Lakhani, K. (January 2017). The Truth About Blockchain. *Harvard Business Review.*
Blue Ocean Strategy	After analyzing more than 150 strategic moves, Chan Kim and Renée Mauborgne argued that the most successful companies were able to create *uncontested market spaces*. By reframing their existing belief set, these companies unlocked new customer demands instead of fighting for dominance in existing markets. The latter is compared to a red ocean and the first with a blue ocean. Their book is called *Blue Ocean Strategy* and was first published in 2005.
Boundary spanning	To collaborate, individuals, teams, and companies must reach across physical, virtual, and/or social borders. The stronger the relationship and interdependence, the more effective and sustainable the business model.
Bring-your-own-electricity (BYOE)	The commoditization of solar panels and batteries allows houses to go *off the grid*. In most cases, the houses would still be grid-tied to mitigate extensive periods of no sun. *Smart grid* technologies allow consumers to both buy and sell electricity. See also Smart grid.
Build-operate-transfer (BOT), Build-own-operate-transfer (BOOT)	In the context of this book, BOT refers to an external IT partner receiving a concession from the client company to realize and operate a facility to deliver IT outsourcing or business process outsourcing services. At the end of the term, the external IT partner transfers the facility as a captive center to the client company.

Build to order (BTO)	Also called made to order, BTO is a manufacturing approach where the production starts after receiving a confirmed order. *Build to order* is typically used for highly customizable or perishable goods and *build to stock* for low-cost mass production of similar goods.
Business process management (BPM)	Part of operations management, BPM focuses on optimizing the performance of the company's business processes using a combination of management frameworks (e.g., lean), software tools, and change management practices. See also Business process reengineering.
Business process outsourcing (BPO)	BPO refers to the decision of a company to outsource both the business process and the underpinning IT systems to an external business partner. In return, the client company receives a predefined service (e.g., processed salary slips) or physical product (e.g., bottles of water).
Business process reengineering (BPR)	With a BPR initiative, the company's business process and operating model are radically redesigned to dramatically increase the performance. Compared to business process management, BPR is more risky, and continuous change is replaced by one big high-impact change.
Business-IT alignment (BITA)	Henderson and Venkatraman are the founding fathers of the BITA paradigm. Since its inception, BITA has evolved into a broad set of frameworks, models, and best practices to close the gap between the business and IT in relatively stable environments.
Business model canvas	The business model canvas and the lean business model canvas are templates that companies can use to develop new business models and optimize existing business models. The templates enable a coherent and structured approach to translate strategic objectives into the key organizational building blocks of a company. This so-called *business model* answers questions like: Who is your customer? What customer need are you going to fulfill? How do you differentiate from your competitors? How will you generate more revenue than cost? Which activities should we perform internally and which can be sourced from external partners? The business model canvas was introduced by Alexander Osterwalder in 2008.
Capital expenditure (CAPEX)	Capital expenditures are the financial resources that are used to buy physical assets (e.g., buildings, machines, servers) or to invest in the creation of intangible assets (e.g., patents, new core competencies). If an expenditure is labeled CAPEX, it needs to be capitalized on the balance sheet, allowing the company to spread the cost of the investment over the life cycle of the asset.
Chapter 11	Refers to Chapter 11 of the U.S. bankruptcy code. This part of the bankruptcy code protects a company from its creditors for a limited period, allowing the company to reorganize its business and renegotiate the contracts with its creditors.

Client-server	The client-server model is the most popular way to distribute an application to a user. The applications can be native or based on web technology. In the latter case, the application runs in the web browser, relying on the server to do the heavy lifting. In both cases, the centralized system serves many clients and the power, memory, and storage must be sized accordingly. An alternative to the client-server architecture is a peer-to-peer architecture (see also Peer networking).
Cloud computing	According to Wikipedia, the cloud is "*a model for enabling ubiquitous, on-demand access to a shared pool of configurable computing resources (e.g., computer networks, servers, storage, applications, and services*"). Cloud providers promise flexibility, pay-per-use, service-orientation (e.g., no worrying about underlying infrastructure or updates), and data security (e.g., multiple networked backups). Cloud-enabled value propositions include business process as a service (BPaaS), software as a service (SaaS), platform as a service (PaaS), and infrastructure as a service (IaaS). A key characteristic of the cloud is the use of centralized servers to do the heavy lifting. Siri (Apple), Cortana (Microsoft), and Google Now (Google) sends our question or command to one of its data centers for processing. It minimizes the workload of our mobile device and allows for more complex interactions. Sony uses a similar mechanism to stream PS3 games to the owners of PS4 game consoles. Google's Marketplace and Salesforce.com's AppExchange provide app developers all the resources they need to build, test, deploy, integrate, promote, and service their apps. All the developer needs is a broadband internet connection and a laptop or desktop with moderate specifications. In 2016 alone, IBM received 2,700+ patents to cognitive and cloud computing, reflecting the cloud's strategic importance to International Business Machines. Source link: https://en.wikipedia.org/wiki/Cloud_computing (retrieved August 2017).
Control Objectives for Information and related Technology (COBIT)	COBIT was first published by ISACA and the IT Governance Institute in 1996, and stands for Control Objectives for Information and Related Technology. It provides a set of practices to increase the maturity of IT Governance and IT management, and as a result, the collaboration with the business and regulatory compliance. Version 5 of COBIT integrates COBIT 4.1, Val IT 2.0, and ITGI's Risk IT frameworks into one model. Val IT is the IT Governance Institute's response to the need to optimize the realization of value from IT investments. Val IT focuses on the investment decision (*are we doing the right things?*) and the realization of benefits (*are we getting the benefits?*). COBIT addresses the execution of initiatives (*are we doing them the right way?* and *are we getting them done well?*).

Commercial off-the-shelf (COTS)	Standardized software or hardware solutions that are sold to companies (e.g., Exact) or customers (e.g., Microsoft Office). Compared to custom software or hardware, these solutions have either no or limited customization options.
Common business-oriented language (COBOL)	COBOL is a program language that was designed in 1959 as part of a U.S. Department of Defense initiative. It is now considered legacy and new applications are written in more modern languages. A survey from Computerworld in 2012 reported 48% of the companies still used applications written in COBOL. Source: Computerworld, Cobol brain drain: Survey results, 2012. Link: http://www.computerworld.com/article/2502430/data-center/cobol-brain-drain-survey-results.html.
Composite risk	Composite risk refers to longer term risks, such as losing the capability to insource previously outsourced business processes again due to a lack of employees with the required knowledge and expertise. Signing a build-operate-transfer (BOT) is one way to mitigate this risk.
Compounded average rate of growth (CARG)	It measures the average year-over-year or mean annual growth rate of an investment over a multi-year period.
Concentration risk	A paper on managing outsourcing risk from the Division of Banking Supervision and Regulation Division of the Consumer and Community Affairs Board of Governors of the Federal Reserve System states that "concentration risks arise when outsourced services or products are provided by a limited number of service providers or are concentrated in limited geographic locations." Source link: https://www.federalreserve.gov/supervisionreg/srletters/sr1319a1.pdf.
Conflict management	Conflicts are a source of waste; the process to limit their negative aspects and increase their positive aspects is called conflict management.
Consumerization	According to Gartner, "consumerization is the specific impact that consumer-originated technologies can have on enterprises. It reflects how enterprises will be affected by, and can take advantage of, new technologies and models that originate and develop in the consumer space, rather than in the enterprise IT sector." Source: Gartner, IT Glossary. Link: http://www.gartner.com/it-glossary/consumerization.
Control, hard and soft	Managers are hired to plan, organize, and staff activities to achieve certain goals or objectives. To detect deviations between planned and actual performance, control mechanisms are needed. These allow those responsible for a team, product, or process to check for errors, issues, or other problems and take corrective or preventive action. Most control frameworks prescribe *hard* or formal controls as they are tangible [e.g., delegation of power, organizational structure, function descriptions, policies, segregation of duty (SoD), access controls (e.g., locks), and reporting procedures]. As hard

	controls were unable to prevent scandals at Enron and Société Générale, many companies redesigned their control strategy to balance the pursuit of economic values (e.g., profit, growth) with organizational values (e.g., hierarchical and collegial structures), and social values (e.g., relationships of trust). The latter is the least tangible control—focusing on ethical climate, empowerment, competencies, morale, integrity, openness, and culture to align individual and company interests. The aim of soft or informal controls is stimulating self and (informal) peer control, thus creating a culture that has a positive influence on two of the three preconditions of fraud—motive and rationalization (opportunity is the third).
Convergence	Within the context of this book, convergence refers to the union of several domains enabled by the commoditization and democratization of technology. Typical examples are the convergence of business and IT, the convergence of customer-oriented IT and business-oriented IT (see Consumerization), and the convergence of administrative IT and industrial IT.
Core activity	Sustainable success requires directing valuable resources toward those activities and capabilities that determine the company's long-term success. These are core to the company and should be retained. Non-core activities are often outsourced to free up capital and management attention.
Core competency	Prahalad and Hamel introduced this concept, and they defined it as "*a harmonized combination of multiple resources and skills that distinguish a firm in the marketplace.*" To be considered core, the competency should provide the company with: (a) potential access to a wide variety of markets, (b) a significant contribution to the added value perceived by the customer, and (c) protection against competitors (e.g., difficult to substitute). A core competency reflects particular strengths relative to competitors, and includes the collective learning of the company, how the company coordinates and integrates expertise and technology, and effective collaboration with its external partners and customers. Another important aspect of core competencies is choice: the company must decide in which areas it wants to excel and in which it doesn't. Closely related is the term *distinctive capability*. Source quote: Prahalad, C. and Hamel, G. (1990). The Core Competence of the Corporation. Archived. *Harvard Business Review*.
Crowdsourcing	The act of an organization redistributing activities from internal employees to the general public is called crowdsourcing and "*takes place when a profit-oriented firm outsources specific tasks essential for the making or sale of its product to the general public (the crowd) in the form of an open call over the internet, with the intention of animating individuals to make a contribution to the firm's production process for free or for significantly less than that contribution is worth to the firm.*" The main reasons that companies crowdsource include: (a) increasing

	the capability to create and innovate and (b) outsourcing small discreet tasks (e.g., Uber drivers). Source quote: Kleemann, F., Voß, G. and Rieder, K. (July 2008). Un(der)paid Innovators: The Commercial Utilization of Consumer Work through Crowdsourcing. *Science, Technology & Innovation Studies.*
Customer experience (CX)	Customer experience is the end result of the interaction between a company and a customer over the whole life cycle of the relationship (e.g., reach, acquisition, conversion, retention, loyalty, and exit). The more channels and touch points, the more important the company invests in a coordinated and seamless customer journey. The perceived value, attitudes, and emotions of a person after using a single IT value proposition, service, or product is known as user experience (UX).
Customer relationship management (CRM)	CRM is more than a tool. It refers to the organizational practices, guidelines, and policies to follow and interact with customers through their life cycle. Effective CRM is an important precondition to enhance the overall customer experience.
Customer segment	Customers have different characteristics (e.g., needs, age, buying behavior, or spending power). By identifying them and grouping customers with similar characteristics, a company can optimize both the CX and SoW (see Share of wallet).
Dead code	Those parts of the application that are executed, but whose output is never used. The older the application, the more likely that it wastes CPU cycles and memory. Dead code should not be considered an error and compilers can be optimized to eliminate or strip the dead code.
Deming cycle	The Deming cycle is the oldest and most widely known continuous quality improvement model. The cycle consists of four repetitive steps: • **Plan** (e.g., sense and plan ahead for change, define desired results) • **Do** (e.g., take steps to achieve the desired results according to the plan) • **Check** (e.g., analyze the progress, issues, and results) • **Act** (e.g., adjust the plan, activities, or desired results) The Deming cycle is also known as the PDSA cycle: plan, do, study, and act.
DevOps	An agile Scrum team with a high-frequency feature flow alone is not enough. Only when the operations team can support the feature flow is the customer able to build business processes on top of the application. To do so, the operations team should adopt a mix of lean and agile practices. Furthermore, DevOps emphasizes close collaboration and effective communication between product management, software development, and operations.

Digital strategy	Digital strategy is a plan to realize the company's vision and key objectives in hybrid and digital markets. It is only relevant for companies with a hybrid business model or companies with an analog business model that want to enter digital markets. Hence, digital strategy does not equal IT strategy. For companies with a native digital business model, the digital strategy is the same as the overall company strategy.
Discounted cash flow (DCF)	A widely-used method to *estimate* the value a project or any other investment by using the time value of money. The result of a DCF calculation is the net present value (NPV), which is the sum of all discounted positive and negative cash flows over multiple years. The discount rate depends on the cost of capital, which in turn, is a proxy of the company's risk profile. See also Weighted average cost of capital (WACC).
e-Health	Also written eHealth, this term captures the digitalization of healthcare processes. Here, too, consumerization and the convergence of administrative IT and healthcare technology result in fading boundaries between both domains. Also related is m-Health, solutions that are optimized for mobile devices like tablets and smart phones.
Economies of scale	The transportation cost of a container on board of a container ship with a capacity of 15,000 containers is lower than a container ship with a capacity of 5,000 containers. Size, the scale of the facility (e.g., data center), and productivity drive down the cost per unit of output (e.g., product, service) as the fixed costs are spread out over more units.
Ecosystem	In biology, an ecosystem is a community of living organisms and components such as soil and minerals that act as a coherent, and often interdependent, system. In the IT space, *"ecosystems are product platforms defined by core components made by the platform owner and complemented by applications made by autonomous companies in the periphery. [. . .] In successful technology ecosystems it is easy to connect to or build upon the core solution in order to expand the system of use and allow new and even unanticipated end uses."* Source quote: Ft.com/lexicon. Link: http://lexicon.ft.com/Term?term=technology-ecosystem.
Electronic data interchange (EDI)	EDI is a set of standardized formats allowing IT systems to exchange information. Some are industry specific (e.g., ODETTE in the European automobile industry and HL7 in healthcare) while others allow companies to exchange electronic data across industries (e.g., EDIFACT to send standardized invoices, GS1 EDI for supply chain management).
Embedded software	Software is not limited to computers. Hardware used to control industrial equipment, cars, robots, and pacemakers requires specific software to function. With the convergence of administrative IT, industrial IT, and the software used to operate desktop computers, laptops, tablets, smart phones and smart watches, the term embedded software becomes less relevant.

Emotional quotient (EQ)	Children act on impulse, but adults can recognize and control their own emotions and sense the emotions of others (also known as *emotional intelligence*). To be effective, people in leadership roles must sense the emotional state of their team and its individual team members and act accordingly. The emotional quotient captures the level of a person's emotional intelligence. See also Situational leadership.
Enhanced telecom operations map (eTOM)	eTOM is a process framework for telecom providers that consists of three sections: 1. Strategy, infrastructure, and product (e.g., infrastructure and product life-cycle management) 2. Operations (e.g., CRM, service management) 3. Enterprise management (e.g., R&D, financial management, HRM) Its initial objective was improving the interoperability of telecom-related products. Over the years, both the breadth and depth of the framework increased. The most recent version is Version 14, and was published in 2014.
Enterprise resource planning (ERP)	Offered by external IT partners, ERP is a suite of closely integrated applications to automate and control primary business processes (e.g., production, supply chain, customer relations) and secondary business processes (e.g., human resources, accounting).
Enterprise risk management (ERM)	ERM acts as an umbrella for the frameworks (e.g., COSE, COBIT), processes, and tools used by companies to manage risks from strategy setting to operations.
Enterprise service bus (ESB)	An ESB is a communication solution for companies with an extensive application portfolio. It provides the applications with a standardized and structured *bus* to exchange information, replacing one-on-one interfaces between individual applications.
Entrepreneurial IT	In hybrid and digital markets the IT and business domains converge or even fuse. Combined with the rapid rate of change and competitive forces, the IT team must demonstrate entrepreneurship. Being an entrepreneur means '*one who undertakes an endeavor*' or an '*enterpriser*,'[1] a suitable term when business and IT are together in pursuit of more revenue, profit, or less strategic risk. Related are the terms strategic IT and enabling IT. Both fail, however, to capture the key competencies that are required to operate effectively in hybrid and digital markets.
Fast follower	Companies with a highly developed capability to (a) recognize other's good ideas and (b) turn the good idea to the companies own advantage. Fast followers are often companies that wait until a new emerging technology or business concept becomes mature enough for a value proposition targeting a large and

[1] Technically, the term should be intrapreneur as IT would be acting as in entrepreneur within the company. As this term is not widely used, this book will use the more common term.

	demanding customer segment (e.g., Apple was not the first company to enter the smart watch market). The fast follower strategy is often compared to first movers: companies that are part of an early wave of pioneers. First movers are called prospectors in the Miles and Snow strategy model.
Foundation IT	To innovate and grow, the company needs a reliable and scalable foundation. Foundation IT is the traditional sweet spot of the IT department. Even though most consider it less sexy than entrepreneurial IT, the majority of a company's revenue and margin is generated by business processes that were enabled by this part of the IT portfolio. Entrepreneurial IT is, in most cases, a source of expected *future* cash flows, funded by *current* cash flows, enabled by foundation IT. Related are the terms *transactional IT* and *factory IT*.
Freemium	It is one of the three revenue models that fueled the rapid growth of the internet-based business model: • **Free**: Advertisements or cross subsidization by complementary value propositions are used to generate the necessary revenue to cover the cost. • **Freemium**: The company gives part of the value proposition away for free to attract customers. Revenue is created by offering these customers value-added features they are willing to pay for. Think of access to unlimited amounts of data, unrestricted access to metadata, higher quality of data (e.g., resolution of photos), and early access to new features and data sets. Related is a dual licensing approach whereby, for example, individuals have access free of charge and commercial companies must pay. • **Premium**: Premium is closely related to brand image as quality and other sources of customer surplus are partially subjective. Examples include access to more and/or more-capable features or enriched data sets, and better customer service (e.g., support via phone number instead of web page).
Full service provider	External partners can be divided in two categories: partners with a best-of-breed strategy and partners with a one-stop-shop strategy. The latter is known as a full service provider and offers its customers a broad portfolio of generic value propositions. Niche players with a best-of-breed strategy are the best choice for very specific and discrete business and IT challenges.
Game theory	Game theory is a branch of mathematics used by economists to predict the events and outcomes of a group of people and/or companies if they act on what they perceive as their best interest. Due to the large number of variables, Game theory relies on complex computer models. The theory assumes that all stakeholders make intelligent and rational decisions.

	However, experiments showed that decisions made by humans are more complex (e.g., include regret in their decision-making process). The theory seeking to understand this phenomena is called behavioral game theory.
Governance	Corporate governance provides the necessary high-level guidelines to ensure the company's objectives and strategy are realized according to plan. Within the IT domain, IT governance provides *"the leadership and organizational structures and processes that ensure that the organization's IT sustains and extends the organization's strategies and objectives."* IT governance defines who is allowed to make which decision, including the accompanying control framework. In comparison, IT management is more operational in nature, as its focus is execution. Source quote: Board Briefing on IT Governance, 2nd Edition, IT Governance Institute (2003).
Governance, risk management, and compliance (GRC)	Similar to ERM, GRC acts as an umbrella for the frameworks, models, and tools to manage corporate governance, enterprise risk management, and regulatory compliance.
Greenfield	A start-up has no legacy systems or other constraints imposed by previous decisions. An application developed by an incumbent for a new customer segment lacking any ties with the existing application portfolio and infrastructure can also be considered a Greenfield project. When the new application has to interface or interact with existing applications, it is called a Brownfield development.
Habit-forming technologies	Addiction is the most powerful source of customer retention. Games and social media platforms are two examples of value propositions that are able to hook their users. According to Eyal, these value propositions manufacture desire and *"habit-forming technology creates associations with 'internal triggers' which cue users without the need for marketing, messaging, or other external stimuli."* Source quote: Eyal, N. (2014). *Hooked: How to Build Habit-Forming Products*.
Hyper-personalization	Consumers want products that reflect their desire for individualism. Companies like Netflix and Amazon have already mastered the skill of selling a large number of unique items in relatively small quantities, while still making a profit. Chris Anderson described this concept in his book *The Long Tail: Why the Future of Business Is Selling Less of More*. The *Long Tail* in the book title refers to the statistical argument that a larger share of consumers rests within the tail of a probability distribution than is observed under a *normal* or Gaussian distribution. Hyper-personalization refers to the use of data to analyze and predict the desire of individual customers, allowing for more personalized and targeted value propositions.

Hypervisor-based virtualization	A hypervisor is a piece of software that creates and runs virtual machines. It allows for multiple instances of a variety of operating systems to run on one physical machine, improving efficiency. A virtual machine emulates the hardware that is required by an operating system and/or business application in order for it to run.
Industrial IT	PLC (programmable logic controller), DCS (distributed control system), and SCADA (supervisory control and data acquisition) share many properties with computers used for administrative IT. They are attached to a network, have a graphical user interface, and are used to automate business processes. However, the systems that are used to automate business processes that are related to manufacturing, oil and gas facilities, and chemical process equipment require a specific control architecture. As a result, administrative IT systems and industrial IT systems are not interchangeable.
Information Age	From 1760 to somewhere between 1820 and 1840, the world migrated from manufacturing that was based on labor, wind, and water to steam engines and combustion engines (the *Industrial Revolution*). Today, we are amid another revolution as we are shifting toward an economy that is based on information and automated computing.
Information Technology Infrastructure Library (ITIL)	To support IT departments in their effort to become more business-oriented and reduce the amount of resources spent on maintenance, the British government agency CCTA (now OGC) collected from companies the best practices that performed above average in these areas. These were bundled in ten processes: five service-support processes (day-to-day focus) and five service-delivery processes (medium-term focus). With version 3, the set was expanded considerably in both detail and process scope.
Internet of Things (IoT)	Due to the miniaturization of electronic, mechanical, and optical devices, every physical device eventually becomes *smart*. The Internet of Things refers to the network infrastructure required to (a) control these devices and (b) allow these smart devices to exchange data between each other and with centralized servers.
Investment risk	Investment risk is the likelihood and impact of undesired events affecting the expected return of an investment. The higher the perceived investment risk, the higher the discount rate used to calculate the net present value.
ISAE 3402	In 2007, the International Auditing and Assurance Standards Board (IAASB) initiated a rationalization initiative for auditing standards and third-party assurance statements for external IT partners. The initiative resulted in two new international standards for reports: one for client companies and their internal auditors (ISA 402), and one for external IT partners and external auditors (ISEA 3402).

(ISO) Standards and Certifications	Due to the distance between the buyer and the supplier of a product or service, it is difficult for a buyer to observe the qualifications of a potential supplier. Standards, in combination with certifications, are used to reduce this so-called *information asymmetry*. The International Standards Organization (ISO) is an important source of standards, and everybody can participate in the committees that are responsible for the 21,378 published ISO standards or 4,938 ISO standards that are under development (note: data retrieved May 2017 from https://www.iso.org/technical-committees.html). The most widely adopted standard within the IT industry are ISO 9001 (quality management) and ISO 27001 (information security management system).
IT business model	The introduction of the business IT model is a logical consequence of the convergence of business and IT. To manage this trend, the business and IT need a common, business-oriented model to protect existing company value and create additional company value. For this growing part of the IT and business portfolio, the traditional business-IT alignment paradigm does not yield the desired result anymore. At a more operational level, this gap has led to the introduction of concepts like agile (Scrum), DevOps, and continuous deployment. However, they are only some of the necessary puzzle pieces. There are several others, and they all have to fit together, requiring a more strategic view. The IT business model aims to fulfill this need. The IT business model canvas is based on the business model canvas from Alexander Osterwalder.
IT outsourcing (ITO)	ITO refers to the decision of a company to outsource part of its IT function to an external business partner. In return, the client company receives a predefined service (e.g., ERP functionality) and/or physical product (e.g., laptops, tablets).
IT positioning	Positioning at the company level refers to *"the place that a brand occupies in the mind of the customer and how it is distinguished from products from competitors."* It is a powerful marketing concept and, due to the digitalization of business models, is increasingly relevant for the IT team. Positioning is closely related to strategy, as it includes the distinctive features (e.g., lowest price, most innovative) that shape the image in the market. IT positioning refers to the need and the process to remain in tune with the positioning of the company as a whole. IT positioning is not equal to digital positioning, as the latter refers to the specific positioning of the company in digital and hybrid markets. Source quote: https://en.wikipedia.org/wiki/Positioning_(marketing).
Just-in-time (JIT)	JIT was introduced by Japanese car manufacturers to optimize their production process. It emphasizes flow, minimal inventory levels, and customer-pull, thereby reducing waste. As JIT *leans out* manufacturing and production processes, it shares many properties with lean and agile development.

Kaizen	This term is related to continuous improvement and quality management. Like lean and JIT, Kaizen initiatives strive to minimize waste from the board level all the way down to the operational teams. Kaizen is the Japanese word for *continual improvement*.
Key partner	The distinction between key partner and supplier is based on added value. Delivering standard servers is done by a supplier. When the business and IT require help to realize a new cutting-edge e-business model, they source for a key partner. Among others, net present value (NPV) can be used to categorize an external business partner.
Labor arbitrage	The economics of many traditional outsourcing deals were based on differences in labor costs. A combination of deregulation and advances in IT allowed companies to shift business and IT activities to other countries. Its relevance is decreasing due to the ability to automate increasingly complex administrative and manufacturing tasks.
Lean	The essence of lean is increasing value from a customer perspective while eliminating waste by emphasizing flow efficiency followed by resource efficiency. A widely-used tool to support the implementation of lean is Six Sigma. The name stands for Six Standard Deviations from mean, and thus, has its roots in statistics. The methodology provides techniques and tools to increase quality by enhancing process capability and reducing the number of defects.
Marketing automation	This term refers to a category of practices and technologies to rationalize and streamline the marketing function. It extends beyond CRM and includes the automation of repetitive tasks, social media optimizations, and improved customer analytics.
Massive open online courses (MOOCs)	At universities, MOOCs are disrupting the traditional educational pedagogy that has been the norm for decades. MOOCs can be accessed via the web, allowing for unlimited participation and reuse. They allow students to study at their own pace and remove many of the financial constraints related to the traditional approach (e.g., high tuition fees). Downsides include challenges to track the progress of the student and inability to provide personal guidance.
Moore's Law	Moore's Law refers to an observation made by Carver Mead and Intel co-founder Gordon Moore when exploring the theoretical limits of microelectronic miniaturization. They found that the efficiency of the CPUs in relation to a reduction in scale would increase by the cube of the scale's reduction, instead of a more traditional linear reduction. Until recently, the number of transistors per unit of area, indeed, doubled every 12 to 18 months.

Multi-vendor strategy	Single-vendor or multi-vendor is one of the many topics that should be covered when defining the sourcing strategy. If the business and IT teams face a broad variety of specific technology-related challenges, a multi-vendor strategy is all but unavoidable. Even for commodity solutions (e.g., office furniture, low-end servers), large corporations often opt for a multi-vendor to maintain a competitive environment. If the company wants to source from an external IT partner with a proprietary platform (e.g., AWS Paas, Azure Paas, Oracle Paas) or technology (e.g., Arm Holdings owns all intellectual property required to build ARM processors), it has no choice but to opt for a single-vendor strategy.
Net present value (NPV)	See Discounted cash flow (DCF).
Network effect	Network effects are an economic effect whereby one user of a value proposition has a positive effect on the value of that value proposition for other users. In that case, the value proposition has *network externalities*. Social networks (e.g., Facebook), COTS software (e.g., Adobe pdf), and hardware (e.g., x86 CPUs) are some examples of the winner-take-all effect of positive network effects.
Nonfunctional requirements	An often-overlooked category of requirements, especially in immature and feature-focused agile development teams. In contrast to the functional requirements that describe specific behaviors or functions, nonfunctional criteria cover the context that the application should operate in. Think of the relative importance of scalability, maintainability, reliability, flexibility, and security. For this reason, nonfunctional requirements are a key input for the solution architecture and restrict the amount of user stories that can be dedicated to functional requirements.
Open Web Application Security Project (OWASP)	A widely-used set of best practices and open standards that is focused on improving the security of software. The most widely adopted and implemented practice, it is the so-called *OWASP Top 10*, a yearly evolving list of most critical web application security risks.
Operational expenditure (OPEX)	These are the costs that a business team or IT team incurs through its normal day-to-day activities. OPEX include the operational costs related to CAPEX investments (e.g., recurring yearly license cost after implementing Oracle ERP). Other examples include payroll, rent, SaaS and IaaS invoices, marketing, and server lease contracts.
Order-to-cash (O2C)	This is the most important flow within any commercial company because it involves those business activities that are required to receive and process a sales order by a customer and his or her payment. Sooner or later, every function within a company is affected, either directly or indirectly, by this flow.

Organic light emitting diodes (OLED)	OLED is a flat light-emitting technology that is used to make displays. Other popular light-emitting technologies include liquid-crystal display (LCD) and light-emitting diodes (LED). OLED displays are made by placing one or more films of an organic compound on top of each other.
Original equipment manufacturer (OEM)	OEMs are the result of companies focusing on their core competencies. Companies including Coca Cola, Procter and Gamble, Unilever, Apple, Google, and Microsoft outsource parts of their value chain to external partners. Original equipment manufacturers are, therefore, companies that produce parts and products that are, in most cases, marketed by other companies. Microsoft uses OEMs to build its Surface hardware devices, but is at the same time an OEM for Dell, Lenovo, and HP, as these latter install the Windows operating systems on their devices, but sell them under their own brand name.
Payback period	This term used in the context of business cases and DCF/NPV calculations and refers to the period of time required to recoup an investment.
Peer networking	This term has two meanings. The first is technical and refers to a type of distributed network architecture (*peer-to-peer infrastructure*) that partitions tasks between systems using APIs. A *peer* is also somebody with a similar experience or background. The second meaning, therefore, refers to the social network that people use to climb the corporate ladder or find a more challenging and rewarding job.
Performance management	Performance management is a process to improve the value of the company or an individual investment. There are many definitions including this one from Gates: "*A strategic performance measurement system translates business strategies into deliverable results. Combine financial, strategic, and operating measures to gauge how well a company meets its targets.*" Consequently, performance management includes: • Setting objectives and results; • Motivating employees to achieve the set objectives and results; • Planning, organizing, and executing activities; • Providing resources and information to execute those activities; and • Defining and implementing management controls to check deviations from set objectives and results. Source quote: Gates, S. (1999). Aligning Strategic Performance Measures and Results, The Conference Board. New York.
Pilot	Instead of investing $1 million in a full-blown platform, a company can also opt for investing in a small-scale project to test and evaluate several key assumptions. Based on the information that was collected during the pilot project, the team can refine the

	scope, cost, time, and key risks of the main project. See also Real options. Closely related is a proof of concept, as it, too, is a mini project to realize one or more ideas of key features of a new application or value proposition to demonstrate its feasibility.
Predictive analytics	See Big data.
Product market combination (PMC)	A PMC is a unique combination of a value proposition that is targeting a specific market. It fulfills a specific need or want of a customer. The better the value proposition satisfies a strong customer demand, the higher the so-called *product/market fit*. In the IT business model, the PMCs of the IT team are reflected by the building blocks value propositions, customer segments, customer relations, and channels.
Proof of concept	See Pilot.
Real options	The typical DCF calculation assumes a static scenario, ignoring the financial value represented by the flexibility to change course during a project. In real life, people learn during a project and want to adjust their decisions accordingly, effecting the business case. Real options provide a way to calculate the value of managerial flexibility and add that value to the business case. In real options terminology, the decision to invest in an initiative is a *call option*; the right but *not the obligation* to spend valuable company resources.
Robotic process automation (RPA)	Robots are not only used to automate increasingly complex manufacturing and production tasks, but software robots are also replacing knowledge workers. In the latter case, the software robot is trained to replicate the actions of a human being, and more advanced versions even include the ability to learn and adapt. See also Artificial intelligence.
Scenario planning	Also called scenario analysis or scenario thinking, scenario planning is a strategic method to make flexible long-term plans. It provides senior decision makers with a structure to think about the future. See also the real options.
Search engine optimization (SEO)	SEO refers to a set of practices and tools to optimize the visibility of a website in a service engine's unpaid results. The desired result of SEO is an increase in the number of visitors.
Secure sockets layer (SSL)	The default technology used to secure the communication between the web server and the web browser of a user. SSL encrypts all data being transferred, and combined with an SSL certificate (digital cryptographic key binded to a specific company), the user is ensured of a private communication channel.
Segregation of duties (SoD)	To prevent fraud or other undesired behavior and errors, companies require more than one person to perform sensitive tasks (e.g., approve invoices, raise salaries). SoD is a control that is part of the overall governance framework and can be found in most business applications.

Service level agreement (SLA)	The professional demand-supply relationship between the business and IT, propagated by the business IT alignment paradigm, inevitably resulted in a desire for some kind of *contract* between both parties. SLAs cover the operations and support phase of the IT life cycle and typically cover, among others, the scope (e.g., office automation), service levels (e.g., response times), reporting, and escalation. More recent is the introduction of the experience level agreement (XLA), focusing on the performance of the internal IT team or external IT partner, as perceived by the end user.
Service-profit chain	Until the introduction of chatbots, artificial intelligence, and other technologies to automate business processes, helping or doing work for a customer always required one or more employees. According to Heskett et al., the human interaction between the customer and employee that is inherent to a service is a key value driver. The service-profit chain concept argues that high employee satisfaction leads to customer loyalty and consequently higher revenue and profitability. The service-profit chain was first introduced in the following article: Heskett, J., Jones, T., Loveman, G., Sasser, W. and Schlesinger, L. (July–August 2008). Putting the Service-Profit Chain to Work, *Harvard Business Review*.
Shareconomy	Sharing, or *using instead of owning*, is driven by customers faced by: • An abundance of choice (read: supply outstrips demand), • A desire for instant gratification, • A decline of stable and full-time employment, and • A decline in purchasing power. Technology is an important enabler of sharing because it reduces the friction between *customers* and *suppliers*. Apps, in combination with a scalable back-end platform, allow for a free flow of information providing the necessary convenience and trust (e.g., via reviews). Using instead of owning gave rise to a whole new industry, including companies like Uber (car), Airbnb (house), TaskRabbit (labor), Kickstarter (funding), Wallapop (used goods), Udacity (education), Repair Cafe (repair), and Facebook, Twitter, and Instagram (personal content). Some are mission-driven, but most are profit-driven or at least a hybrid.
Share of wallet (SoW)	This concept helps managers to understand how much individual customers spend on the company's products and services. According to Keiningham et al., SoW *"is the percentage of a customer's spending within a category that's captured by a given brand, or store, or firm."* Source quote: Keiningham, T., Aksoy, L., Buoye, A., and Cooil, B. (October 2011). Customer Loyalty Isn't Enough. Grow Your Share of Wallet. *Harvard Business Review*.

Singularity	In the context of this book, singularity represents the ultimate fusion of humans and technology, made popular by technology-guru Ray Kurzweil in 2005 with his book *The Singularity Is Near*. He borrowed the term *singularity* from physics, where it is used to describe the center of a cosmic black hole—a place where all energy and mass are compressed to an infinite small point. The book indicates that the combination of Moore's law and the convergence of IT, robotics, nanotechnology, and biology will eventually lead to conscious computers and humans living without a body.
Situational leadership	There is no single *best* style of leadership. Everybody is blessed with a unique set of strengths and development points. A leader must determine the willingness and ability of every individual team member to perform a certain task. This is called *situational leadership*, a concept developed by Paul Hersey and Ken Blanchard.
Smart grid	Adding a wide variety of sensors and computers (e.g., smart meters, smart appliances) turn a *dumb* electricity network into a *smart* one. Key benefits for the utility providers include improved reliability (e.g., better fault detection enabling self-healing), security and efficiency of the electric grid, while the customers with solar panels can look forward to bidirectional energy flows.
Specific, measurable, acceptable, relevant, and time-bound (SMART)	Part of the performance management body of knowledge, SMART provides an easy-to-remember acronym to set objectives. The most popular interpretation of SMART is specific, measurable, assignable, realistic, and time-bound. In Chapter 7, I took the liberty to use the Dutch interpretation of SMART, whereby assignable is replaced by acceptable. SMART objectives are: • **Specific**: Is the objective unambiguous for all team members and other stakeholders? • **Measurable**: What are the metrics used to determine that the team has achieved the objective? • **Acceptable or Assignable**: Are the objectives and the accompanying metrics acceptable for all stakeholders involved?—or—specify who will do it. • **Realistic**: Can the team reasonably be expected to reach the objective (e.g., considering budget)? • **Time bound**: When should the objective be realized?
Spiral model	The spiral model was introduced by Barry Boehm in 1986 to reduce the risk of a project step-by-step. A new initiative would, for example, start with developing one or more small-scale prototypes or proof of concepts to *test the water*, followed by a larger effort when the uncertainty cone has been sufficiently reduced. The spiral model is neither a strong opponent of iterative development (e.g., agile) or sequential development (e.g., waterfall), but expects the practitioner to think. Source: Boehm, B. (August 1986). "A Spiral Model of Software Development and Enhancement." *ACM SIGSOFT Software Engineering Notes, ACM, 11(4)*:14–24.

Software-defined data center (SDDC)	Part of a category of technologies that also include software-defined networks (SDN) and software-defined infrastructure (SDI), SDDC refers to a concept whereby all of the hardware in one or more data centers is virtualized, pooled, and delivered as a service to the developers and operations engineers. Using a combination of tools and scripting, the developers and operations engineers access those resources they need to run for their applications, releasing them back to the pool when the application has finished using them.
Strategy	Every company wants to grow and become more profitable. As markets have a finite size, companies have to compete for their share. Strategic thinking means understanding the key success factors of the business that the company is in and performing a competitive analysis to understand the strengths and weaknesses of the competition. The basic strategies to do so are competing on: • **Cost**: Selling value propositions with an acceptable feature set and quality level at the lowest possible price-point. • **Differentiation**: Competing by creating new and difficult-to-copy value propositions. Another form of differentiation is segmentation, whereby value propositions are tailored to the specific needs of a group of consumers within a market. Strategic thinking can be top-down (*intended strategy*), or bottom-up (*emergent*). The top-down approach translated the company's mission into objectives, which in turn lead to strategies and tactics to realize them. An emergent strategy is more bottom-up, whereby actions taken over time condense into a strategy, often in response to unexpected opportunities and problems at the operational level. According to Mintzberg and Waters, five kinds of strategies can be identified: emergent strategy, intended strategy, deliberate strategy, realized strategy, and unrealized strategy. Source: Mintzberg, H. and Waters, J. (1985). Of Strategies, Deliberate and Emergent. *Strategic Management Journal, 6.* pp. 257–272. Another important topic related to strategic thinking is the choice between a market-driven strategy versus resource-based strategy. With a market-driven strategy, the market trends and customer needs dominate, instead of the company's capabilities or product portfolio. Tapping into any market segment that is not yet recognized or served adequately by competitors is the starting point of a new strategy. With a resource-based strategy, the key input for any new strategy is the application of the valuable resources (e.g., knowledge, skills) at the company's disposal. Based on the available resources and core competencies, suitable market segments are identified and products are designed and produced.
Supplier	See Key partner.

Theory of Constraints (TOC)	The Theory of Constraints, also known as management by constraints (MBC), got widespread attention with the book *The Goal* from Goldratt and Cox published in 1984. TOC has its roots in manufacturing and logistics, and seeks to identify and address bottlenecks in the workflow. The assumption is that the slowest link of the chain sets the speed for the whole concept-to-cash process, or any other process. The capacity of the weakest link (e.g., functional testers) determines the amount of output the upstream part of the chain can produce without creating a backlog (e.g., how fast developers can write code and the frequency at which new software is released to production). After identifying the weakest link, the team tries to maximize the throughput by analyzing and optimizing the constraint. This approach is similar to agile (Kanban) software development, where the aim is also to create a constant flow without any *inventory*. After *widening* one constraint, the team addresses the next bottleneck, resulting in a continuous improvement process.
TOGAF	See Architecture.
Transaction costs	In the context of outsourcing, transaction costs include searching for a suitable source of supply, deal making, and contract enforcement. More generally, transaction cost is an economic concept that captures the cost of any economic transaction in a market.
Value chain, value network, and value shop	The company's value chain is a high-level model of the activities that a company performs to deliver a value proposition to one or more customer segments. This concept was introduced by Porter in 1985 and differentiates between primary activities (e.g., inbound logistics, operations, outbound logistics, marketing and sales, and service), and support activities (e.g., firm infrastructure, human resource management, technology, and procurement). In an article published in 1998, Stabell and Fjeldstad pointed out that Porter's model had a perfect fit with manufacturing companies, but less so for professional service firms as found in law, engineering, and medicine. The same applies to companies that link customers to each other—like telecom providers, retail banks, and logistics companies. For this reason, Stabell and Fjeldstad introduced two additional value configurations: the value shop for professional service companies and the value network for companies that provide connectivity. With the rise of digital platform business models (e.g., Facebook, Twitter, eBay, and Kickstarter), differentiation between value chain, value shop, and value network gained in importance. Contrary to more traditional value chain or *pipe* business models, value networks or *platforms* "*do not just create and push stuff out. They allow users to create and consume value. At the technology layer, external developers can extend platform functionality using APIs. At the business*

	layer, users (producers) can create value on the platform for other users (consumers) to consume." The users of Facebook create the content consumed by other users, while news agencies provide the content for readers of Flipboard. Sources: • Porter, M. (1985). *Competitive Advantage: Creating and Sustaining Superior Performance.* • Stabell, C. and Fjeldstad, Ø. (1998). Configuring Value for Competitive Advantage: On Chains, Shops, and Networks. *Strategic Management Journal, 19.* pp. 413–437. • Choudary, S. (2013). Why Business Models Fail: Pipes vs. Platforms. Link: http://www.wired.com/2013/10/why-business-models-fail-pipes-vs-platforms/.
Value proposition	A value proposition articulates the value of a product or service from a customer perspective. It is a promise that has to be communicated, delivered, and acknowledged by the customer. Hence, the customer has to believe and experience the statement in order for it to be effective.
Value-based management (VBM)	Value-based management (VBM) is a result-oriented performance management model, consisting of the following key activities: • Defining and implementing strategies that provide the highest potential for shareholder value creation; • Implementing information systems that are focused on value creation and the underlying *drivers* of value across a company's business units, products, and customer segments; • Aligning management processes, such as business planning and resource allocation, with value creation; and • Designing performance measurement systems and incentive compensation plans that reflect value creation. The focus of VBM on shareholder value creation allows for a relatively simple performance management framework when compared to measuring and balancing value creation for multiple stakeholders. The downside of solely focusing on share price includes an incentive to focus on the short-term profit (e.g., leading to Kodak's downward spiral), excessive risk taking (e.g., highly leveraged acquisitions), uneven distribution of value creation (e.g., excessive layoffs), and lack of transparency (e.g., keep underperforming subsidiaries off the books). Source: Ittner, C. and Larcker, D. (2001). Assessing Empirical Research in Managerial Accounting: A Value-Based Management Perspective, *Journal of Accounting and Economics 32.* pp. 349–410.

Virtual reality	According to Wikipedia, *"virtual reality (VR) is a computer technology that uses virtual reality headsets, sometimes in combination with physical spaces or multi-projected environments, to generate realistic images, sounds, and other sensations that simulate a user's physical presence in a virtual or imaginary environment."* Virtual reality and augmented reality are closely related, but they are not the same. Virtual reality is more immersive, as both the users' vision and hearing are stimulated, but augmented reality provides more freedom (e.g., no head-mounted display or headphones). According to Augment.com, *"augmented reality (AR) is a technology that layers computer-generated enhancements atop an existing reality in order to make it more meaningful through the ability to interact with it."* Sources: • Virtual Reality, Wikipedia.org. (Retrieved August 2017.) Link: https://en.wikipedia.org/wiki/Virtual_reality. • Virtual Reality vs. Augmented Reality, Augment.com. (Retrieved August 2017.) Link: http://www.augment.com/blog/virtual-reality-vs-augmented-reality/.
Waterfall	Waterfall development was created more than half a century ago to structure and professionalize software development. All other models are either based on it or created to mitigate its weaknesses. Like waterfall, the V-model development process is sequential. Where waterfall is linear from beginning to end, the V-model bends upward after the coding phase. It makes the necessary verification and validation between the first and second part of the process more transparent.
Weighted average cost of capital (WACC)	The cost of capital or the WACC reflects the riskiness of the company. *"Weighted average cost of capital (WACC) is a calculation of a firm's cost of capital in which each category of capital is proportionately weighted. All sources of capital, including common stock, preferred stock, bonds, and any other long-term debt, are included in a WACC calculation."* See also Discounted cash flow. Source: Investopedia. Link: http://www.investopedia.com/terms/w/wacc.asp.

INDEX

Page numbers followed by "*f*", "*n*", and "*t*" indicate figure, footnote, and table, respectively.